What
SELF-MADE MILLIONAIRES
Really Think, Know and Do

THINK

In the UK 50 per cent of adults have an income of £26,000 per annum or less. Ninety per cent have an income of less than £34,000. Those in the top one per cent have incomes in excess of £91,000 per annum.

A 1995 survey in the USA reveals that out of 100 citizens who start work at age 25, by the age of 65, 29 per cent are dead and 63 per cent are dependent on handouts from Social Security, friends and relatives. Amazingly, in the richest country in the world, 92 per cent are either dead or relatively poor. Of the remaining 8 per cent, 3 per cent are still working, 4 per cent have 'adequate' capital for retirement, and 1 per cent are 'wealthy'.

Would you like to be in the top 1 per cent, earning more than £91,000 per annum and retiring 'wealthy'? Are you prepared to set it as a goal? Are you prepared to pay the price? READ THIS BOOK.

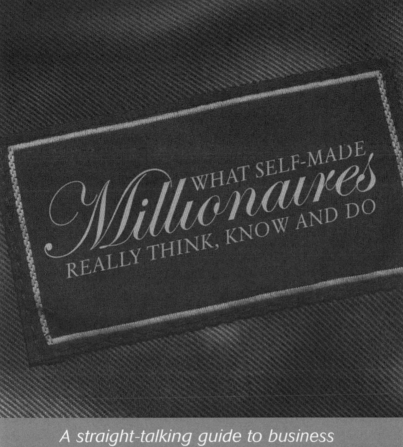

WHAT SELF-MADE Millionaires REALLY THINK, KNOW AND DO

A straight-talking guide to business
success and personal riches

RICHARD DOBBINS &
BARRIE O.PETTMAN

CAPSTONE

First edition published 1999
Second edition published 2002
Third edition published 2006
Capstone Publishing Limited (a Wiley company), The Atrium, Southern Gate Chichester, West Sussex, PO19 8SQ, England Phone (+44) 1243 779777

Copyright © Richard Dobbins and Barrie O. Pettman 1999, 2002, 2006

Email (for orders and customer service enquires): cs-books@wiley.co.uk
Visit our Home Page on www.wiley.co.uk or www.wiley.com

Other Wiley Editorial Offices
John Wiley & Sons, Inc. 111 River Street, Hoboken, NJ 07030, USA
Jossey-Bass, 989 Market Street, San Francisco, CA 94103–1741, USA
Wiley-VCH Verlag GmbH, Pappellaee 3, D-69469 Weinheim, Germany
John Wiley & Sons Australia, Ltd, 33 Park Road, Milton, Queensland, 4064, Australia
John Wiley & Sons (Asia) Pte Ltd, 2 Clementi Loop #02–01, Jin Xing Distripark, Singapore 129809
John Wiley & Sons Canada Ltd, 22 Worcester Road, Etobicoke, Ontario, Canada, M9W 1L1

Wiley also publishes its books in a variety of electronic formats. Some content that appears in print may not be available in electronic books.

British Library Cataloguing in Publication Data
A catalogue record for this book is available from the British Library

ISBN13   978-1-84112-680-7 (pb)

Typeset in 11/15 pt Dutch 801 by
Sparks, Oxford
http://www.sparks.co.uk
Printed and bound in Great Britain by T.J. International Ltd, Padstow, Cornwall

This book is printed on acid-free paper responsibly manufactured from sustainable forestry in which at least two trees are planted for each one used for paper production.
10 9 8 7 6 5 4 3

DEDICATION

For Richard Robson,
Tasha, Vicky,
Samantha, Joseph,
Victoria, Jessica and Chris,
Maureen and Marie

'The ideas I stand for are not mine. I borrowed them from Socrates. I swiped them from Chesterfield. I stole them from Jesus. And I put them in a book. If you don't like their rules, whose would you use?' – *Dale Carnegie*

CONTENTS

Acknowledgements   *xi*
To the Reader   *xiii*
About the Authors   *xix*

1   Everything Starts With Ideas   1
    How to think creatively

2   You Can Have It If You Want It   27
    How to set and achieve your goals

3   Strategy Will Get You There   97
    How to implement a winning business strategy

4   Marketing Is The Key   133
    How to implement a winning marketing strategy

5   Sales Skills Will Make Your Fortune   159
    How to be excellent at selling

6   Everything Is Negotiable   197
    How to negotiate better deals

7   We All Need Leadership   215
How to lead a winning team

8   Everything You Do Affects Sales, Costs and Profits   235
How to understand the financial implications

9   Never Use Time As An Excuse   277
How to focus on the 20% that brings in the 80%

Further Reading   *295*
Index   *301*

ACKNOWLEDGEMENTS

We wish to thank:

- Gordon Wills for 30 years of strategy, marketing and leadership
- Richard Branson for being a portrait in positive thinking
- Tom Peters for his contribution to management thinking
- Napoleon Hill for his observations on successful people
- Brian Tracy and Jay Abrahams for great insights and presentations
- Andy Lothian for being the student who taught us more than as academics we could teach him
- All those philosophers, theologians and prophets who contributed to the Gita, Koran, and the Bible.

TO THE READER

Would you like to change your life dramatically? Are you tired of doing a crummy job for peanuts? Are you tired of being a macho dickhead moron? Would you like to have a more successful life? Would you like to be more, have more, do more? Would you like to spend your life doing something which is more worthy? Would you like to earn a lot more money? Are you in the public sector, knowing that you should be in the private sector? Are you suffering from justification and identification? Are you suffering from negative emotions: blame, stress, self-pity, worry, anger, envy, fear of failure, fear of rejection? Are you suffering from self-limiting beliefs? Do you imagine that there are rocks standing between you and what you really want? Would you like to be the master/mistress of your own destiny?

This book is for you. We offer you your freedom.

This book is for those who would like to be winners in a competitive world.

- Set clear goals.
- Learn what you need to know.
- Be more positive.
- Find your area of excellence.

- Establish a competitive advantage.
- Find your market segment.
- Concentrate.

An entrepreneur is someone who is determined to improve the life of a customer in a competitive world.

A customer is someone who is willing and able to purchase the improvement you offer in a competitive world.

Even if you take only a few ideas from this book and develop a few new habits, it will make a dramatic difference.

CHANGE YOUR LIFE

We know that you want to change your life. Be honest with yourself. You know that you want to change. This is totally natural and totally predictable. Everybody wants to be more, have more, and do more. This is your birthright. In order to be more, have more and do more, you have to change. Being the way that you are now, got you where you are today. If you do not change, you will probably stay exactly where you are now, forever. This is probably a painful prospect for you. You must change to move forwards. Fortunately, there are only two ways in which you can change. Firstly, you can learn more, and secondly you can be more positive in your attitude.

This book teaches you how to be successful in business, although the principles of success are the same in all areas of human activity. If you set clear goals and resolve to pay the price in advance by learning what you need to know and thinking more positively, then you will become more successful. Other people will call you 'lucky'. You can certainly join the top three per cent. You can join the top one per cent. You are the master/mistress of your own destiny. You are responsible for you own happiness. This book teaches you how, with special emphasis on success in business.

SELF-MADE MILLIONAIRES

Millionaires become millionaires by improving the lives of their customers in a competitive world. Some time ago, we learnt that there are approximately one million self-made millionaires in the world. Apparently, 80 per cent of them took at least twenty years to get there. This is therefore the normal route, Route 1. This slow but sure route requires you to set goals and to resolve to pay the price in advance of achieving those goals. It requires you to establish a specialisation, an area of excellence, a mission. It requires you to be creative, implement a winning business strategy, get the marketing right, be excellent at selling, negotiate sensible deals, give leadership to others, understand the financial implications, and manage your time well, manage your life well. Most of this book is directed at giving you the necessary knowledge and attitude to take Route 1, the twenty-year route to success and achievement. This book teaches you how to get what you want by using the law of belief, the law of cause and effect, the law of attraction, and the law of accumulation.

A small section of this book is directed at Route 2, the six-year route, i.e. How To Get Rich Quickly, dealt with mainly in Chapter 3. For some people it is extremely good news that twenty per cent of self-made millionaires get there in less than twenty years; usually around six years. Route 2 requires you to buy somebody else's 'dog', or beat the other guy by ten per cent, or market somebody's wonderful product in a new market. This route includes the management buy-out, the franchise, and creative imitation. Route 1 and Route 2 are not mutually exclusive. Once you begin to see life as full of opportunities, then all sort of opportunities suddenly arise.

You can switch from the twenty-year route to the six-year route, and you can just as easily switch from the six-year route to the twenty-year route. Once you begin the process of setting clear goals, learning what you need to know, and thinking very positively, then things do begin to improve very quickly. All sorts of opportunities suddenly open up to you.

There is, of course, Route 3 – the chosen route of the millions of people who will achieve nothing in their lifetimes, the millions of people for whom life is just another day another dollar, the millions of people who accept that they are born into a world of low expectations and low achievement. You leave school or university. Somebody gives you a job. You may get 'lucky' enough to get a couple of promotions, you retire on a peanut pension, and you die shortly afterwards with just enough cash to cover the funeral bill. These people go to their graves with their music still inside them. They have used about two per cent of their mental capacity.

They go through life with the one great hope which is … come on, be honest … you know the answer … to win the National Lottery! We understand that the probability of winning the lottery is about fourteen million to one. If you enter the National Lottery once each week, then you can expect to win, on average, about once in every two hundred and seventy thousand years. You can reduce the expected winning period to about only one hundred and thirty five thousand years by doing the lottery twice each week.

By reading this book you will fully understand why the vast majority of people take Route 3. This route requires no goal-setting, no resolution to pay the price, no specialisation, no competitive advantage, no market segmentation, and no concentration. This route requires no creativity, no strategy, no marketing, no sales skill, no negotiation skill, no leadership skill, no financial understanding, and no time/life management.

Route 3 allows people to be lazy, ill-informed, selfish, greedy, ruthless, disloyal, impatient, irresponsible, unreliable and vain. Route 3 allows people to watch television for twenty-six hours per week, prop up a bar for two or three hours every night, and spend their lives totally absorbed by sex and football. Route 3 requires no reading of books, no educational courses, and Route 3 allows you to spend you life with other people who are equally lazy, ill-informed, selfish, greedy, ruthless, disloyal, impatient, irresponsible, unreliable and vain. Route 3 requires no information, no decision-making, and no action.

Most of the current generation's fathers did the football pools. Every year they 'knew' that this was going to be their lucky year. It never happened. All were perfectly capable of becoming millionaires by Route 1 or even Route 2, but they chose Route 3. If only they had known and used the rules of success in this book! In this book we ignore Route 3.

Happiness is striving to achieve your most desired goals,
living a life consistent with your highest ideals.
Your are the hero/heroine of your own story.
Enjoy the journey.
Enjoy every minute.

ABOUT THE AUTHORS

Richard Dobbins made his first £ million in management development. He is a management consultant, a practising chartered Certified Accountant and editor of the journals *Managerial Finance* and *Management Research News*. He qualified as a Certified Accountant in 1968 after several years' experience in professional offices, industry and public service. He studied for his MSc and PhD in management at the University of Bradford where he was appointed lecturer in finance in 1973 and senior lecturer in financial management in 1979. He has written over 90 articles and books and has lectured as a Visiting Professor of Management on MBA programmes in western Europe, eastern Europe, the Far East, the Middle East, Africa, Australia and North America. He has extensive experience in management development and as a management consultant in over 100 companies both in the UK and overseas. He now spends his time/life encouraging other people to be more, have more and do more. His other interests include a publishing company, a small accounting practice, early furniture and old master paintings.

Barrie Pettman made his first £ million in publishing. He is a management consultant, registrar and professor of human resource management at the International Management Centres, director of the International Institute of Social Economics, chairman of MCB University Press, president of Emerald Group Publishing, and a Vis-

iting Professor at the Canadian School of Management. He lectured at the University of Hull and the University of Rhodesia 1970–82. He is editor of the *International Journal of Sociology and Social Policy, Equal Opportunities International,* the *International Journal of New Ideas* and co-editor of *Managerial Law*. He was awarded a Distinguished Fellowship of the International Society for Intercommunication of New Ideas in 1991. For 'fun', he owns a restaurant, a publishing company, and a small oil-delivery company. He has the distinction of having recently accepted an offer of £22 million for his stake in one business. He acceded to the title of Baron of Bombie in 1999.

One

EVERYTHING STARTS WITH IDEAS

How to think creatively

So you have this vague idea: 'I would like to be more, have more, do more.' You want to achieve certain results ... in a world of constant change. Change is inevitable. Change is opportunity. If you stay as you are, you stay where you are. The world belongs to those who are in love with the new. In such a world there is a strong relationship between the quality and quantity of new ideas and your success in achieving results. Business is all about the implementation of ideas which improve the life of your customer and could result in profit for you. You are a creative genius.

'Find out everything everybody else knows, and then begin where they left off.' – *Thomas Edison*

1   A DEFINITION OF CREATIVITY

> Success is related to the quality and quantity of new ideas.

Creativity is the ability to improve. We all came into the world being creative, innovative, and inventive. Approximately ninety-seven per cent of children are highly creative at the age of five, thirty-six per cent are highly creative at the age of ten, with only twelve per cent scoring highly creative at age fifteen. Our birthright is to improve our condition. We all behave in a manner consistent with improving our condition. For most of us our creativity has lain dormant since childhood. We must all now learn to tap into our own creativity. We can all learn to tap into the creativity of others.

One of the mental laws which govern all our lives is the law of habit. The law of habit states that almost everything we do is habit. The ways in which we walk, talk, respond to situations and the ways in which we use our creativity are all habits. Make a habit of using your creativity. Make a habit of trying to improve situations by ten per cent. There are many ways in which we can improve sales by ten per cent, reduce costs by ten per cent, and increase profit by ten per cent.

Everything can be improved in some way. The success of the organisation is directly related to the quality and quantity of new ideas generated and implemented. Many companies have been saved by using the techniques in creativity discussed later in this chapter. In all aspects of the business there are ways of being better, cheaper and faster. The competitive advantage of our business is that we are better, cheaper or faster than our competitors in some way.

> Everything can be improved by at least 10 per cent.

Furthermore, there are always ways in which we can be more pleasant in our dealings with customers, suppliers, bankers, etc. Being 'nicer' is the fourth way in which we can establish competitive advantage. Continuous improvement through creativity is one of the keys to success in business.

2   DETERMINANTS OF CREATIVITY

'The brain is a wonderful organ: it starts working the moment you get up in the morning and it does not stop until you get to the office.' – *Robert Frost*

The world of success and failure in business is a mental world in which everything starts with ideas. Unfortunately, most of us have a strong tendency to stifle our own creativity or to dismiss our own creative ideas as worthless. For individuals, the level of creative activity and the value which an individual places on his or her own creativity tend to be determined by past experience, the present situation and the self-concept. We tend to be more creative if in the past we have worked in a positive environment where creativity has been encouraged. Creativity is encouraged by enthusiasm, excitement, love, joy and acceptance of responsibility.

Unfortunately, many of us have worked in negative environments where creativity was stifled by fear of failure, fear of rejection, self-doubt, self-pity, failure to accept responsibility, hate, envy and blame. If our present situation is dominated by positive emotions, then this encourages creativity. Finally, from the law of belief we know that we always behave in a manner consistent with our beliefs. If we believe we are creative, then we behave in a manner consistent with being creative.

We have a self-concept or belief about each aspect of our lives. Each individual has a self-concept level of income, a self-concept level of creativity, a self-concept as a manager, a self-concept as a sales person, a self-concept as a negotiator, a self-concept as a squash player, cook and lover. The self-concept is the bundle of beliefs an individual has about his or her ability. In short, if you believe you are creative, you behave in a manner consistent with being a creative person.

The most exciting part of the law of belief is that beliefs are not based on reality. If you believe you are a Christian, you are a Christian. If you believe you can swim, you are a swimmer. If you believe you can ride a bicycle, then you will always behave in a manner consistent with being able to ride a bicycle. Make a decision to believe that you are a creative genius. Visualise, emotionalise, and affirm. Visualise yourself as a creative person. Imagine how well you would feel if you were a creative person. Finally, make a habit of the affirmation: 'I am a very creative person.' If you believe you are creative, then you will behave in a manner consistent with being creative.

So far as your organisation is concerned, happy, open, optimistic, encouraging environments stimulate creativity. Low levels of creativity are associated with a negative environment. Positive emotions are strongly associated with creativity. Managers should provide a work situation which is encouraging, enthusiastic and exciting. These are the great positive emotions. Finally, high self-esteem is strongly associated with creativity. Self-esteem is the extent to which an individual feels valuable and worthwhile. One aspect of a manager's job is to make people feel important, to make people feel valuable and worthwhile. We must all encourage others to repeat the affirmation: 'I am a valuable and worthwhile person.' Many people suffer from low self-esteem believing that their ideas are of little value. A high self-esteem environment is a creative environment.

3   STIMULATE YOUR CREATIVITY BY GOAL SETTING

Creativity is stimulated by clear goals with specified deadlines for achievement. Think about your business goals. Where would you like to be one year from now? Where would you like to be three years from now? What business would you like to be in at some specified future date? How much money would you like to be earning three years from now? What sort of a company car will you have? What are the skills you must acquire in order to achieve those goals? What are your personal and family goals? Where would you like to be 20 years from now? What are your most urgent goals during the next 12 months? What are your three most pressing problems or challenges at this moment? At this stage you may have only a fairly vague idea that you would like to be more, have more, do more. We shall go for much greater clarity in Chapter 2.

We use the following exercise to stimulate the creativity of our audience, including the self-employed.

Career/business goals

In an ideal world, what business would you like to be in three years from now? What position will you hold in the company? What will your salary be? What level of sales and profits will you achieve? What sort of a company car will you have? Write down five career/ business goals for achievement within three years.

Personal development plan

One of the simple truths we all have to face up to as adults is that wherever we are in life at the present time is where we deserve to be. If we had greater knowledge/skills and a more positive attitude then we would be in a better position. If we had less knowledge and a more negative attitude, then we would not even be where we are today. In order to advance in business, we must change in some way. We must increase our knowledge/skills and/or we must be more positive in attitude. Which additional skills must you acquire as a manager to be in the position you would like to be in three years from now? Do you need to be more creative? Do you need to learn more about strategy, marketing, sales skills, negotiation skills, finance, leadership? Be honest with yourself and write down five skills which you must acquire over the next three years to achieve your career/ business goals.

Personal and family goals

Why do you want to be successful in business? What are the personal and family goals that drive you forwards? Do you want to be happily married with two children in private school? Do you want a beautiful home in the country? Do you want a trip around the world, an expensive motor car, status, admiration, your own private swimming pool? By focusing and concentrating on these goals, defining them with crystal clarity, and setting deadlines for their achievement, you will stimulate your own creativity.

> ## GOALS
> Set personal and family goals.
> Set business/career goals.
> Set personal development goals.
> Stimulate your creativity.

'The business of life is to go forwards.' – *Samuel Johnson*

4   STIMULATE CREATIVITY BY IDENTIFYING ROCKS

What are the rocks that stand between you and achieving your desired goals? What are the limiting factors? What are your self-limiting beliefs? What are the negative emotions which are holding you back? There are always obstacles which stand between an organisation and the achievement of its goals. There are always obstacles which stand between you and achievement of desired results.

By facing up to the rocks, with a great deal of self-honesty, we can stimulate our creativity. What are the obstacles that stand between the organisation now and its ideal future? Define the ideal future, i.e. goals, and then identify the rocks. Use your creativity either to overcome the rocks or avoid them. What is the factor which is limiting the organisation in achieving its goals. Is it lack of finance? Is it lack of leadership? Is it lack of a coherent strategy? Is it failure in marketing, selling, negotiating, people-skills? Is it lack of focus, poor advertising, poor human relations, lack of information, failure to maintain competitive advantage? As a manager, what are your own self-limiting beliefs? Do you believe that you are incompetent in leadership, in marketing, in selling, in negotiating, in strategy? Do you feel that you cannot achieve more because you are inadequately qualified, because you did not go to university, or perhaps because you are a woman? Which negative emotions are holding you back? Is it an inability to accept responsibility, a propensity to blame others for your condition, envy, self-pity, fear of failure, fear of rejection, jealousy, anger or self-doubt? Use your self-honesty and

Identify the then your creativity to change your self-limiting beliefs
rocks that stand and overcome negative emotions. Negative emotions can
between you be replaced with the positive emotions of excitement,
and success. enthusiasm, love, joy and acceptance of responsibility.

These positive emotions can be stimulated by clear goals. Focus and concentrate on what you want. Focusing on your desires stimulates positive emotions and creativity.

'The individual who is able to perceive a glimmer of possibility in a situation that seems, at first glance, full of insurmountable obstacles, is the one most likely to reap the greatest benefits.'
– *John Paul Getty*

---

5   CREATIVE AND UNCREATIVE THINKING

Mechanical thinking

Do you tend to see things as either black or white? Are you inflexible in your thinking? Are you generally pessimistic? Do you have fixed attitudes? Do you tend to blame others for your condition? If you do tend to indulge yourself in this kind of mechanical thinking, then you will also tend to be uncreative. Make the necessary efforts to change your thinking.

'For most people, thinking is just a re-arrangement of their prejudices.' – *William James*

Adaptive thinking

Do you tend to have an open mind on most issues? Are you flexible in your thinking? Are you generally optimistic? Is your thinking solution-oriented rather than problem-oriented? Do you generally suspend judgement until all the facts have been collected and analysed? Do you avoid attachment to one idea? If you can practise adaptive thinking rather than mechanical thinking, then you will be more creative. Do not take it personally if someone holds a different opinion from yours. Do not make a habit of justifying being exactly as you are. If you stay as you are, you stay where you are. The more you do of what you do, the more you get of what you have got!

'Criticism is never inhibited by ignorance.'
– *Harold Macmillan*

'Faced with the choice between changing one's mind and proving there is no need to do so, almost everyone gets busy on the proof.' – *John Kenneth Galbraith*

6 I AM A CREATIVE GENIUS

Intelligence is a way of behaving. If you behave intelligently, then you are intelligent. Alternatively, if you behave as an idiot, then you are an idiot – even if you have a university degree. Your IQ is a measure essentially of your verbal and mathematical skills. There are many different kinds of intelligence, which are more relevant to success in business than verbal and mathematical skills, e.g. intuitive intelligence, social skills intelligence. Use the affirmation: 'I am a creative genius.' This will become part of your belief system. Once you believe that you are a creative genius, then the law of belief tells us that you will behave in a manner consistent with being a creative genius. The following four characteristics of genius can all be learned.

Clarity

Try to see the big picture. Try to identify causal relationships. Identify specific, measurable goals. Decision-making becomes much easier when the goal is clear. Be honest in identifying problems, rocks, negative emotions, self-limiting beliefs.

Focus and concentration

Focus on outcomes. Define the perfect outcome. Describe the perfect outcome. Focus and concentrate on the issue. All highly creative people have the ability to focus and concentrate on the issue. Avoid the butterfly mentality of those who consistently jump from one issue to another, resolving nothing. Make lists. Keep notes. Investigate all the possible routes.

Adaptive thinking

Avoid attachment to one idea. Be adaptive and flexible. Keep an open mind. Ask questions. Stand back and consider the ideas of others. Keep questioning your assumptions. Ask others who have faced the same problems. A different point of view from yours is not an attack on your integrity or ability.

'There is a natural opposition among men to anything they have not thought of themselves.' – *Barnes Wallis*

'When a fixed idea makes its appearance, a great ass also makes its appearance.' – *Nietzsche*

Use systematic methodology

Use the systematic methods of problem solving discussed in this chapter – the 20-idea method, the systematic method, brain-storming, finish the statement, the standard approach, lateral thinking and access the superconscious.

7   MAKING A NEW START IN CREATIVITY

Creativity is a skill which can be learned and developed. We can all make improvements, especially in those areas which are closest to us. Make a start as below.

1   *Desired goals.* Begin to focus and concentrate on achievable goals within a specific time period.
2   *Urgent problems/challenges.* Identify your most pressing problems/challenges, and focus and concentrate on those issues.
3   *Use focused questions.*
    • How can we increase sales by 25 per cent over the next three months?
    • How can we reduce our heating costs by 15 per cent?
    • How can we improve our customer care?
    • How can we make our advertising more effective?
    • In any situation what are our assumptions?
4   *Start being adaptive/flexible.* Make a habit of saying: 'I was completely wrong on that occasion'; 'I changed my mind completely'; 'I don't know anything about that'; 'I need a great deal of help in this area.'
5   *Bombard your mind.* Bombard your mind with the information which is consistent with being highly creative. Read books, listen to tapes, attend courses, and most of all, spend time with people who are creative. Form a mastermind alliance of creative people. We are very much influenced by the people around us, our reference group. If you spend time with very creative people, this will encourage you to be creative.

8   USE THE THREE TIERS OF THE BRAIN

The brain seems to be divided into at least three sections: the conscious, the subconscious and the superconscious. The conscious mind is where our daily thinking takes place in making decisions and trying to solve problems. The conscious mind can call up ideas, experiences and beliefs from the subconscious which is where all our experiences and beliefs are stored. The subconscious operates 24 hours a day and can handle any number of problems. One way to stimulate creativity is to consider all aspects of a problem, and then ask the subconscious to find the answer by 3 p.m. the following Friday, i.e. sleep on it! The subconscious can be used to solve problems or rise to challenges or instructions from the conscious mind.

The superconscious mind has access to knowledge and experience beyond one's own knowledge and experience. The superconscious is the source of creativity, excitement and intuition. The superconscious mind is stimulated by clarity, strong desire, solitude and strong emotions. It is maintained by some people that any desire that can be transmitted to the superconscious must be brought into reality by the superconscious mind.

Focus and concentrate on your crystal-clear goals. Drive those goals into the superconscious. Desire to achieve your goals in life. Reflect in solitude on goals, problems, challenges, opportunities. Drive a great deal of emotion into your desires. The superconscious will reward you with blinding flashes of the obvious, the people, information, and circumstances required to achieve your goals, and unexpected chance events which will enable you to get the results you require. Remember that any goal or desire which you can drive into the superconscious must be brought into your reality.

9   CREATIVE THINKING ALTERNATIVES

We do not all think in exactly the same way. Some people think in pictures, others in words, others depend on their emotions. Faced with a problem/challenge, those who visualise tend to draw or map out the possible solutions. They conclude: 'it looks good to me.' Those who think auditorially talk through the various alternatives, using words, and conclude 'this sounds like a good idea.' Those who think kinaesthetically rely on their feelings about a situation and conclude: 'I feel this is the right way forward.'

In order to stimulate our creativity, we should each approach the same situation by trying to draw solutions, work out solutions in words, and examine our emotional responses to situations. We should also try to understand that we may be able to see an answer, but others need to have it spelt out in words. Try not to be too hard on those who cannot see or even work out the answer verbally. Some people need to feel it is the right way forward. You can stimulate your creativity by trying an approach which does not come easily to you.

10   THE STANDARD APPROACH TO PROBLEM-SOLVING

Faced with a problem, many people do not know what to do. Those who think they know what to do often stick to the one obvious solution. Many of us suffer from identification in that we take it very personally if somebody offers an alternative. Many of us continue to justify making the same mistakes we have always made. The following standard approach solves many problems:

1   Define the problem with great clarity. Simply defining the problem precisely is believed to solve about 50 per cent of problems.

> **PROBLEM-SOLVING**
> It's a challenge/opportunity.
> Keep defining the problem.
> Most problems are solved by clear definition.

'A problem is a chance for you to do your best.'
– *Duke Ellington*

---

2   Collect information. Collect all the facts together, not just the convenient facts. Avoid identification, i.e. taking it personally if some of the facts do not fit with preconceived solutions. Practise detachment, i.e. separate people from the problem. Detach yourself from the personalities involved, and focus on the problem.

3   Ask others for advice. Tap into the creative genius of others. Tap into the experience of others. Do not be afraid to ask your way to success.

4   At first, try to find the conscious solution. If a conscious solution cannot be found, then feed all the information into the subconscious/superconscious sections of the brain. Demand a solution by 3 p.m. next Friday. Express the desire with great clarity, desire a solution with intensity, use solitude and put a tremendous amount of emotion into the desired goal. Wait for a blinding flash of the obvious.

5   Go through the problem, information, desired outcomes, etc., last thing at night before sleeping. The answer could appear in the middle of the night or first thing in the morning. If the answer occurs at 4.30 a.m., then catch the idea on a tape, or jot it down in a notebook. Always keep a notebook or a dictaphone at hand on journeys and at night. Many blinding flashes of the obvious will occur to you when you are extremely tired or fast asleep. You must catch the moment. The answer which is obvious at 4.30 a.m. may be unavailable at breakfast.

> **CATCH THE MOMENT**
> Always write down or tape record useful thoughts,
> new ideas, blinding flashes of the obvious.

11   ASK FOCUSED QUESTIONS

In business we face many problems/challenges/opportunities often associated with increasing sales, reducing costs and increasing profits. In any situation, we should ask a series of focused questions along the following lines:

1 What is the perfect outcome?
2 What exactly are we trying to achieve?
3 How are we trying to achieve the perfect outcome?
4 How else could we achieve the same result?
5 Is there a better way of achieving the same outcome?
6 What are our assumptions?
7 Could our assumptions be wrong?
8 What would be the effect if our assumptions are wrong?
9 Who else has faced the same problem?
10 What are the alternatives?
11 What do our competitors do?
12 Can we ignore the problem?
13 Has anyone else achieved a better result?
14 What mistakes have we made in the past?
15 What mistakes have others made in the past?

12   A ZERO-BASED APPROACH

A very simple way of looking to the future is to take what happened last year and add on a few percentage points. This approach has been found to be unsatisfactory in a dynamic economy. A different approach is to assume a zero base and then justify all future activities. One way of approaching zero-based thinking is to ask the question: 'knowing what we know now, would we ...?' For example, 'knowing what we know now, would we have launched this product?' If the answer to the question is 'no', then make a decision to drop that product and take the necessary action. Sell it, franchise it, close it down, but get rid of it.

• Knowing what we know now, would we have opened this department?
• Knowing what we know now, would we have entered into the joint venture?

- Knowing what we know now, would we have started legal proceedings?
- Knowing what we know now, would we have employed this person?
- Knowing what we know now, would we have entered into this relationship?

If the answer to any of these questions is in the negative, then make the necessary decision, take the necessary action, to bring the matter to a close.

13   SOLVING PROBLEMS USING THE SYSTEMATIC METHOD

- How can we increase sales by 25 per cent over the next six months?
- How can we make our advertising more effective?
- How can we gain an extra 5 per cent market share?
- How can we double our effectiveness in selling?

The systematic method is a very powerful tool in fighting off threats, solving problems, rising to challenges and taking advantage of opportunities.

1 Assume that there is a logical, workable solution and confidently expect that you will find the answer.
2 Use positive language, i.e. avoid the words 'threat' and 'problem', and use the words 'challenge' and 'opportunity'. At least use the word 'situation' which is neither positive nor negative.
3 Define the situation with great clarity. Make notes. Make lists. Make use of paper.
4 Identify and list all the possible causes of the problem. A great many problems are solved simply by identifying the causes.
5 List all the possible solutions, not just the obvious solutions, but all the solutions. Even after finding the right answer, make the necessary effort to find a second right answer. At this stage, focus and concentrate on the solution and stop focusing on the prob-

lem. Many people can never solve a problem because they insist always on talking about the problem. In fact, many people fall in love with their problems and seem at times to talk about nothing else. Winners focus on solutions, talk about the future, focus on opportunities. Losers fall in love with their problems, talk about the past and blame other people for their condition.

6 Make a decision or set a deadline for making a decision. Remember, making a decision is much better than making no decision at all. Indecisiveness is a major cause of stress and anxiety. Most problems are solved at this stage, but even if you only set a deadline, then the superconscious should come up with a solution at the appointed time.

7 Assign responsibility for taking the necessary action which will give the desired result. Only action gets results. Making a decision is not enough. Somebody must accept 100 per cent responsibility for taking the necessary action. Many problems remain unsolved because nobody takes the necessary action after a decision has been made.

8 Set a deadline by which the necessary action must be taken.

9 Take the necessary action. Only action gets results. In order to take action, we need to make decisions. In order to make decisions we need information. The sequence is: information–decision–action–results. A manager's job is to get results.

Use deadlines on yourself and others.

10 Inspect what you expect. What gets measured gets done. We must develop the habit of inspecting what we expect from other people. We must find a way of measuring the key result areas of employees. If it does not get measured, then it probably will not get done. When assigning responsibility for action to somebody else, this is delegation not abdication. As the manager or proprietor, you are still responsible for the result, even if somebody else is taking the appropriate action.

The answer to most problems, worries, anxiety, boredom is
PURPOSEFUL ACTION.

14   THE 20-IDEA METHOD (MIND-STORMING)

Of all the techniques for solving problems, rising to challenges, taking advantage of opportunities, the 20-idea method is probably the most powerful and most widely used. There are 20 ways of increasing sales by 25 per cent over the next six months; there are 20 ways of getting to work everyday; there are 20 ways of making our advertising more effective; there are 20 ways of doing just about anything. The key to using this method is to force yourself to come up with 20 ideas. Managers often find that ideas 17 to 20 are the best ideas. Clearly, you have probably already considered 1 to 6. These obvious ideas, which you have already decided are inappropriate, can be quickly dismissed.

There are 20 ways of achieving anything

You can use this method alone or in groups. This method is used by many wealthy and successful people.

1   Write down the problem/challenge/opportunity.
2   Generate 20 possible answers. Force yourself to go the distance and create 20 solutions; not 10, not 16, but 20. It is usually the last few ideas which are the best ones.
3   Select the appropriate answer and take immediate action.

> **THERE ARE 20 WAYS IN WHICH YOU CAN:**
> improve quality (better)
> improve on price (cheaper)
> make buying easier (faster)
> improve customer relations (nicer).

15   BRAIN-STORMING

> **TAP INTO THE CREATIVITY OF OTHERS**
> Thousands of businesses have been transformed
> by ideas from employees.

> 'Many ideas grow better when transplanted into another mind than in the one where they sprang up.'
> – *Oliver Wendell Holmes*

Many companies use this method on a regular basis to achieve goals and solve problems. Quality circles meet on a regular basis to improve quality, solve other specific problems and rise to other specific challenges.

1   The group should consist of four to eight people meeting in a spirit of co-operation.
2   Define the question/problem with clarity, e.g. how can we increase sales by 25 per cent over the next six months?
3   The group should be given 50 to 60 minutes to generate a recommendation.
4   The leader should encourage the group in the first instance to generate as many ideas as possible. Quantity is more important than quality at this stage.
5   Every idea must be recorded by the facilitator/leader.
6   The leader should allow no criticism or ridicule of ideas.
7   The appropriate decision should be made selecting the best course of action which may well be a superconscious solution from one of the participants.
8   Assign responsibility, set a deadline, and take the necessary action as listed earlier under section 13.

USE QUALITY CIRCLES
to exploit opportunities
to rise to challenges
to improve situations
to solve problems
to overcome threats.

> 'A good idea is the enemy of a better one. You stop looking for alternatives.' – *Tudor Rickards*

16   FINISH THE STATEMENT
(ORGANISED BRAIN-STORMING)

One of the most effective ways of generating ideas is to make statements which need to be finished.

- We could double our sales over the next 12 months if ...
- We could reduce our distribution costs by 15 per cent if ...
- We could double our profits next year if ...
- We could reduce the time it takes to grant a loan by 15 per cent if ...
- We could double car-parking facilities if ...
- We could get 50 per cent more output from our existing facilities if ...

The results of this simple technique can be astonishing. We are forced to be creative. We come up with superconscious solutions. The technique can be very powerful used with small groups of people.

> **FINISH THE STATEMENT:**
> I could be successful in business if ...

17   LATERAL THINKING

Instead of trying to solve the same old problem using the same old method, why not try a completely different approach? Why not *step out of the box*?

Reversal

Instead of thinking of the problem as a problem, think of it as an opportunity. An opportunity is something from which we benefit. What benefits can we generate from this situation? How can we use this situation to increase sales, reduce costs, increase profits? Losing your biggest customer sounds like a major problem. It is really an opportunity to demonstrate that you can replace that customer with three new customers of equal size to the greater benefit of your business.

> You have just lost your job. Your husband has walked out on you – with your best friend and the kids. The house has burned down and your insurance policy has lapsed. The company keeps the car.
>
> • Write down 20 reasons why this is the best sequence of events that ever happened.
> • Write down 20 lessons that you have learned from this experience.
> • It's a challenge, an opportunity.
> • It's not a threat or a problem.

Random association

'Our business is like a tree because ...', 'Our business is like an apple because ...', 'Our business is like a fairground because ...', 'Our business is like a motorway because ...', 'Our business is like a helicopter because ...', etc. This mind-stimulating exercise allows us to see the business in a completely different light. It stimulates our creativity. We make mental connections which we are not in the habit of making.

Shift the dominant idea

We are often asked the question: 'why should only ten per cent of the market buy our product?' We could ask a different question: 'why should 90 per cent not buy our product?' Instead of asking the question: 'how can we increase sales by 25 per cent over the next six months?', we could ask the question: 'what action would we have to take for us to lose 25 per cent of our sales during the next six months?' Doing the complete opposite of what we would have to do to lose sales helps us to generate ideas about what we should do to win sales.

> We have been advising a supermarket chain which has only 2–3% market share. They keep asking the question: 'How can we increase our market share to 4, 5, 6%?' This has proved to be a tough question. We recently asked the same question, but in a different way: 'Why do 97–98% of housewives not shop at your store?' Managers immediately respond: 'because our stores are pretty unpleasant places to be, we do not carry a wide enough range of products, and we simply do not have enough stores to cope with 5–6% market share.' Our advice to the company is to make it a more pleasant shopping experience, carry a wider range of products, and open more stores.

Argue the case for the opposition

If only lawyers would learn to do this, there would be far fewer appearances in court. Use your creativity to generate an argument from the point of view of the competition or adversary. This gives greater understanding of the situation and can tell us exactly what we must do to win.

Fantasise

Instead of trying harder and harder to solve the problem, ask the question: 'if I could wave a magic wand in this situation, what would be achieved?' By fantasising, waving the magic wand, visualising the perfect outcome, we can use our creativity to find a way forward. We can imagine that the problem is already totally solved and then ask the question: 'how did we actually get to this perfect solution?'

18   ASK INNOVATIVE QUESTIONS

Stimulate your creativity by asking innovative questions relating to marketing, selling, etc. If our customers are buying products A, B, and C, which D, E, F products can we add to our product list? Which additional benefits can we provide for our existing customers? Where can we find additional customers for our present benefits? Can we put our existing products to other uses? How can we creatively imitate our competitors? Can we develop our product to make it more attractive? Can we reduce our product to make it more attractive? Can we make a substitute for our existing product? Can we combine our product with another product? How can we change our existing product to make it look like something else? Which additional products do our competitors sell?, etc.

Stimulate your creativity by asking innovative questions.

19   SOURCES OF INNOVATION

Unexpected events

Surprise events can lead to the demand for new products/services.

Incongruity

New products sometimes occur when the search for an answer to one problem results in the unexpected. The unexpected discovery can be a new product which results in benefits for customers.

Process need to overcome difficulty

Innovation sometimes becomes necessary when an organisation or an individual hits a rock which appears to prevent the achievement of a desired result.

Change in industry structure

When a major industry has to change its products, this can lead to lots of spin-offs for other businesses, e.g. the move towards smaller cars.

Demographic changes

The fact that people move in numbers from one area to another means that there is increased demand for all sorts of products/ services in the newly-occupied territories.

Changes in values

Changes in customer values necessitate innovation, e.g. the move away from meat products to vegetarian products.

New knowledge

Research and development provides a constant stream of new knowledge. From this knowledge, new products in which customers see a real benefit can emerge. When managers find these sources of innovation, they should ask the question: 'how can this situation be used to produce benefits for which customers are willing and able to pay?'

20   NEW IDEAS

The world is full of new ideas. Very few of these ideas are ever turned into profitable products. When faced with new ideas, we should adopt the following approach:

1 Define clearly what the idea is.
2 What is the benefit it produces?
3 What does it do?
4 What does it cost?

5 Does it make at least a ten per cent difference to customers?
6 Why should anybody buy this benefit from me?
7 What else could produce exactly the same benefit?
8 What does the alternative cost?
9 How will our competitors react?
10 Will it do the job it is intended to do?
11 Is it at least ten per cent better than the existing alternative?
12 Is it a significant improvement?
13 Is it compatible with human nature?
14 Would you recommend it to your family and friends?
15 Would you buy it yourself?
16 Is anybody prepared to be a product champion for this product/ service?
17 Is it too soon for this product, or is it too late for this product?
18 Is it worth the expense?
19 Will people understand it? Can the benefit it provides be easily summarised in 20 words?

21   BENEFITS FOR CUSTOMERS

Remember that we are all in business to provide benefits for customers – at a profit. We are not in business to make products and provide services. The world is full of products and services in which customers see no benefit and for which they are neither willing nor able to pay. Benefits that customers seek include an increase in self-esteem, new knowledge, companionship, additional wealth, success, power, influence, self-expression, better health, better relationships, social status, popularity, self-actualisation, recognition, admiration, prestige, security, safety, self-preservation, a decent meal, a good laugh and excitement.

Everything starts with ideas.

Remember that customers are lazy, ignorant, selfish, greedy, impatient, disloyal, ruthless, irresponsible, unreliable and vain. Use your creativity to generate benefits which are consistent with customer characteristics.

CREATIVITY IS THE ABILITY TO IMPROVE.
CREATIVITY IS A SKILL.
USE THE IDEAS AND TECHNIQUES IN THIS CHAPTER
TO STIMULATE YOUR CREATIVITY.
SEEK AND YE SHALL FIND.

'Imagination is more important than knowledge.'
– *Albert Einstein*

Two

YOU CAN HAVE IT IF YOU WANT IT

How to set and achieve your goals

Success is achieving one's goals. To become successful you have to set clear goals. Winners set goals, losers don't! The very small number of people who set believable goals are the same very small number of people who become successful. These successful people use the mental laws which prevail in the world of achievement to get what they want. You can join them!

'Men are born to succeed, not to fail. – *Henry David Thoreau*

> A manager's job is to get results in a world of constant change.

1   SUCCESS IS GOAL-SETTING

Anybody can have a Rolls-Royce. Set it as a goal. The people who set goals are the people who become successful. Set goals for your career, set goals for your own self-development and set goals for your private life. Think ahead at least three years into the future. Set five goals for your business career. In an ideal world, in which business would you like to bring benefits to customers? What is your area of excellence? For which products are you prepared to be a product champion? What is it that makes you feel valuable and worthwhile? What is your core business? What position would you like to hold in three years' time in that business? What will be your salary? How many people will be working for you? If you choose to be self-employed, what will your sales and profits be?

The people who set goals are the people who become successful.

Set five goals for your personal development. The reason why you do not hold that position in that business at the moment is that you are not prepared for it. You have not learnt the skills, paid the necessary price in advance. If you were ready for that position, you would already have it. Be honest with yourself. Self-honesty is one of the key ingredients of happiness. Do you need to learn creative skills, goal setting, strategy, marketing, sales skills, negotiation skills, leadership skills, finance, time-management? Make a decision to learn the skills you need to achieve that job, in that industry, earning that amount of money. Remember three years from now somebody will hold that position. That somebody could be you, but you must acquire the necessary skills and be very positive in your attitude. Make a decision to launch your own business and achieve your desired level of sales and profits.

By setting goals you become a different person from the person you used to be who did not set goals.

Finally, set at least five personal goals. Why do you want to be successful in your career? What are your personal and family goals? Do you desire admiration, respect, a house in the country, a happy family, two children in private education, happy relationships with friends and family, travel, a yacht, an expensive motor vehicle? Set at least five personal goals you will achieve in the next three years.

The meaning of life is to enrich the lives of others.

This is a challenging exercise. It requires self-knowledge and courage. Remember, whatever goals you write down you can have, provided you believe it, you are prepared to set it as a goal, and you are prepared to pay the necessary price in advance. Unfortunately, you always have to pay the price for success in advance. You have to make the necessary efforts to learn the skills, be positive and take the necessary action. Collecting information is important, making decisions is important, but only action gets results. A manager's job is to get results. Your job is to achieve the results you desire.

Never use time as an excuse.

"Heaven never helps the individual who will not act."
– *Sophocles*

Write down your goals. Make lists. Be very clear as to exactly what you desire. Clarity always defeats vagueness. Review your goals every day. Mentally rehearse achieving your goals. Mentally rehearse the great joy of your success.

"The discipline of writing something down is the first step toward making it happen." – *Lee Jacocca*

---

2   WHAT SUCCESS MEANS TO YOU

One important part of your journey towards self-knowledge is discovering what is important to you. What do you want out of life? Many people have suggested that the following are the ingredients of success:

1   *Happiness/peace of mind.* Peace of mind is top of the list for many
    people. This includes freedom from fear, freedom from worries,
    freedom from ill-health, freedom from any kind of limitation,
    from financial troubles, etc. It is the feeling that you are the
    master/mistress of your own destiny, a feeling that you are in
    control.
2   *Excellent health.* Many people put excellent health at the top of
    their list. Health is energy, not fitness. If you have a tremendous
    amount of energy, then you are extremely healthy. Your birth-
    right is to enjoy lots of energy, excellent health. Your body has a
    natural bias towards health.
3   *High quality of loving relationships.* Those of us with families
    understand that we would not sacrifice our loving relationships
    for all the money in the world. This is perfectly natural. Enjoy-
    ing excellent relationships with family and friends is an essential
    ingredient of human happiness.
4   *Adequate finance.* Many people assume that money equals hap-
    piness. This is clearly not the case since many people place a
    much higher value on their health and the quality of relation-
    ships than on the amount of wealth they hold. Nevertheless,
    money is important. We all need to feel that we have enough
    money not to worry about money.

'Happiness seems to require a modicum of external prosperity'
– *Aristotle*

---

5   *Worthy goals.* As human beings we all need to feel that what we
    are doing is important. As managers and business people we
    must strive to work in those areas which make us feel valuable
    and worthwhile. The extent to which an individual feels valuable
    and worthwhile is known as 'self-esteem'. Success is highly cor-
    related with high self-esteem. Unfortunately, millions of people
    are doing jobs which they themselves believe are unworthy,
    unsatisfying and undemanding.

6   *Self-knowledge.* We all need to go on a journey of self-knowledge to discover our desires, our needs, our goals. What is your area of excellence? What is your self-concept level of income? What is it that makes you feel valuable and worthwhile? What do you need to include in your personal development plan? How much money do you really want?

'We do not deal much in facts when we are contemplating ourselves' – *Mark Twain*

---

7   *Self-fulfilment.* To what extent are you fully stretched in your career? To what extent are you fully stretched in striving to achieve excellent health, enjoy your relationships, earn your self-concept level of income, pursue worthy goals and discover who you are and what you want? The self-fulfilled person is the person who is fully stretched in striving to achieve worthy goals. Unfortunately, millions of people do not know what they want. Millions of people feel that they are stuck in comfort zones, and uncomfortable zones.

'You will give yourself peace of mind if you do every act of your life as if it were your last.' – *Marcus Aurelius*

One of the first steps we must all take to be successful is to accept responsibility for our condition. Accept 100 per cent responsibility for your health, for the quality of your emotional life, for the amount of money that you earn, for pursuing goals which are worthy of you, for finding out who you are and what you want, and for getting a tremendous feeling of satisfaction out of your life. All successful people accept responsibility for themselves. If you accept responsibility, then you must be in control. This is why throughout history people have claimed that you are the master, you are the mistress, of your own destiny. The key ingredients in health are positive mental attitude, diet and exercise. Accidents do happen, but you must accept responsibility for your level of energy. The only person who can adopt a positive attitude for you is you. The only person who can eat sensibly for you is you. The only person who can exercise regularly for you is you. The National Health Service can patch you up, but the National Health Service cannot adopt a positive mental attitude for you, diet, or exercise for you.

Whether you like it or not, you decide the extent to which you get along with other people. Whether you like it or not, you decide how much money you earn. The amount of money you earn is decided by the quality and quantity of what you do. At the same time, we all strive to earn our self-concept level of income. If you believe you are a £20,000 per annum person, then you will always earn close to £20,000. If you believe you are a £50,000 a year person, then you will do whatever is necessary to earn approximately £50,000 per annum. People who earn a lot of money are not necessarily more clever or more highly qualified than people who earn very little money. People who earn a lot of money offer a higher quality and quantity of benefits, and they have a higher self-concept level of income.

The only person in this world who can work out worthy goals for you is you. The only person in the world who can give you the self-knowledge you need to discover who you are and what you want is you. You are the only person in the world who can see to it that you are fully stretched in striving to achieve your goals. In short, you are responsible for achieving your own happiness, you are responsible for achieving your own peace of mind. You can blame other people for your condition, but this does not improve your condition. You can only improve your condition by accepting responsibility for yourself, setting clear goals, and then resolving to pay the necessary price in advance. Your success in life is determined by your knowledge and your attitude. Again, since you have **You cannot set** infinite capacity for learning and you can adopt as posi- **goals for other** tive or as negative an attitude as you wish, then you must **people.** accept responsibility for your own success or lack of it. In short, nobody else can be successful for you!

We stress the importance of a little courage and self honesty. So many men insist on pretending to be James Bond, Elvis Presley, James Dean and Eric Cantona. They will not accept responsibility for being the way that they are. A rich man spending time in prison for a drug offence observed that he was the only guilty person in the prison. Apparently, everybody else had been framed. It was not their fault. Of course, these people will always be criminals. They blame others. They refuse to change. They insist on staying as they are. Criminals can stop being criminals by having the self-honesty to recognise that what they have done is unacceptable, and then by making a decision to change. Unsuccessful people can become successful by having the courage and self-honesty to recognise that they have been held back by their own self-limiting beliefs, negative emotions, and imaginary rocks. Unsuccessful people can make decisions to change. You can change.

'Most people are about as happy as they make up their mind to be.' – *Abraham Lincoln*

'Look to your health: and if you have it, praise God, and value it next to a good conscience; for health is the second blessing that we mortals are capable of; a blessing that money cannot buy.' – *Izaak Walton*

'Money is better than poverty, if only for financial reasons.' – *Woody Allen*

'If you can actually count your money then you are not a really rich man.' – *John Paul Getty*

'He that will not apply new remedies must accept new evil; for time is the greatest innovator.' – *Francis Bacon*

'There is only one success – to be able to spend your life in your own way.' – *Christopher Morley*

> Happiness is striving to achieve your most desired goals

> Happiness is a journey from the person you are now (your self-image) to the person you want to be in the future (your self-ideal).

Why are so many people so unhappy? They are unhappy because they are not striving to achieve their most desired goals. They do not set goals. They will not define where they want to be in the future. They are not prepared to pay the price they must pay to achieve their goals. It is so much easier to watch television, go down the pub, and lose your tiny savings on the lottery. We are lazy creatures. This is the great tragedy of the human condition. Everybody wants to be more, have more, and do more, but members of the crowd cannot be more, have more, and do more because they are too lazy, ill-informed, self-ish, greedy, disloyal, impatient, ruthless, irresponsible, unreliable and vain. If we were designed by God, then we must conclude that she has a sense of humour (or that she enjoys our suffering).

3   I AM RESPONSIBLE

Most people blame their inadequacies on their education, their qualifications, the boss, the company, the economy, the government, their families, their friends, the neighbourhood in which they grew up. As human beings we are all geniuses at justification. We are all brilliant at justifying being exactly as we are. Unfortunately, once you justify being as you are, this becomes your excuse. You will probably hang on to the same excuse for the rest of your life. Unfortunately, the price we pay for justification is that we stay exactly as we are. If we do not change, but stay as we are, the penalty is that we stay where we are. If we want to move forward in life, then we have to change in some way.

I am responsible.
I am in control.

All successful people accept responsibility for themselves. They do not blame others for their condition. The only person who can learn to play the violin for you is you. The only person who can learn to speak Russian for you is you. The only person who can earn £50,000 per annum for you is you. If you accept responsibility, then you take control. You become the master, the mistress, of your own destiny. Accept responsibility for your level of energy, for adopting a positive mental attitude, for what you eat, and for taking regular exercise. Accept responsibility for the quality of your family life, for the amount of money you earn, for pursuing goals which make you feel valuable and worthwhile, for acquiring self-knowledge and self-fulfilment. Accept responsibility for setting goals and resolving to pay the price in advance. Accept responsibility for being creative, for setting goals, for implementing a successful business strategy, for implementing a successful marketing strategy, for being excellent at selling, excellent at negotiating. Accept responsibility for giving leadership, for understanding the financial implications of your activities, and managing your time in a manner consistent with achieving your goals.

Most people are extremely averse to change. Most people think about the pain of learning and taking the action which arises from the energy generated from being more positive. We encourage these people to think of the pain of not changing. Think about the pain of staying exactly as you are which means staying exactly where you are. Focus and concentrate on this pain for some time. For the rest of your life do you want the same job, the same money, the same recognition, same house, same car, same people in your life, same holidays, same negative emotions? Focusing and concentrating on all this pain should give you the will to strive for change.

Just imagine how great life will be when you change. Imagine the better job, greater satisfaction, better house, greater recognition, respect etc. Whenever you find yourself doing what you know you should not be doing, then think of the pain of staying as you are – same house, same relationships, job, income etc. Successful people are people who do what unsuccessful people know they should do but can't be bothered. There really is a reason for everything. When people do not have any money, then there are reasons for it.

Link that which you do not want with pain. Staying as you are is probably going to be very painful. Link what you do want with pleasure. When studying and forcing yourself to think more positively, focus on the pleasure of achieving your goals. It's easier to change yourself than change the world. Millions of people wish that the world would change to accommodate them. It does not work.

'Nobody can make you feel inferior without your consent.'
– *Eleanor Roosevelt*

Is it worth making the effort? People are motivated by desire and fear. Once you have set your goals, ask the question: is it worth paying the price to achieve that which I desire? Are you prepared to pay the price to achieve that level of health, those wonderful relationships, that amount of money, etc.? Then ask a different question: can you afford not to pay the price? Do you want to stay as you are and where you are for the rest of your life – the same job, same salary, same house, same car, same colleagues. Perhaps this prospect will generate motivation from the fear of your life always being the same.

4 STOP MAKING EXCUSES

We all have to accept that wherever we are in life at the present time is a direct result of our knowledge/skills and our attitudes. If you want to be somewhere else three years in the future, then you must go to work on your knowledge/skills and your attitude. Stop making excuses. Make a decision to change. If you stay as you are, you stay where you are. Why is it that so many people stay many years in jobs which they dislike and find undemanding and unrewarding? The answer is simply that they stop learning and they hang on to the same attitudes which got them into those undemanding and unrewarding jobs in the first place. Even hard work is not enough. The more you do of what you do the more you get of what you've got. Working very, very hard at the job which you are doing right now will not lead to success in the future. If you want to earn more, then you have to learn more. If you want to have the job that you desire three years from now, then you have to change your attitude and go to work on a self-improvement plan.

Adopting a positive mental attitude will dramatically and very quickly increase your success rate. The good news is that attitudes can be changed in seconds. Most of us assume that to be successful you must be intelligent, be highly qualified, be good looking, be of sufficient height, have a great deal of luck, have excellent connections, and be in the right place at the right time. These factors have been studied over many years and have been found to be irrelevant to success in general and success in business in particular.

We all suffer from self-limiting beliefs and negative attitudes. Go to work on your self-limiting beliefs. We think that we can't ride a bike, can't sell, can't be creative, can't do presentations, can't understand marketing, can't develop our leadership skills, can't understand strategy, can't understand the financial implications of our actions. These are simply examples of self-limiting beliefs. Question your beliefs about yourself. Your beliefs are not based on reality. They are based on all sorts of strange ideas which have been planted in your mind over the years either by others or by yourself. You can remove your self-limiting beliefs immediately if you make the necessary effort. Negative emotions hold us back more than anything else. Most people adopt a very negative attitude. They blame others for their condition. They feel that they do not deserve to be successful. They suffer from envy, hate, self-pity, worry, stress, anxiety, fear of failure and fear of rejection.

Make a tremendous effort to rid yourself of negative emotions. Try to substitute negative emotions with positive emotions. Focus and concentrate on the positive emotions of willingness to accept responsibility, being excited about what you do, being enthusiastic, having positive expectations about yourself and others, bringing joy and love to your work and others. Accept responsibility for setting goals and achieving them, and stop making excuses.

'Can't is a four letter word.' – *John Clements*

We recently experienced an investigation by the tax man. He told us, 'We always investigate people with Rolls-Royces.' Everything turned out to be satisfactory. As we were about to wave him farewell, he looked up the drive and said, 'You know, it does not matter how hard I work at my job in the Inland Revenue, I will never be able to afford a house like that or a car like that.' This is music to our ears. We asked him, 'Would you like to own a house like that and a car like that?'. 'Oh, yes. I'd do anything', he replied. We quickly established that his area of excellence is taxation. We suggested that he get out of the public sector, spend two years with a firm of accountants, discovering how they argue the case for the other side, and then set up his own tax planning advisory service. He immediately came up with three reasons (rocks) for not taking our free advice. 'Firstly', he said, 'I could not give up the pension scheme in which I have already accumulated 22 years' contributions. Secondly, if I go to work for a firm of accountants, I could be made redundant, something which will not happen in the Revenue. Thirdly, I think people should pay more tax, not less.' We reminded him that he did say that he would do anything. Of course, he was not prepared to leave his comfort zone, or change his attitude towards taxation.

We are all geniuses at inventing reasons why we cannot have what we really want. The answer is to set it as a goal, and resolve to pay the price in advance. If you are not prepared to pay the price, then you cannot have it – but you decide.

If you stay as you are, you stay where you are.

The world is full of people who are suffering because they refuse to change. Millions of people want to be rewarded in advance. Unfortunately, nature does not work that way. Nature requires that you pay the price of success in advance. Learn how to delay gratification. Do not reward yourself until you have achieved the desired result. Do not expect customers to reward you until you have improved their lives in the required way.

'To do nothing is in every man's power.' – *Samuel Johnson*

'You said "but." I've put my finger on the whole problem.
You're a "but" man. Don't say "but." That little word "but" is
the difference between success and failure.' – *Sgt. Ernie Bilko*

The meaning of life is to improve. In business, customers pay for improvements in their lives. You can improve your helath, your relationships, your self-knowledge, your self-fulfilment. You can start with something simple. You can improve your hair, your smell, your clothes, your garden, the state of your car, the way you conduct yourself, your attitude, your knowledge, and so on.

5   THE SUCCESS FORMULA

Many people make the incorrect assumption that their success depends on paper qualifications, general intelligence, height, connections, good looks, and the wheel of fortune. In fact, the two key determinants of human potential are knowledge and attitude. The success formula is as follows:

$$\text{Knowledge/skills} \times \text{attitude} = \text{results/performance.}$$

If you want to earn more you have to learn more and be positive. We all came into this world with infinite mental capacity, an infinite capacity for learning. We can all be creative, set goals, learn strategy, marketing, sales skills, negotiation skills, leadership, finance and time-management. We are all capable of becoming experts in our area of specialisation, our area of excellence. If we make the necessary efforts to study our area of excellence, take action, think about our results, question what we have learned and the actions we have taken, then we are ready to learn even more. Over a five-year period, we are all capable of becoming experts in our own chosen areas of excellence. We can all blame others for the extent of our knowledge, in particular our family and the educational institutions we attended. However, at the age of 18 we all become adults. From the age of 18 onwards we must all accept responsibility for our own learning.

Most people are very surprised to learn that our knowledge/skills probably account for less than 20 per cent of all the success we ever enjoy. The world is full of geniuses who cannot even earn a living. The world is full of geniuses doing jobs which they find undemanding and unrewarding. The staff common rooms of universities we have visited all over the world are full of geniuses who can barely earn a living. They fill their lives with negative criticism of others, they play bridge for 'only' two hours each day, they rush into coffee at 10.25 a.m. complaining that they had difficulty getting their cars parked, and you can never find them on Wednesday or Friday afternoons, or during the months of December, April, July, August and September. As for attitude towards customers, we thank one professor for the quote: 'Working in a university would be a good job if we did not have any students.'

The first recommendation we always make to universities is that all signs should be removed which read 'Staff parking only'. These should be replaced with signs which read 'Student parking only'. Can you use this idea in your business? Can you make the customer the focal point of your business? Attitude accounts for over 80 per cent of the success we enjoy. The good news is that attitudes can be changed in seconds. Positive mental attitude means being excited, enthusiastic, bringing love, joy and encouragement to situations.

Unfortunately, most of us love to indulge ourselves in the negative emotions of blame, guilt, fear of failure, fear of rejection, self-pity, anger, worry, self-doubt, hate, envy, etc. All positive emotions give us energy. All negative emotions drain us of energy. Although we would like to blame others for our condition, the simple fact is that you are the master, you are the mistress, of your own destiny. You can learn just about anything you want, and you can adopt any attitude you wish. An alternative but similar success formula is as follows:

Understanding × effort = results

A great deal of understanding multiplied by a low level of effort gives a very poor result. A limited amount of understanding multiplied by a great deal of effort gives much better results. Again, we all have infinite capacity for learning and we all decide the efforts we choose to make. The amount of energy we bring to a situation depends on the positive emotions of excitement, enthusiasm, etc. Whether you like it or not, the simple fact is that once you are an adult, you become master/mistress of your own fate. Once you are an adult, you can accept responsibility for your learning and your attitude. By accepting responsibility you take control.

We have all met people who are extremely well-read. They are often regarded as well-educated. They have qualifications. Unfortunately, many well-read people still hang on to their negative emotions – fear of failure, blame, self-pity etc. They also hang on to their self-limiting beliefs, and often have negative attitudes towards enterprise. They are also brilliant at imagining that rocks stand between them and their desires. If education does not change your behaviour, then what have you learned? If you enter the school system as a macho dickhead kid, and emerge ten years later as a macho dickhead grown-up, then what have you learned?

Unfortunately, politicians are in the habit of referring to schooling as 'education'. When they throw money at schooling, they call it 'investing in education'. We often try to figure out what we learned at school that changed our behaviour in adult life. We struggle. What do school teachers know? Did they teach you how to be successful in life, how to earn a living, how to make a marriage work, how to get along with other people, how to bring up children, how to be creative, set goals, implement a winning strategy, get the marketing right, be excellent at selling, excellent at negotiation, give leadership, understand the financial implications of your actions, manage your time well, get a mortgage, be more, have more, do more?

Unfortunately, the great majority of people stop learning when they leave school or university. Learning is a process which should continue throughout life. When you stop learning, you stop growing. If you stay as you are, then you stay where you are. The great news is that if you make the necessary effort to set those goals for your self development, business, and private life, then a whole series of mental laws will come to your assistance. People who set goals become successful. It's automatic!

'If you always do what you have always done, you will always get what you always got.' – *Ralph Waldo Emerson*

'It is not enough to have a good mind. The main thing is to use it well.' – *René Descartes*

Knowledge/skills × attitude = results
20%   80%   100%
Understanding × effort = results
20%   80%   100%

'The only good is knowledge and the only evil is ignorance.' – *Socrates*

'Life is like a ten speed bicycle: most of us have gears we never use.' – *Charles M. Schulz*

---

6   MENTAL LAW NUMBER ONE: THE LAW OF BELIEF

The fundamental law of human achievement is the law of belief. It postulates that you always behave in a manner consistent with your beliefs. If you believe you are a Roman Catholic, then you are a Roman Catholic. If you believe you are a Buddhist, you are a Buddhist. If you believe you can swim, you can swim. If you believe you can't swim, then you can't swim. Even if you can't swim, as long as you believe you can swim, then you will persist in failing until you can actually swim. Unfortunately, once you decide you can't swim, then you can't swim. Even though we are all capable of swimming, once you believe you can't swim, you can't swim. You suffer from the self-limiting belief that you just can't do it. Your belief is not based on fact, it is just a belief.

Nevertheless, even though our self-limiting beliefs are not based on fact, we always behave in a manner consistent with our beliefs. If you believe you can ride a bicycle, then you can ride a bicycle. If you believe you can't, you can't. If you believe you can drive a car, be creative, set goals, implement a successful strategy, implement a successful marketing strategy, sell well, negotiate, give leadership, understand the financial implications, manage your time well, etc., then you can master all these skills. Even if at the present time you have not mastered these skills, so long as you believe you are excellent at business skills, then you will make the necessary efforts. You will set goals and resolve to pay the necessary price. You will set career goals, design a personal development plan, and set personal and family goals.

Another vitally important aspect of the law of belief is that you can believe anything that you want to believe. You can believe that you are brilliant at marketing, selling, strategy, finance, time-management. You can believe that you are successful in business management. You can believe that you are a millionaire/millionairess. As long as you truly believe, then you will hang on to that belief, despite setbacks, until your beliefs become your reality. Your beliefs are your reality. Make a decision to adopt beliefs which are consistent with achieving your goals. All successful people have beliefs consistent with what they want to achieve. Join them! Make a decision to change your beliefs. The beliefs you hold at the moment are largely responsible for the position you hold at the moment. If you change your beliefs, then you change your reality.

Changing your beliefs about yourself, means changing your self-concept. Your self-concept is your bundle of beliefs about yourself. Make a decision to adopt the self-concept which is consistent with achieving your business and personal goals. Everything starts with ideas or thoughts. Thoughts and ideas become feelings which eventually become beliefs. Your beliefs have a powerful effect on your expectations. Your expectations have a powerful effect on your attitude. If you believe you are destined to become successful, then this has a strong effect on your expectations, which become very positive. Your positive expectations are translated into a very positive attitude. Your attitude is the major determinant of your success in achieving goals. Everything comes back to beliefs. Successful people have the beliefs of successful people, unsuccessful people have the beliefs of unsuccessful people. Make a decision to shake off self-limiting beliefs and negative emotions. Replace them with positive beliefs, positive expectations and positive emotions.

I always behave in a manner consistent with my beliefs. I can believe anything I want.

'Reality is created by the mind. We can change our reality by changing our mind.' – *Plato*

'They can because they think they can.' – *Virgil*

'You see things as they are: and ask "why?" But I dream things that never were: and I ask "why not?"' – *George Bernard Shaw*

'When dealing with people, let us remember we are not dealing with creatures of logic. We are dealing with creatures of emotion, creatures bustling with prejudices and motivated by pride and vanity.' – *Dale Carnegie*

'Whether you think you will succeed or not, you are right.' – *Henry Ford*

'The greatest pleasure in life is doing what people say you cannot do.' – *Walter Bagehot*

7   MENTAL LAW NUMBER TWO: THE LAW OF CAUSE AND EFFECT

This mental law is sometimes called the iron law of the universe or the law of sowing and reaping. As ye sow, so shall ye reap. The law of cause and effect tells us that nothing just happens. Everything happens for a reason. The most important application of this law is that in a mental world, thoughts are causes, and conditions are effects. If you want anything to happen in life, then think about it. Concentrate and focus on it. Thinking about it is the first step in making it happen. There has to be a reason why people buy your product/service. There are reasons why you are where you are right now. There have to be reasons why you will be somewhere else in the future. The most important reasons are your thoughts because thinking about something is the first step in making it happen.

Most people spend a great deal of time complaining about the conditions in their lives, but do not tackle the causes of these conditions. Complaining about the company, the boss, your spouse, your income, your health, the quality of your relationships, etc., is a national pastime. People fall in love with their suffering, talk about their suffering, focus and concentrate on their suffering, and inevitably draw even more suffering into their lives. Remember that thoughts are causes. Whatever you think about, you tend to draw into your reality.

The present conditions in your life are the result of thoughts you have thought in the past. Make the effort to focus and concentrate on your goals. Just thinking about your goals is an important step in bringing your goals into your reality. Think about the house you want, the salary you want, the position you would like to hold in the company, the weekly jog you would like to make, the goals you would like to pursue, the strategy you want to implement, the level of sales you would like to make, the deals you would like to negotiate, the admiration you want from other people, the mountain you would like to climb. You will never achieve anything unless you think about it. Make the first step in success by determining your goals, and then focusing and concentrating on those goals. Change your future by changing your thoughts. Successful people think about what they want. Unsuccessful people think about what they don't want.

We are told that in the Universe there is only matter and energy. Thoughts are energy. Thoughts are the start of making things happen. When we study the way in which people spend their lives, we find that their lives are a series of distractions from the main event. Most people do not even have a main event. Most of those who do have goals focus on distractions – the daily bad news, the daily good news, TV programmes, the public house, gossip. Most people's lives are a series of distractions from their major definite purpose.

EVERYTHING HAPPENS FOR A REASON
In a mental world thoughts are causes,
conditions are effects.
Your thoughts are your future.

'What you would not want done to yourself, do not do to others.' – *Confucius*

'We must believe in luck. For how else can we explain the success of those we don't like.' – *Jean Cocteau*

'Success is simply a matter of luck. Ask any failure.'
– *Earl Wilson*

8   MENTAL LAW NUMBER THREE: THE LAW OF ATTRACTION

The law of attraction postulates that there is an almost magnetic force which draws into our lives the information, circumstances and people in harmony with our dominant thoughts. If you think about increasing sales, then you automatically attract into your life the information, circumstances and people to assist you in increasing sales. Unfortunately, if you think about drugs then you automatically stumble across information relating to drugs, circumstances in which you can take drugs, and people who are prepared to push drugs in your direction. By focusing on your personal goals, business goals and your own self-development plan, you automatically attract into your life all the information required, the circumstances

I attract into my life people, circumstances and information consistent with my dominant thoughts.

and opportunities necessary to achieve your goals. Most important of all, you will attract into your life the people with the knowledge, experience, money and the positive mental attitude required to help you succeed. Serendipity means stumbling across exactly what you are seeking. If you are not looking for anything, serendipity will not work for you!

9   MENTAL LAW NUMBER FOUR: THE LAW OF CORRESPONDENCE

The law of correspondence postulates that the world we see around us is a reflection of our own thoughts. Each individual likes to believe that he or she sees reality. In fact, your beliefs are your reality. The outside world conforms to your inside world. Is Roman Catholicism the true faith, or is Islam the true faith? Is life full of opportunities, or are there no opportunities in life? Is Juventus the greatest football club in the world, or is it Manchester United? Your own truth is a reflection of your beliefs. Whatever you believe on the inside, you perceive as your reality on the outside. In order to change the conditions in your life, you must change your thoughts, you must change your beliefs. If you wish to be excellent at selling, then you must believe you are excellent at selling before you become excellent at selling. You must believe that you are excellent at communication before you become excellent at communication. You must believe that you can run your own business before you actually run your own business. You must believe you are a £50,000-per-annum person on the inside before you earn £50,000 per annum on the outside. You must believe you are a thin person on the inside before you become thin on the outside.

You can use this mental law to believe whatever is necessary on the inside before you achieve your goals on the outside. People do not like to use the word 'brainwashing'. The fact is that you are already brainwashed in that you already have a set of beliefs. These beliefs are not based on reality, they are just beliefs. Make the effort to feed into your mind the ideas, information, circumstances, people, books, tapes, courses, etc., to help you get what you want. As with many other people, you have probably spent many years feeding into your mind information, people and circumstances which have failed to get you what you want. Use visualisation, emotionalisation and affirmation to assist you in succeeding in the achievement of your goals.

Visualise the perfect outcome. See yourself at the helm of your beautiful yacht, see yourself driving the car you desire, see yourself winning the prize as best salesperson of the year. Many athletes use this version of mental rehearsal. You are simply rehearsing success in advance. Remember you have to be successful on the inside before you become successful on the outside.

**'The greatest revolution of our generation is the discovery
that human beings, by changing the inner attitudes of
their minds, can change the outer aspects of their lives.'**
– *William James*

Another kind of mental rehearsal involves emotionalisation. Imagine how good you would feel if you could swim, if you earned £50,000 per annum, if you could launch your own successful business, manage your time well, be brilliant at selling, be excellent at negotiation, be brilliant at strategy and marketing. Imagine how happy you would feel if you could achieve your personal and business objectives. As with visualisation, this kind of mental rehearsal drives the desire into the subconscious. Keep pictures in your diary of the beautiful home you would like, the car you desire, the magnificent body you would like to develop. Follow this visualisation with emotionalisation. Imagine how good you would feel if you achieved that home, that car, that level of business success. Mental rehearsal acts as a stimulant to success in the outside world.

Finally, use affirmations to change your beliefs. Whenever your subconscious hears the words 'I am', your subconscious knows that it is about to receive an important message. Your beliefs are stored in the subconscious. Many people tell themselves that they are lazy, stupid and undeserving of success in a competitive world. The subconscious accepts these messages as beliefs, and these low expectations people achieve very little in life. Use affirmations to drive beliefs into the subconscious. Tell yourself over and over again: 'I am creative, I set goals, I am brilliant at strategy, I am brilliant at marketing, I am brilliant at selling, I am brilliant at negotiating, I am a leader, I am a good listener, I am a high-expectations boss, I understand the financial implications, I am brilliant at managing my time, I am a loving, caring parent, I am a £50,000-per-annum person, I am a brilliant swimmer, I am a jogger, I am 11st 6lb, I am free from negative emotions, I am free from self-limiting beliefs, I am a non-smoker, I am punctual, I am a smart dresser, I am an intelligent business person, I am achieving my goals, etc.'. Successful people have positive affirmations, unsuccessful people have negative affirmations. Use visualisation, emotionalisation and affirmations to achieve your personal and career goals. People have difficulty in imagining how effective this is – until they give it a try!

> ## MENTAL REHEARSAL
> Visualise: see the perfect outcome.
> Emotionalise: imagine the feeling.
> Affirm: I am the best in the business.

'Immense power is acquired by assuring yourself in your secret reveries that you were born to control affairs.'
– *Andrew Carnegie*

'Pleasure lies in being, not becoming.' – *St Thomas Aquinas*

'The way to gain a good reputation is to endeavour to be what you desire to appear.' – *Socrates*

PAIN
You can never remove a remembered pain.
Whenever you remember something painful,
get into the habit of immediately replacing the painful thought
with an enjoyable, pleasant thought or experience.
Forget the pain.
Remember the pleasure.

10   MENTAL LAW NUMBER FIVE: THE LAW OF EXPRESSION

The law of expression postulates that whatever is impressed into your mind is expressed into your reality. In other words, all information fed into your mind has some effect. Nothing is neutral. Every idea or thought either drives you towards the achievement of your goals, or takes you away from the achievement of your goals, but nothing is neutral. Everything starts with ideas, thoughts, feelings. These are translated into beliefs, expectations, and finally positive or negative attitudes.

This extremely powerful mental law is very inconvenient for most people. Most people will fill their minds with over 20 hours of television every week. Millions of people spend many hours each week drinking alcohol with their friends. Millions of people spend several hours each week reading utter nonsense in daily newspapers. Millions of people spend hundreds of hours every year sitting in a motor car listening to Radio Idiot. These people tend to be low achievers. They don't have time to be successful. If you dramatically cut down the number of hours you spend watching television, the time you spend drinking, the time you spend listening to Radio Idiot, then you will have all the time in the world to focus on your personal development plan, your personal and career goals. Make a decision and a plan to read the books necessary to give you the information which will help you to achieve business success. Make a decision and a plan to attend the necessary courses. Make a decision to acquire the necessary educational tapes to play in the car.

AVOID:

television

wasting hundreds of hours driving

wasting time in public houses

newspapers

negative people.

'Learning, improving, growing … You can do it with cassettes!
– *Joel H. Weldon* (author of *Winning with Cassettes*)

Excellent tapes are available on marketing, strategy, time-management, selling, negotiating, creativity, etc. Most important of all, spend time with the people who can give you the information, knowledge, experience, the positive mental attitude required for you to be successful. Make a decision to bombard your mind with the books, courses, tapes and people which are consistent with what you want to achieve in life. Stop bombarding your mind with information, people and circumstances which are inconsistent with what you want.

The vast majority of people will achieve little in life because they bombard their minds with self-limiting beliefs, negative emotions, television, newspapers, radio, and they spend their time with other low achievers. We are all very much affected by other people around us, i.e. our reference group. We pick up their values, their beliefs, their expectations and their attitudes.

Attitude is the key determinant of success. If you want to be more creative, spend time with creative people. If you want to be brilliant at selling, then spend time with people who are brilliant at selling. If you wish to accumulate a great deal of money, then spend time with wealthy people. If you wish to be successful in business management, then spend time with people who are successful in business management. If you must get drunk, get drunk with high achievers! If you must behave badly, then behave badly with complete strangers, not with family, customers, employees, suppliers or your bank manager!

> ## RECOMMENDED:
> reading relevant books
> going on educational courses
> listening to/making tapes
> forming a mastermind alliance.

The law of expression can be used to put yourself in the top achievers in any area of human activity. Goal-setting immediately puts you in the fast track. You can use the law of expression to put yourself in the top one or two per cent in any area of human activity. Make a decision and take the necessary action to bombard your mind with the books, tapes, courses and the people consistent with being excellent in your chosen field. Implement a programme for continuous self-improvement. Develop a personal network. Fight off those self-limiting beliefs and negative emotions. Go to work on a positive mental attitude and keep learning, learning, learning. True learning leads to a change in behaviour. Keep programming your mind with new information. Take the necessary action to use that new information. Review the action that you take, and then ask more questions. When you ask more questions, then you are ready to programme your mind with more information from those books, tapes, courses and people.

If you keep adding to your knowledge and improving your attitude, then you will become more successful. There are always better things to do with your time than watching television, propping up a bar, listening to junk radio and spending time with low achievers. Bombard your mind with museums, stately homes, art galleries, theatres. Bombard your mind with educational books, inspirational poetry, uplifting paintings, top quality porcelain, beautiful furniture, the world's finest music, exhilarating scenery, interesting plays and operas, stimulating films, everything which inspires and makes us appreciate that life is precious and beautiful.

> Is the life you are leading now
> consistent with what you really want?
> Are you bombarding your mind
> with appropriate information?
> Are you putting yourself
> in the appropriate circumstances?
> Are you spending time with appropriate people?

'We are more than half of what we are by imitation. The great point is to choose good models and study them with care.'
– *Lord Chesterfield*

'He that walketh with wise men shall be wise: but a companion of fools shall be destroyed.' – *Proverbs 13:20*

---

11   ADDITIONAL MENTAL LAWS 6–17

Mental law number six: the law of expectations

In the world of achievement, we all get what we confidently expect. We do not achieve what we would like to achieve, we do not achieve what we try to achieve, we do not achieve what we wish we could achieve. We all achieve what we confidently expect to achieve. The good news is that you can confidently expect to achieve whatever you want to achieve. The higher your expectations, the more positive will be your attitude. Positive mental attitude is the key determinant of success. The vast majority of people suffer from very low expectations of themselves, of the people around them, of the company, of the government. These low expectations people are low achievers. Expect yourself to perform excellently. Confidently expect that those around you will perform at levels of excellence. As a manager, let people know that you confidently expect that they will perform at the highest level. Being a high expectations boss is one of the key skills in leadership. Make a decision to expect with confidence that you will achieve all your business and personal goals.

We all get what we confidently expect.

'It's a funny thing about life; if you refuse to accept anything but the best, you often get it.' – *W. Somerset Maugham*

Mental law number seven: the law of control

One of the characteristics of successful people is that they assume that they are controlling circumstances and events which will lead to success. Unfortunately, most people assume that their fate is decided by factors beyond their control – the economy, the company, the boss, the spouse, the schooling, the neighbourhood in which they grew up. The simple fact is that as an adult you have control over the ideas and information fed into your own mind. You have the power to feed into your own mind the knowledge/skills and the positive mental attitude required to achieve your full potential. Take control of your own life. Feed into your own mind the information, knowledge, skills and attitude required to be successful. Remember that knowledge and attitude are the two key determinants of success. Feed into your mind the courses, books, tapes, experiences and people necessary to achieve your goals. Use visualisation, emotionalisation and affirmations to be successful.

The only person who can acquire the necessary knowledge for you is you. The only person who can adopt the necessary positive mental attitude for you is you. You are the only person who can learn creativity, goal-setting, strategy, marketing, sales skills, negotiation, leadership, finance, and time-management. You decide your own level of energy/health because you decide whether or not to adopt a positive mental attitude, you decide what you eat and you decide whether you take regular exercise. You decide whether or not you get along with other people. You decide whether or not you pursue worthy goals. You decide whether or not you are fully stretched. You got yourself into that relationship, into that business, into that job.

If the situation is unsatisfactory, then you must take the necessary action to get the result you desire. Happiness is strongly associated with the feeling that you are the master/mistress of your own destiny. Be happy, achieve peace of mind by accepting responsibility for your own life and taking control. Once you accept responsibility, then you are in control.

If what is going on inside your head is exactly the same as what is going on inside Richard Branson's head, then you are where Richard Branson is. If what is going on inside your head is exactly the same as what is going on in side the head of the bin man, then you are where the bin man is. Everything depends on what is going on inside your own mind – knowledge and attitude.

> The only thing over which you need total control is
> what is going on inside your own mind.
> By a remarkable coincidence the only thing over which
> you have total control is what is going on inside your own mind.
> Is nature wonderful?
> So give yourself a head start.

Mental law number eight: the law of accumulation

Wherever you are in life right now is a result of the ideas, experiences and people you have accumulated in your life to date. Make a decision that as from today you will start accumulating the knowledge, attitude, experiences and people to help you achieve your goals. Creativity begets more creativity, money begets more money, knowledge begets more knowledge, positive mental attitude begets more positive mental attitude, success begets even more success. Unfortunately, ignorance begets ignorance, negativity begets more negativity, failure begets even more failure. Be honest with yourself. How many evenings of watching television have you accumulated? How many evenings propping up a bar have you accumulated? How many years of self-limiting beliefs and negative emotions have you accumulated? How many years have you accumulated of low expectations, fear of failure, fear of rejection, envy, hate and self-pity? Is all this accumulation consistent with what you really want? Make a decision right now to start accumulating the sensible diet, regular exercise, positive mental attitude, loving relationships, articles, books, tapes, experiences and the people consistent with achieving your goals. Make a decision to accumulate beautiful period furniture, beautiful books, paintings, metal work, arms and armour, sculpture, beautiful artefacts from the ancient world. We observe people who spend a fortune on new furniture. This is almost certainly worth nothing, once it is delivered to your home. As one antique dealer put it: 'If you can buy the antique one for the same price as the new one, then buy the antique!'. If you want to accumulate wealth, then get into the habit of accumulating artefacts which move forward in value. Would you rather lose £10,000 per annum on a new car, or acquire a classic car which will retain its value? You must accept responsibility for what you accumulate. By focusing and concentrating upon your own goals, you will also acquire mental toughness. You will stop envying the success of others. You will no longer care who drives more quickly than you do. You will not be destroyed by the insults of others. You know that you are a valuable and worthwhile person. When insulted, you can always ask the question: 'And how do you think I can improve myself?'.

Kaizen is a way of life. It is constant improvement. Keep asking these questions. How can I improve my home? How can I improve my furniture? How can I improve my paintings, my garden, my relationships, my knowledge, my attitude, my sales, my profits, my creativity, goal-setting, strategy, marketing, sales skills, negotiation skills, leadership skills, financial awareness, time-management? Everything can be improved – by at least ten per cent. If you constantly improve, then you will constantly accumulate.

Unfortunately, during the course of a working life of 40 years, most people accumulate just about nothing. Here are a few simple ideas which should ensure that you retire comfortably. Always buy a home that you can improve by extending the property, adding additional bedrooms and bathrooms, splitting into two or three units, building a larger house on the plot etc. Always buy antique furniture which should double in value every seven or eight years. New furniture is worth just about nothing the moment it is delivered to your home. Accumulate early porcelain, early jewellery, whatever gives you enjoyment and interest. Acquire paintings that can be restored and reframed, either as Old Masters or by listed artists. Invest in equities through your pension scheme, your contributions being tax deductible. Acquire bits of land strategically positioned between two or three neighbours. Accumulate classical rock music etc. Acquire classic cars with high mileage for very small amounts of money. The depreciation on new cars is, in our opinion, absolutely horrendous. How many times have we seen people driving round in new cars every five years, to end their careers with absolutely nothing.

What have you accumulated to date? Look around you. Have you accumulated the people, house, car, opportunities, which you desire? Have you accumulated self-honesty? Have you accumulated the lifestyle consistent with your self-concept, consistent with the life you would like to lead? Which information do you need to accumulate? In which circumstances do you need to put yourself – trade shows, discussion groups, seminars, colleges, universities, courses? Who are the people? Where are they? Make a decision to use the law of accumulation to accumulate that which you desire.

Mental law number nine: the law of concentration

The law of concentration postulates that the more you focus and concentrate on your goals, the quicker will your goals be achieved. Make a habit of reviewing your personal and career goals every day. Visualise, emotionalise and affirm every day. Look at pictures of the home, car or yacht you desire. Concentrate on the target sales, costs and profits of the business. Focus and concentrate on your personal development plan. This focus and concentration will activate the subconscious and the superconscious. You will draw into your life the information and people necessary to achieve your goals. Your thoughts are your future.

'The only reason some people get lost in thought is because it is unfamiliar territory.' – *Paul Fix*

'The true art of memory is the art of attention.'
– *Samuel Johnson*

'Memory is the treasury and guardian of all things.' – *Cicero*

'Concentration is my motto. First honesty, then industry, then concentration – *Dale Carnegie*

'The harder you work, the luckier you get.' – *Gary Player*

'Genius is one per cent inspiration, ninety-nine per cent perspiration.' – *Thomas A. Edison*

Mental law number ten: the law of reversibility

On planning for the future, the usual process is to ask the question: 'where are we now?'. The next usual step is to define the ideal future. Third, we devise a plan to get from where we are now to our ideal future. This is perfectly logical and satisfactory. However, there is a second approach. We can visualise the perfect outcome. Visualise winning the contract, visualise an excellent presentation, getting the job you want, driving the car you want, earning the amount of money you want, enjoying the house that you want, enjoying the family life you desire, achieving the level of fitness you desire. Focus and concentrate on the perfect outcome. Then, ask the question: 'how did I achieve this perfect outcome?'. By reversing the planning process, the steps you must take to achieve your goals are often revealed instantly. Imagine you are totally successful, then use your creativity, use the law of reversibility to identify the actions you must have taken to achieve your goals. Imagine you are totally successful, and that you have been asked to write the story of your success for a forthcoming film.

Mental law number 11: the law of substitution

The conscious mind can only hold one idea at a time. This is extremely convenient in the world of achievement. It means you can always remove a negative emotion with a positive emotion. You can always remove a self-limiting belief by replacing it with a positive belief. Many people complain that they cannot overcome their negative emotions or their self-limiting beliefs. One very simple and very effective technique is to focus and concentrate on your personal and career goals. Thinking about your personal and career goals fills you with the positive emotions of excitement and enthusiasm. You can use this excitement and enthusiasm to overcome self-pity, envy, fear of failure, fear of rejection, hate, anger, etc. Carry a photograph of the adult or child you love. You cannot think about how much you love that person and be angry at other motorists at the same time. You cannot think about that beautiful house, wonderful car, or that yacht you desire and indulge in negative emotions at the same time. You can always remove a negative thought with a positive thought. Use your self-knowledge to recognise your self-limiting beliefs and your negative emotions, then use your goals to remove those negative emotions and self-limiting beliefs from your thinking. With practice, it becomes a new habit. You will spend a great deal of your time thinking about what you want. Take a good look into the face of Richard Branson.

Mental law number 12: the law of habit

Successful people have the habits of success; failures have the habits of failing. As adults, almost everything we do is habit. We are already in the habit of indulging ourselves in negative emotions and self-limiting beliefs. If we stay as we are, then we will stay where we are. If we wish to move forwards, then we have to learn new habits. The habits of success include acquiring the knowledge/skills required to achieve our goals and adopting a positive attitude. Make a decision that as from today you will make the necessary efforts. If you want something, make a decision to set it as a goal and resolve to pay the necessary price in advance. The price you will have to pay is the acquisition of the knowledge and the adoption of positive mental attitude. Make a habit of thinking about what you want – the achievement of your goals. You will find that you will gradually suffer less from envy, hate, road rage, the negative criticism of others. You will develop mental toughness.

Mental law number 13: the law of emotion

The law of emotion postulates that the stronger your desire to achieve a goal, then the more quickly it will be achieved. Put a great deal of desire into your visualisation, emotionalisation and affirmations. Avoid using the words 'try' and 'wish'. 'I wish' means 'I can't.' 'I wish I could give up smoking' means 'I can't give up smoking.' Yet how often do we hear people say 'I wish I could earn more money', 'I wish I could get a better job', 'I wish I could lose weight', 'I wish the boss would be more pleasant towards me.' 'I'll try' means, 'I am almost certainly going to fail.' How often do we hear people say, 'I'll try and get there on time', 'I'll try and finish that report by Friday', 'I'll try for promotion.' The expectation is, 'I won't succeed.' Use the expression: 'I am.' 'I am a non-smoker', 'I am always punctual', 'I am a £100,000-per-annum person.'

PROGRESSION

1 I wish I could launch my own business, earn more money, learn more, be more positive, have better friends, take more exercise, do something valuable with my life, understand myself, be fully stretched, read books, attend courses, listen to educational tapes, stop watching television.

Remember 'I wish' means 'I can't'.

2 I'll try to launch my own business, earn more money, etc.

Remember 'I'll try' is advanced notice of failure.

3 I am launching my own business, earning more money, etc.

'I am' is a belief. Drive it into the subconscious by repeating it over and over again with great intensity until it becomes a belief.

Your beliefs are your reality.

Call it 'brainwashing' if you wish. Alternatively, call it 'making my beliefs consistent with my self-ideal'.

Mental law number 14: the law of superconscious activity

The law of superconscious activity has several other titles including the law of cosmic understanding. It postulates that any thought, wish, desire or goal which you can hold consistently in your mind must be brought into your reality by your superconscious. The superconscious mind has access to knowledge and experience beyond your own knowledge and experience. It is the source of innovation, creativity, excitement and blinding flashes of the obvious. This powerful and controversial third stage of the brain exists beyond the conscious and subconscious. The superconscious responds to clarity, strong emotion or desire, authority and positive affirmations. It is activated by solitude and concentration. Spend one hour sitting quietly in the countryside focusing and concentrating on any problem, challenge or goal, and the superconscious will yield a complete solution.

The superconscious mind is also stimulated by strong visualisation, strong positive affirmations, day-dreaming and meditation. The superconscious does not give clues; it gives 100-per-cent answers, 100-per-cent solutions. Nobody really believes it until they try it!

Strong desire is important in goal-achieving. Do you sincerely want to achieve your target levels of income and wealth? Do you sincerely want to achieve your ideal weight? Do you sincerely want to be the best in the business? Do you sincerely want that yacht, that house, that Jaguar car?

Clarity is also extremely important. You don't just want a Jaguar car. You want the Westminster blue one with the doeskin interior, three years old, one lady owner with 32,000 miles on the clock. In response to desire, clarity, positive affirmations, concentration, solitude and visualisation, the superconscious will generate blinding flashes of the obvious. You must catch the moment. Keep a notebook or tape recorder with you at all times. That which is obvious at 4.30 a.m. will not be available to you at 9.30 a.m. Ideas in creativity, innovation, poetry, music, answers to problems and challenges, must be captured when they occur. Otherwise they may not subsequently be available for recall.

'The memory is always present; ready and anxious to help – if only we would ask it to do so more often.' – *Roger Broille*

"When mind is comprehended, all is comprehended.' – *Buddha*

Mental law number 15: the law of compensation

In life, we all get rewarded for what we do. We all get rewarded in direct proportion to the quantity and quality of service we give to others. If you want to increase your financial rewards, then you must increase either the quality or the quantity of what you do for other people. Increasing the quantity will make some difference. You can work longer hours, sell more, produce more. However, given your present level of skills, and your existing attitude, you will not usually greatly improve your condition by working harder at what you are doing at the present time. Remember the more you do of what you do, the more you get of what you've got! If you wish to improve your circumstances to a great extent, then you must improve the quality of what you do. You must increase your skills and/or be more positive.

The market pays a premium price for a premium product/service, an average price for an average product/service, and a low price for a poor quality product/service. Very few people understand this. Most people would just like to be paid more money for doing exactly what they are doing at the present time, preferably for an even shorter working week. They do not understand that it is what you do before 9 a.m. and after 5 p.m. that makes a difference. They do not understand that to earn more you have to learn more, to be more successful you have to go to work on positive mental attitude, i.e. accept responsibility, encourage others, be excited and enthusiastic. They do not understand that our commitment to help others depends on the self-concept. They do not understand that they must increase their value to the business. They do not understand that we all get rewarded for what we do for others. They do not understand the law of compensation.

We all get rewarded for the quality and quantity of what we do for other people.

Fight the comfort zone. Make a habit of stepping out of the box. If you want to be rewarded for your time, then your are doomed to work for an hourly rate. Your are doomed to work for peanuts. If you expect to be rewarded for your qualifications, then you are doomed to earn in the average range. If you expect to be rewarded for your experience, then you are doomed to laziness and low achievement. These are all comfort zones. Millions of people settle for the comfort zone. High achievers get rewarded for results. High achievers expect to be rewarded for the quality and quantity of what they do to improve the lives of others in a competitive world.

Mental law number 16: the law of reciprocity

The law of reciprocity postulates that as human beings we tend to want to help those who help us. You are not a go-getter, you are a go-giver. Help other people to get what they want. Encourage others. Offer people the information, advice, circumstances and introductions to people to help them to achieve their objectives. We all want to be led by those who encourage and help. We all want to reciprocate when others help us. Use the law of reciprocity to be helped by others by helping them. The purpose of business is to improve the lives of others by providing them with products and services, i.e. benefits which are worth more than they cost. Nobody buys anything unless they see it as an improvement in their condition. In short, they prefer the product/service to the money. If they prefer the money, they do not purchase the product/service. You succeed in life and business to the extent to which you improve the lives of other people. Enrich your own life by enriching the lives of others.

Mental law number 17: the law of inertia

This law postulates that in the mental world of achievement, as in the physical world, a body stays where it is until something comes along to move that body. Wherever you are now in life is where you deserve to be, given your present skills and attitude. If you stay as you are, you stay where you are! Millions of people make virtually no progress in 20 years of their working lives because they do not change. They are the same people at 50 years of age as at 30 years of age. Make a decision to change. Make a decision to set goals, learn the skills, adopt the positive attitude, pay the price in advance, believe the necessary beliefs. Adopt the values consistent with achieving your goals.

Inertia is the price people pay for staying as they are. Inertia is the price people pay for justifying being as they are. Justification and identification (taking it personally) are the fertilisers of negative emotions. Negative emotions are the excuses we make for failing to set and achieve goals. Whatever you are reaping today is the result of what you have sown in the past. Start sowing the seeds today that will reap you the rewards you desire in the future. As ye sow, so shall ye reap.

'A man grows most tired while standing still.'
– *Chinese proverb*

'Even if you're on the right track, you'll get run over if you just sit there.' – *Will Rogers*

---

12   GOAL ACHIEVING AND THE MENTAL LAWS

It should be clear to the reader that we can all use the mental laws to achieve our goals. In fact, goal achieving is automatic if we decide to put ourselves in the top three per cent or even the top one per cent of achievers. We can now briefly summarise the 17 mental laws. From the law of belief, we know that our beliefs must be consistent with the achievement of our goals. The law of cause and effect tells us that thinking about our goals is an important step in bringing our goals into reality. From the law of attraction, we know that we automatically attract into our lives the people, circumstances and information consistent with achieving our goals.

The law of correspondence tells us that if we mentally rehearse achieving our goals, then that achievement will be brought into our reality. The law of expression tells us that if we impress into our minds the skills, knowledge and attitude consistent with achieving our goals, then such goal achievement will be expressed in our reality. From the law of expectations, we know that we must confidently expect to achieve our goals. The law of control tells us that we can control the events, circumstances and information which will lead to the achievement of our goals. We must accumulate the knowledge, skills and attitudes consistent with achieving our goals. We must focus and concentrate on achieving our goals. From the law of reversibility, we know that if we imagine we have already achieved our goals, then the steps we must take to achieve those goals will be revealed to us. The law of substitution tells us that we can eliminate negative emotions by focusing on our goals. We must develop the habits of successful people.

The more emotion we put into desire or achievement of a goal, the more quickly will that goal be achieved. We can use the law of super-conscious activity to achieve any goal. If the quality and quantity of the service we offer is great enough, we shall be compensated with the achievement of our financial goals. If the quality and quantity of the service we deliver is great enough, then our customers will reciprocate by rewarding us in equal amount. Finally, from the law of inertia we know that we must increase our knowledge and go to work on positive thinking to achieve higher levels of performance in the future than the levels of performance we have achieved in the past. Finally, goal-setting is extremely difficult, but goal-achieving is automatic. All successful people use the mental laws to achieve their goals.

One cautionary note we always add, especially for younger readers, is that you cannot set goals for other people. We cannot set a goal that you should learn to play the violin. You cannot set a goal that we should learn to speak Russian. Although we cannot set goals for other people, we can use our leadership skills to encourage people to become committed to common goals. It is widely accepted that fewer than five per cent of people in the Western world set goals. Even fewer people resolve to pay the necessary price in advance. Resolve to pay the price. Resolve to do whatever is necessary. If you wish to be excellent, then practise, practise, practise; be patient, persist, and eventually you will achieve perfection.

Fritz Kreisler, after a performance, was approached by a woman who said 'I would give my life to play as you have!' He smiled and said, 'I did!'

---

13   THE SELF-CONCEPT

'To love oneself is the beginning of a lifelong romance.'
– *Oscar Wilde*

Your self-concept is your bundle of beliefs about yourself. You have a belief, a vision of yourself as a squash player, as a lover, as a friend, as an employee, as a cook, as a manager, as an achiever. You also have a self-concept level of income. It is widely believed that you cannot earn more or less than a few percentage points of your self-concept level of income. If you want to earn a great deal more money, then you must change your self-concept level of income. From the law of belief, we know that your beliefs determine almost everything that happens to you in life, since your beliefs determine your expectations, and your expectations determine your attitude, and your attitude determines over 80 per cent of all the success you will ever enjoy.

Part of your self-concept is your level of self-esteem. Self-esteem is the extent to which you feel you are a valuable and worthwhile person. It is the extent to which you accept and enjoy being yourself. There is a strong relationship between achievement and self-esteem. Remember that you are an extremely valuable and worthwhile person. All successful people have high self-esteem. They do not believe that they are superior to other people, but they do not believe that they are inferior to other people.

> The more you do of what you do, the more you get of what you've got.

'High self-esteem is like money in the bank.'
– *Marilyn Ferguson*

All change begins with a change in the self-concept, a change in your beliefs about yourself. Use affirmations to convince your subconscious. 'I am a valuable and worthwhile person. I am excellent at creativity, goal setting, strategy, marketing, selling, negotiating, leadership, finance, and time-management, I am a £100,000-per-

annum person. I am a loving parent, I am a brilliant cook, etc.' Use
the law of belief to convince yourself that your beliefs are consistent
with achieving your goals. Is the life you are leading now consistent
with your self-concept? If not you will always be unhappy,
dissatisfied, doing a job which you find undemanding   You have to get
and unrewarding, probably blaming somebody else for   rid of yesterday,
your condition. Adopt a bundle of beliefs about yourself   before you can
consistent with achieving your goals. You are the hero/   move on to
heroine of your own story.   tomorrow.

'It's no good running a pig farm badly for thirty years while
saying "Really I was meant to be a ballet dancer." By that time,
pigs will be your style.' – *Quentin Crisp*

MY SELF CONCEPT IS MY BUNDLE OF BELIEFS ABOUT MYSELF.
My present beliefs got me where I am today.
If I wish to be somewhere else,
I must change my beliefs about myself.

Make a decision that as from right now you will raise your standards in all aspects of your life. You will raise your standard of dress,
jewellery, garden, cleanliness, furniture, food, car, home, music,
people, knowledge etc. Everybody has problems – job problems,
boss problems, people problems, legal problems, husband and wife
problems, school problems, problems with kids, car problems, etc.
The difference between winners and losers is the way in which they
respond to their problems. Winners see them as challenges and
opportunities. Losers see them as threats and problems. Winners
do not focus on the seedy aspects of life. They focus on the stars,
the mountains, trees, opportunities. They think about their goals.
As Oscar Wilde put it, 'We all live in the gutter, but some of us are
looking up at the stars.'

Most important of all is to remember that within every disappointment or setback is the seed of a tremendous advantage. In adversity, in depression, at the lowest point, search for the learning insight, the tremendous opportunity, the seed of a great future advantage.

'To fall in love with yourself is the first secret of happiness.'
— *Robert Morley*

---

14   YOU ARE A GENIUS

We all have the intelligence to perform at the highest levels in at least one area. This is your specialisation, area of excellence, and will normally be an activity which makes you feel valuable and worthwhile, resulting in high self-esteem. There are many different kinds of intelligence. It is not possible for you to be below average in all of them. We all have areas of excellence in which we can perform at high levels of achievement, providing we are prepared to set it as a goal and resolve to pay the necessary price in advance, provided we are willing to learn the skills and adopt a positive mental attitude. You can run a wonderful restaurant, a wonderful hairdressing salon, a wonderful fuel delivery service, a wonderful taxi service, a wonderful market garden, etc.

Some people excel in verbal intelligence. Others excel in mathematical intelligence. These are important in establishing your intelligence quotient or IQ. Do not be deterred or misled by your IQ. You could excel in artistic intelligence or mechanical intelligence. You may be gifted with musical intelligence. Finally, you could have excellent social-skills intelligence and perhaps even intuitive intelligence. We all know people who are very successful in business, because they have excellent judgement and because they have excellent social skills. Many of these people were poor performers at school, about 20% suffering from dyslexia (including Richard Branson and Alan Sugar).

The above seven kinds of intelligence are not exhaustive. Furthermore, there are many kinds of intelligence within each area of intelligence. For example, in music you might be excellent on the clarinet, but a poor performer on the guitar. You could be excellent at writing music but a poor performer. You could be excellent at arranging other people's music, etc. The point we are making is that you do have areas of excellence in which you can perform at very high levels of achievement. Make a decision to find your area of excellence. You will usually find it is whatever you enjoy doing. You will usually perform at high levels doing something which makes you feel valuable and worthwhile, doing something which gives you high self-esteem. Make the effort to find your area of excellence, your specialisation, that which makes you feel valuable and worthwhile, while at the same time enriching the lives of your customers.

We all know people who are academically brilliant, but who have no social skills at all. These people do not succeed in the competitive world of business where co-operation from others is essential. In short, the world is full of geniuses who cannot even earn a living. In the world of business, intelligence is a way of behaving, not IQ. If you behave intelligently, you are an intelligent person. If you behave as a fool behaves, then you are a fool – even if you have two university degrees.

In business, intuitive intelligence or judgement is important, particularly where people are concerned. Being a good judge of other people is critically important. Most of us can learn fancy business techniques to help us collect information, make decisions, take action, hopefully to get the desired results. However, despite all the techniques, good judgement is critical in business. Judgement can be derived from intuitive intelligence or from experience. In fact, in management studies we examine successful and unsuccessful businesses. From their successes and failures we devise rules of thumb to give good advice in creativity, goal-setting, strategy, marketing, sales skills, negotiation, leadership, finance and time-management.

By making the necessary efforts we should ensure that the ability to take intelligent action (which gets results) is not necessarily correlated with IQ or formal qualifications. In addition to learning the basic managerial skills we can also use our creativity to answer the following questions:

- In this situation, what action would be taken by Jesus of Nazareth?
- In this situation, what action would be taken by Richard Branson?
- In this situation, what action would be taken by Alexander the Great?

15   POSITIVE MENTAL ATTITUDE

Millions of people believe that there are no opportunities in life. You leave school, somebody gives you a job, you do that job until you retire, and then you die.

'I'm not bragging, I am simply trying to show that there are always occasions where business people can make a good profit if they could only recognise and seize the moment and if they could ignore the negative sentiments expressed by those who become prophets of doom.' – *John Paul Getty*

Being positive rather than negative simply means that we take an optimistic, constructive, forward-looking, winning view of life rather than a pessimistic, destructive, backward-looking, losing view. It means seeing situations as challenges and opportunities, rather than as threats and problems. It means mentally rehearsing success rather than failure, confidently expecting success rather than failure, seeing life as being full of opportunities rather than devoid of opportunities, being adaptive and flexible, rather than unadaptive and inflexible. It means bringing the great positive emotions to situations.

The great positive emotions are excitement, enthusiasm, joy, love, acceptance of responsibility, encouragement of others. It means avoiding the great negative emotions of blame, guilt, self-doubt, self-pity, hate, worry, stress, anxiety, fear of failure, fear of rejection, envy and anger. It means looking for solutions rather than somebody to blame. It means focusing on outcomes rather than roadblocks. It means having high expectations of ourselves and others. It means that we focus on making positive statements about other people, rather than focusing on being critical. It means that we bombard our minds with the people, circumstances, and information consistent with achieving our goals, consistent with getting what we want, rather than bombarding our minds with information consistent with failure, unhappiness and underachievement. It means that we have the self-honesty to confess to our weaknesses and mistakes. It means we are willing to learn, to change. It means avoiding justification and identification.

As human beings, we are all geniuses at justifying being exactly as we are. We can always blame somebody else. We can always find reasons for failing to do what we know we should do. We can all blame time, our schooling, the boss, the company, the government, the economy etc. Unfortunately, as long as we are justifying being as we are then we shall stay as we are. If we stay as we are then we shall stay where we are. Identification means making a personal attachment to one solution, one way of doing something. It means taking it personally. It means asking the question, 'why do these things always happen to me?'

The simple fact is that everybody has bad news, everybody has setbacks, everybody has problems. The difference between winners and losers is the way in which they respond to their problems, threats, i.e. their challenges and their opportunities. Many people love to indulge themselves in victim language, claiming that their situation is the result of the evil doings of others. What they are in fact claiming is that they are not in control of their own lives. They tend to believe that they are not the masters/mistresses of their own destinies. They blame others for their conditions. On the other hand, successful people tend to have a condition sometimes referred to as 'inverse paranoia'. They believe and confidently expect that others are conspiring to help them. One of the sad aspects relating to negativity is that it is learned. We all came into the world uninhibited, unafraid, with a success instinct in that we wanted to improve our condition. We all start out with a very positive attitude towards life. Unfortunately we learn negativity from our parents, from our brothers and sisters, from other people in our lives. Nobody came into the world feeling a failure, blaming other people, suffering from self-pity, hate, fear of rejection, etc. We all need to make the necessary efforts to identify our own negative emotions. They hold us back and stop us achieving our goals. We can overcome negative emotions by focusing on positive emotions.

If we focus on our goals, then we are filled with excitement and enthusiasm. We are excited about achieving our goals and cannot at the same time feel self-pity, hate, anger, worry, stress, blame, etc. We can also tackle negative emotions on an individual basis. Blame can be overcome by accepting responsibility for ourselves. We can overcome fear of failure by understanding that failing is essential to success. We keep failing until we succeed. We can overcome hate by forgiving those who have hurt us. We can overcome anger, worry, stress, etc., by understanding that there is no emotion in a situation. In the same situation some people get angry, worry, etc., but others do not. We need to understand that we bring negative emotions to the situation. Once we understand this, we can make the necessary efforts to bring different emotions to the same situation. Every problem is a challenge if you think about it. Every disaster is an opportunity if you think about it.

'Mistakes are the portals of discovery.' – *James Joyce*

'Those things that hurt, instruct.' – *Benjamin Franklin*

One of the marvellous attributes of positive emotions is the free energy we receive from enthusiasm, excitement, joy, love, acceptance of responsibility, etc. Positive people have all the energy they need to achieve goals and happiness. They have all the necessary energy to overcome problems and threats, turning them into challenges and opportunities. Unfortunately, all negative emotions deprive us of energy. Blaming others, self-pity, fear of failure, fear of rejection, anger, hate, worry, etc., all these negative emotions deprive us of energy, deprive us of our peace of mind, and are associated with failing to achieve our goals and happiness. As already indicated, we are all brilliant at justifying our negative emotions. We are all absolutely brilliant at justifying, blaming other people for our condition, justifying our hatred of others, justifying our anger, our self-pity, our worry, our anxieties. We use our own negative emotions to justify our failure to achieve our own happiness.

As a final note in singing the praises of positive mental attitude, we should add that many medical and psychological experts agree that positive mental attitude is strongly associated, not only with physical health, but also with mental health. It is our birthright to be positive. All positive emotions give us energy. This free energy assists us in achieving our goals. Positive mental attitude appears to be the key ingredient in giving us our energy, and our energy levels are equated with physical health.

One leading psychiatrist has made the suggestion that there are no differing degrees of mental health, only varying degrees of irresponsibility. One of the most positive things we can all do is accept responsibility for ourselves. We encourage our audience to focus on those areas of human activity which give us excitement and enthusiasm. Go to work on eliminating negative emotions. We should all focus and concentrate on those goals which excite us. The positive emotions will give us all the physical and mental energy we need to succeed.

POSITIVE EMOTIONS
= free energy
= physical health
= mental health

Positive mental attitudes affect other people. We influence their behaviour through the power of suggestion. Our positive expectations affect the expectations of people around us. They want to help us achieve our high expectations. Our enthusiasm for achieving our goals makes other people enthusiastic. The way we dress, the way in which we adjust our hair, the way we speak, the cars we drive, the body language we use, all affect the people around us. The positive way in which we conduct our lives conveys to others through the power of suggestion that we confidently expect to achieve our goals. This affects their behaviour in that they automatically wish to participate in our inevitable success.

> ## NEGATIVE EMOTIONS
> = drain on energy
> = physical ill-health
> = mental ill-health

'Nothing on earth consumes a man more quickly than the passion of resentment.' – *Friedrich Nietzsche*

Positive mental attitude helps us to be proactive rather than reactive. Millions of people live their lives by reacting to events, people, circumstances and information received. They don't make things happen. They are not proactive. They fail to seek out the information, the circumstances and the people necessary to achieve their goals. In fact, the vast majority of people don't even have goals. Millions of people live their lives hoping that perhaps one fine day they will win the National Lottery or that some wonderful, miraculous event will come to pass that completely changes their lives for the better. Of course, the miraculous event has to happen without any effort from the beneficiary!

Here are a few ideas to help the reader be more proactive rather than reactive.

- In the next two hours write down your career and personal development goals.
- Today set deadlines for the achieving of all those goals, e.g. three months, three years, five years, etc.
- Pick up a telephone today and order the five books and five tapes which are essential to your personal development.
- If you are an employee, make an appointment today with your boss to discuss your three-year goals, your areas of excellence and

the ways in which you can enhance your value to the organisation.

- Form a mastermind alliance today by ringing up the three people you most admire and make appointments to spend time with them on a regular basis.
- Make a decision to work in your area of specialisation to which you can bring excitement and enthusiasm.
- Make a decision to go on a journey of self-honesty so that you can identify your negative emotions and take the necessary steps to substitute positive emotions for negative emotions.
- Pick up a telephone and ask your travel agent to send you the brochures relevant to that round-the-world trip you have always wanted to make.
- Pick up a telephone and acquire details of that Rolls-Royce/Ferrari you have always desired.
- Pick up the telephone and ring five estate agents, giving them details of the house you have always desired. Ask them to forward the appropriate details. Go out today and buy the magazine which contains pictures of the home you have always wanted.
- Pick up a telephone and contact five people who can tell you everything you need to know about the future of your chosen industry.
- Make a list of the 20 things you always wanted to know but never dared to ask. Pick up the telephone and contact the people who can give you all the answers. Ask your way to success. Make a decision to develop a sense of urgency, a 'do it now' approach to life including business.
- Pick up the telephone and obtain the necessary information relating to enrolling in that MBA class, that aerobics class, that course on launching your own successful business, etc.

Successful people make a habit of doing what unsuccessful people could do but never quite get round to doing. Live every moment as if it were your last, but as if you will live forever. At the end of a session on goal-setting, we do not wish people the best of luck. We wish people lots of learning and lots of positive thinking. If you develop

Be proactive. Make it happen. Only action gets results.

an obsession with learning/self-improvement and go to work on positive attitude, then it will appear to others that you have all the luck in the world.

'It wasn't just luck. I *deserved* to win it.' – *Margaret Thatcher* (aged nine)

Be proactive! Do it now! Make a start! Make the first move! Start the ball rolling! Discipline weighs ounces, but regret weighs tons.

'Knowing is not enough; we must apply. Willing is not enough, we must do.' – *Goethe*

'Thinking is easy, acting is difficult. To put one's thoughts into action is the most difficult thing in the world.' – *Goethe*

'To change one's life:
• start immediately
• do it flamboyantly
• no exceptions.'
– *William James*

'The people who get on in this world are the people who get up and look for circumstances they want and if they cannot find them, make them.' – *George Bernard Shaw*

'Character determines men's qualities, but it is by their actions that they are happy or the reverse.' – *Aristotle*

---

16   YOUR NEXT PROMOTION

With a view to gaining advancement in the workplace, in any application or at any job interview the following qualities must be emphasised:

- an ability to set priorities;
- an ability to carry out action plans to completion;
- an ability to accept responsibility for results.

Very few people set priorities. Most people devote their time and effort to the 80 per cent which yields only 20 per cent of the desired result. Set priorities by focusing on the 20 per cent which yields 80 per cent of the desired result. Very few people start, and even fewer finish, tasks which they undertake. To stand out from the crowd, finish that job, complete that training course, gain that qualification, go the extra mile, carry out that action plan to completion. A manager's job is to get results. However, very few people can accept responsibility for results. It is much easier to blame quality control, blame the salesforce, blame marketing, blame the boss, the economy, the competition, etc.

> **There is no traffic jam on the extra mile.**

Ask your way to success. Ask your boss to identify your key result areas, to identify the action plans which must be completed, to help you set priorities. Ask your boss how you can increase your value to the business. Identify your own areas of excellence and set very clear goals for your own career. Most people prefer the comfort zone of avoiding the most problematical area of the business. With a view to rising rapidly, get into the business area which is critical to the future success of the enterprise. Which area of business activity is critical to the future survival and success of your organisation? Is it marketing?

Is it selling? Is it finance? Is it new-product development? Is it quality control? Finally, here is one small tip: dress for success. Dress in the style of management one or two levels above your present level. This conveys the message to the hierarchy that you are ready to proceed to a higher level. Don't dress in a style similar to the chairman of the organisation (yet), as this could give people the impression that you have ideas above your station!

17   GOAL SETTING

You are the master/mistress of your own destiny. You can be, have, or do more or less anything you want in life provided you are prepared to:

1   set it as a goal;
2   focus and concentrate on the goal on a day-to-day basis;
3   resolve to pay the necessary price in advance. (Unfortunately, you always have to pay the price in advance.)

It is generally recognised that fewer than five per cent of people set goals. It is also generally recognised that fewer than five per cent of people consider their lives to be successful. It should come as no surprise that the people who do become successful are the same people who do set goals. The vast majority of people do not realise that goals are important. The vast majority of people do not know how to set goals. This section is designed to help readers to set goals. Remember that you cannot set goals for other people and that they cannot set goals for you. You are responsible for setting your own goals.

We know that success is derived from both knowledge and positive mental attitude. We also know that failure is strongly associated with lack of knowledge and negative attitudes. Focusing on desired goals stimulates excitement and enthusiasm, which are in turn strongly associated with positive thinking. Very few people are prepared to set goals. Most people are not prepared to learn more or make the necessary efforts to be more positive. Millions of people think that 'education' is something that you get at school, or perhaps university. In fact, very few people ever recover from the damage done to their education by going to school. Real learning is a continuous change in behaviour. Winners are happy to change to accommodate the world. Losers wish the world would change to accommodate them.

Here are a few questions and answers which reflect the philosophy of free enterprise:

- *What is life?*
  Life is the time you have between birth and death.
- *What is the meaning of life?*
  The meaning of life is to enrich the lives of other people.
- *So what am I doing on this planet?*
  You are here to enrich the lives of other people.
- *How do I enrich the lives of others?*
  Love your customers. Increase the quality and quantity of what you do for others. Find your area of excellence, set goals, focus and concentrate on goals, resolve to pay the necessary price in advance.
- *What's in it for me?*
  You will enrich your own life to the extent to which you enrich the lives of others.
- *Precisely what should I do?*
  At the corporate level, find your specialisation, establish competitive advantage, identify your market segment, and concentrate all your resources hitting your market segment with your competitive advantage in your area of excellence. At the personal level, find your area of excellence, set goals, focus and concentrate, and resolve to pay the price in advance.

Clear goals are the essential ingredient to success and happiness. People with clear goals do not waste their time watching five-day cricket matches, watching television, or propping up a bar six nights each week. Clear goals make decision-making very easy. With clear goals we tend to collect the relevant information, make sensible decisions, and take the necessary actions which achieve the desired result or goal. We tend to avoid time-wasting opportunities. Procrastination is not just the thief of time, it is the thief of life. When you are killing time, you are killing life. When you indulge yourself in pastimes, you are passing life. Be wise in the ways in which you use your time for time is the stuff of which life is made.

The vast majority of people simply do not know what they want. Here are some questions which should help you to identify your goals. In a perfect world, where would you be three years from now? What are your career or business goals, stated in terms of sales, profits, or salary? What are the skills you will need to learn? What are your personal and family goals?

Focusing on these questions should help you to set goals as indicated at the start of this chapter:

- *If you were successful, what would you be, have or do?*
  Focusing on this question should help you find out what you really want.
- *What do you daydream about?*
  Answering this question should help you to identify your personal goals.
- *What are the three to five aspects of life which you value most?*
  Is it health, is it the quality of your relationships, is it money, is it some worthy goal, self-knowledge or self-fulfilment?
- *What would you do if you knew you had only ten years to live?*
  This question can help you identify what you really want.
- *What is it that holds your attention?*
  This could help you to identify your area of excellence.
- *What were you doing in your career when you were happiest?*
  This also can help you to identify your area of excellence.
- *What do you consider to be your greatest achievements?*
  This should help you to identify those activities which raise your self-esteem.

- *What do you consider to be your areas of excellence?*
  Again, this could help you identify your specialisation.
- *If there were only one achievement you could effect in life, what would that achievement be?*
  Answering this question could help you to identify your most worthy goal.
- *What would you do if you won £10 million on the National Lottery?*
  Answering this question can help you to establish your self-concept level of income. In fact, most people start giving money away as quickly as possible.

The reader of this chapter should now understand that there are clear differences between successful and unsuccessful people. Some of the more obvious ones are listed in Table 2.1.

In conclusion, people who do not have clear goals tend to take whatever comes along. People who do not set goals are usually destined to spend the rest of their lives working for people who do set goals. If you don't know where you are going, just about any road will take you there!

'Since the mind is a specific bio computer, it needs specific instructions and directions. The reason most people never reach their goals is that they don't define them, learn about them or even seriously consider them as believable or achievable. Winners can tell you where they are going, what they plan to do along the way, and who will share the adventure with them.' – *Denis Waitley*

'Our plans miscarry because they have no aim. When a man does not know what harbour he is making for, no wind is the right wind.' – *Seneca*

Table 2.1   The differences between successful and unsuccessful people.

Successful people	Unsuccessful people
Set goals	Do not set goals
Resolve to pay the price in advance	Refuse to pay the price
Focus and concentrate on goals	Focus and concentrate on television, sports news, alcohol and drugs
Expect good things to happen	Expect bad things to happen
Think they are in charge of their own lives	Think their lives are controlled by forces outside themselves
Focus on successes	Focus on failures
Visualise perfect outcomes	Visualise disasters
Mentally rehearse success	Mentally rehearse failure
Emotionalise perfect outcomes	Emotionalise disasters
Make good positive affirmations	Make bad negative affirmations
Do not suffer from self-limiting beliefs	Suffer from self-limiting beliefs
Continue to learn and grow	Have stopped learning and growing
Talk challenge/opportunity	Talk problems/threats
Do not use victim language	Use victim language
Accept that change is inevitable	Fear and fight change
Understand that there is a reason for everything	Believe in luck and accidents
Accept responsibility for themselves	Blame others
Manage their time well	Manage their time badly
Read non-fiction books, go on courses and listen to tapes	Don't read, never go on courses, never listen to tapes
Spend time with their mastermind	Spend their time with people going nowhere
Forgive and forget	Bear grudges
Have high self-esteem	Have low self-esteem
Have high self-concept level of health, income, etc.	Have low self-concept levels of health, income, etc.
Make the necessary efforts	Don't make the necessary efforts
Take action	Procrastinate
Set priorities	Focus on the unimportant
Accept that it takes 20 years to be successful	Want everything now, without effort
Are proactive, make things happen, do it now	Are reactive, wait and see what happens, do it later
Make plans	Don't make plans

Are full of energy, well-informed, unselfish, generous, patient, fair-minded, self-effacing	Are lazy, ill-informed, selfish, greedy, impatient, ruthless and vain
Use deadlines	Will get round to it one day
Use the expression 'I am'	Use the expressions 'I wish' and 'I'll try'
Are excited and enthusiastic	Have no enthusiasm, can't be bothered
Use their time well	Always use time as an excuse
Make lists	Put it at the back of their minds
Ask for help	Refuse to ask for help, know it all
Are flexible, adaptive	Are inflexible, won't change
Question beliefs, assumptions	Hang on to their beliefs, stick to same assumptions
Carry out action plans to completion	Don't finish what little they start
Separate the situation from the person	Take everything personally
Listen to others	Justify the status quo

Personal characteristics

Success	Failure
Energetic	Lazy
Well-informed	Ill-informed
Unselfish	Selfish
Generous	Greedy
Patient	Impatient
Loyal	Disloyal
Forgiving	Ruthless
Responsible	Irresponsible
Reliable	Unreliable
Self-effacing	Vain

'I will study and prepare myself, and someday my chance will come.' – *Abraham Lincoln*

'Everything that irritates us about others can lead us to an understanding of ourself.' – *Carl Jung*

18   GOAL-ACHIEVING

If we were designed by a super-power, then that super-power has a wicked sense of humour. Everybody is designed to want to be more, have more, and do more and, at the same time, people cannot be more, have more, or do more, because they are too lazy, ill-informed, selfish, greedy, ruthless, impatient, disloyal, irresponsible, unreliable and vain.

These characteristics are perfectly acceptable in the great many aspects of you life – but not in your area of excellence, your specialisation, your mission. In this area you must exhibit the opposite characteristics. You must be very energetic, extremely well informed, and unselfish. You must accept reward only where it is earned, you must be generous, patient, loyal, responsible, reliable and self-effacing. We find the statistics on income in the UK for the year 1999–2000 somewhat frightening. Average earnings for men were £23,000 per annum. The richest ten per cent of the population has an annual income of £34,000 and above. Only the top one per cent earns £91,000 per annum. We are all capable of joining the top one per cent.

One of the best-kept secrets of the universe is that goal achieving is automatic, provided you are prepared to set goals and to pay the necessary price in advance, and provided you are content to be in the top 3–5 per cent of achievers. Of course, being the best in the business or winning a gold medal in the Olympic Games means that you finally have to defeat other people who also set goals. Since you cannot set goals for other people, you cannot set goals for people to fail in competition with you. Once you have established your goals, then you can use all the mental laws, together with all the other rules in this chapter to achieve those goals. In this section we provide a list of the 12 steps you should consider in achieving any goal:

1 *Make a decision that you desire to achieve the goal.* It is your goal, not somebody else's goal. You really want it.

2 *Believe that you will achieve the goal.* You always behave in a manner consistent with your beliefs.

3 *Write down your goal on paper.* Look at that piece of paper every day. All successful people are list makers. If you are feeling list-less, make a list!

4 *Be honest with yourself.* Why do you want to achieve this goal? Is it for the admiration, better health, more money, etc.?

5 *Analyse your present position.* Again, be honest with yourself. What are your strengths, weaknesses, opportunities and threats? What is your existing level of knowledge? How positive/negative are you in your attitude?

6 *Use deadlines.* Set targets for three months, three years and twenty years. Make appointments with others to discuss your results.

7 *Identify the rocks that stand in your way.* Be honest in identifying all the obstacles that stand between you and the success and happiness you desire.

8 *Identify the skills you will need.* Again, be honest with yourself. Do you need to be more creative, be more positive in goal-setting, understand strategy, marketing, selling, negotiating, leadership, finance and time-management?

9 *Identify those people from whom you will need co-operation.* You may need the co-operation of your family, customers, suppliers, bank manager, employees, partners, mastermind alliance. Why should these people co-operate with you? What's in it for them?

10 *Make a complete business plan.* A plan is a list of activities. It is a 'to do' list. Make sure the plan includes the names of the people who will carry out the necessary activities. At the end of the plan include the projected financial statements as they will appear if the plan is achieved.

11 *Visualise, emotionalise, affirm.* Visualise the perfect outcome. Imagine how terrific you will feel when the outcome is achieved. Make the necessary affirmations consistent with achieving the goal.

12 *Determine to back your plan with patience and persistence.* Be patient. It usually takes 20 years to be recognised as the best in the business, or to achieve your financial independence. Your persistence is your measure of your belief in yourself. Never give up, never, never, give up. You are not defeated just because you've lost. You are only defeated when you give up.

'The secret to success is constancy to purpose.'
– *Benjamin Disraeli*

'Self-management is the *process* of maximising our *time* and *talents* to achieve *worthwhile goals* based on a sound *value system*.'
– *Paul R. Timm* (author of *Successful Self-Management*)

'I'm against retiring. The thing that keeps a man alive is having something to do. Sitting in a rocker never appealed to me.' – *Colonel Sanders*

'The secret of a happy life is to do work you enjoy and then you'll be too busy to know whether you're happy or not'.
– *George Bernard Shaw*

'Work is much more fun than fun.' – *Noel Coward*

'If it were not for the demands made upon me by my business, I would provide living proof that a man can live quite happily for decades without ever doing any work.' – *John Paul Getty*

19   GREATER SUCCESS: 20 SIMPLE SUGGESTIONS

Simple suggestions include the following:

1 *Tomorrow.* Before going to sleep each night tell yourself that tomorrow will be a terrific day. Prepare yourself to feel positive. Mentally rehearse doing three jobs tomorrow which will make a difference.

2 *Today.* Start each day by telling yourself that you feel very positive. Spend a few minutes each morning reviewing your personal, business and personal-development goals. Read something which results in you feeling very positive, e.g. poetry, life of a sports hero, some inspirational material.

3 *I feel marvellous.* Stay positive by reminding yourself throughout the day that you feel absolutely marvellous, absolutely terrific.

4 *Don't be late.* When you are late, you are telling other people that they aren't sufficiently important for you to make the necessary effort to get here on time.

5 *Dress for success.* Always dress in the manner appropriate for your next promotion. This conveys the message to others that you are prepared to move forward. You never get a second chance to make a good first impression. We are all guilty of judging people on the basis of our first impression. Dress in a manner consistent with winning the business, getting the bank loan, getting the job, etc.

6 *Use deadlines.* Make appointments to present your results to colleagues, publishers, the bank manager, customers, your family.

7 *Don't use time as an excuse.* We all use the excuse that we did not have enough time. Everybody has 24 hours in the day. The reason you did not do something is that you did not set it as a goal and you did not resolve to pay the necessary price in advance.

8 *Look at pictures.* As an aid to visualisation, look at pictures of the home or car or perhaps even the magnificent body you would like to have.

9 *Use lists.* Successful people are compulsive list makers. Leave those lists in your in-tray until you have completed the tasks listed.

10 *I am a valuable and worthwhile person.* To raise your self-esteem, keep reminding yourself that you are a valuable and worthwhile person.

11 *Question your beliefs.* Be sufficiently honest with yourself to question your own self-limiting beliefs.

12 *Question your assumptions.* All business failure, and all failure in life, is based on incorrect assumptions. Keep examining the assumptions in any situation, problem, challenge, opportunity.

13 *Focus on outcomes.* By focusing on the perfect outcome, you will tend not to be obsessed with trivia, obstacles, problems.

14 *Understand that failing equals succeeding.* You have to overcome failure to succeed. Keep failing at selling, negotiating, finance, time-management, etc., until you become brilliant at succeeding.

'Success is 99 per cent failure.' – *Soichiro Honda*

---

15 *Use the law of reversibility.* Use your imagination to visualise the perfect outcome. Then ask yourself the question: 'how did I achieve this perfect outcome?'. This reverse planning often helps you to identify the steps you need to take to achieve the outcome you desire.

16 *Remember the law of reciprocity.* As human beings, we tend to reciprocate when somebody helps us. Make a habit of being a go-giver, make a habit of helping other people, make a habit of enriching the lives of others. If you do this, then other people will want to reciprocate by rewarding you.

17 *Earn your self-concept level of income.* Remember that the amount of money you earn is strongly related to the quality and quantity of what you do for other people. Define your own self-concept, required, believable level of income.

18 $U \times E = R$. Understanding multiplied by effort equals results. To achieve your goals, you must acquire the necessary knowledge and then make the necessary efforts to take the action which

yields the results you desire. The amount of energy you put into achieving your goals is strongly influenced by your level of positive mental attitude.

19 *Acquire self-knowledge.* Be honest with yourself. What do you really want in terms of your personal, career and self-development goals? What are your strengths and weaknesses? Self-honesty is one of the keys to happiness.

20 *Develop a self-improvement plan.* Make a plan to acquire the skills and knowledge you need to achieve your personal and career goals.

20   GREATER SUCCESS: 20 'CAN-DO' SUGGESTIONS

'Can-do' suggestions include the following:

1 *Be a go-giver.* You are on this planet to help other people. You can have anything you want in life provided you help enough other people get what they want.

2 *Find your key results areas.* Identify the 20 per cent of everything you do which yields 80 per cent of the desired result.

3 *Visualise a perfect outcome.* Use your imagination to visualise the achievement of your personal and career goals.

4 *Emotionalise.* Rehearse the feeling of success you will have when you achieve your goals.

5 *Use affirmations.* Keep repeating those 'I am' statements which are consistent with achieving your goals.

6 *Ask for help.* People love to be asked their opinion. People are very happy to help you. Don't be afraid to ask for help. Use your mastermind alliance.

7 *Use the affirmation, 'I am responsible.'* So long as you keep telling yourself that you are responsible for the conditions in your life, then you remain in control.

8 *Use the affirmation, 'I am in control.'* So long as you believe you are in control, then you are in control.

9 *Set priorities.* Try to organise your life so that you are working on priorities, not trivialities.

10 *Carry out action plans to completion.* Make a habit of finishing what you start. This is most unusual among the adult population. Most people do not make a start, and even those who make a start do not usually finish.

11 *Accept responsibility for results.* A manager's job is to get results. If you cannot accept responsibility for results, then you cannot be a leader.

12 *Avoid victim language.* Stop complaining to other people about what somebody else did to you.

13 *Look for the good.* In all situations, look for the good. Most people are satisfied by simply finding somebody to blame.

14 *Do a great job.* Do not be afraid of not taking on a job. However, if you do decide to take on a job, then make an excellent job of everything you do. This raises your self-esteem.

15 *Say 'no'.* Do not do those things which are inconsistent with achieving your personal and career goals. Of course, this may not always be possible, but at least make the effort to focus on those activities which lead you to the achievement of your personal and career goals.

16 *Stop hurrying.* Try very hard to avoid running around like a headless chicken, trying to achieve 15 different tasks at the same time. Take your time and focus on your key results areas.

17 *Avoid being an aggressive driver.* If you think about aggression, you will very quickly draw into your life somebody else who is also thinking aggressively. When driving your car, you should be focusing on your goals and listening to educational tapes.

18 *Be patient.* Try to take a 20-year view. It usually takes 20 years to reach the top of your profession, and it also usually takes 20 years to achieve your financial independence.

19 *Stop justifying yourself.* We are all geniuses at justifying our beliefs, our behaviour, our attitudes, etc. Make a habit of questioning your beliefs and your assumptions. Make a habit of listening to others.

20 *Avoid identification.* Stop taking it personally. Other people have different views from your views. Other people have different ways of doing things. Other people have different values and

beliefs. Everything does not only happen to you. The difference between winners and losers is the way in which they respond to situations.

21 GREATER SUCCESS: 20 DIFFICULT SUGGESTIONS

Difficult suggestions include the following:

1 *Set goals.* This automatically puts you in the top few per cent of achievers.
2 *Set worthy goals.* With a view to raising your own self-esteem, set goals, the achievement of which makes you feel valuable and worthwhile.
3 *Be proactive.* Most people struggle even to respond to situations, i.e. to be reactive. Leaders make things happen. Successful people make things happen, rather than waiting for events to take place, or simply reacting to events.
4 *Read one book per month.* In a world in which knowledge is important, 12 non-fiction books per annum will put you ahead of the rest.
5 *Attend three to five courses per annum.* All successful people make a habit of attending courses. Join them!
6 *Listen to educational tapes.* Listening to educational tapes in the car is a great relief from Radio Idiot! Acquire tapes which teach creativity, goal setting, strategy, marketing, sales, negotiation, leadership, finance and time-management. Think about making your own tapes!
7 *Form a mastermind alliance.* Spend time with people you admire. Learn from them, and adopt their positive attitudes.
8 *Tape your affirmations.* Make a tape of all affirmations consistent with achieving your personal and career goals. Play it in the car. Play it late at night.
9 *Be creative.* In any situation, use the 20-idea method for generating responses to threats, problems, situations, challenges and opportunities.

10 *Use all the mental laws.* Use all the mental laws which guarantee the achievement of your goals.

11 *Access the superconscious.* Your superconscious has access to knowledge and experience outside your own knowledge and experience. Access the superconscious through desire and solitude. Write down and record ideas and responses which occur to you in the middle of the night or in solitude.

12 *Avoid negative emotions.* Identify your own favourite negative emotions and make the necessary efforts to overcome them by focusing on your goals.

13 *Be consistent (television).* Be sure that the ideas, experiences and information fed into your mind are consistent with the achievement of your goals. Is 26 hours of television per week consistent with achieving your personal and career goals? If you stop watching television, you get 3 extra working days per week ahead of the rest.

14 *Be consistent (public houses/bars).* Be sure that the ideas, experiences and people in your life are consistent with achieving your career and personal goals. Is propping up a bar for three or four hours each evening consistent with achieving your goals? How can you better use that time?

15 *Use blind faith/belief.* Your beliefs are not based on fact. Adopt the blind belief that you will achieve your personal and career goals.

16 *Acquire self-knowledge.* Being honest with yourself is one of the keys to happiness. Identify your own strengths and weaknesses. Make a decision to change your knowledge, attitude, actions, etc., in a way which is appropriate to achieving your goals.

17 *Avoid the words 'try' and 'wish'.* 'I wish' means 'I can't.' 'I'll try' means 'I will fail.' Rather than wish you could give up smoking, use the affirmation 'I am a non-smoker.' Rather than trying not to be late for appointments, use the affirmation 'I am always five minutes early for appointments.'

18 *Use the powers of love and suggestion.* You may be able to influence other people through the powers of love and suggestion. Love is the dedication of one person to the self-fulfilment of

another. If someone believes that you are acting in their best interests, then there is a chance that you can influence that person's behaviour. If you suggest to somebody that their condition could be improved by taking a certain course of action, then you may influence that person's behaviour. On the other hand, if you threaten somebody that if they do not do something you will punish them, then that person will probably try to wriggle out of taking the course of action you recommend. These are not universal truths. Some people do respond to threats. Some people do take actions which are clearly not in their own best interests. However, as a general rule you are in with a chance of influencing the behaviour of another person by using the powers of love and suggestion.

19 *Value your relationships.* Most people value their relationships more than they value earning extra money. Make sure you devote enough time and effort to your family and friends.

20 *Look after your health.* Most people value health a great deal more than earning extra money. In your own best interests, look after your own health and appearance.

'All work and no play makes Jack a dull boy – and Jill a wealthy widow.' – *Evan Esar*

YOU CAN BE, HAVE, OR DO
ALMOST ANYTHING YOU WANT IN LIFE,
PROVIDED YOU ARE PREPARED
TO SET IT AS A GOAL AND
RESOLVE TO PAY THE PRICE IN ADVANCE.

Three

STRATEGY WILL GET YOU THERE

How to implement
a winning business strategy

Strategy gets you from where you are now to your ideal future. Strategy is the link between mission and profit. Establish your specialisation, your area of excellence, your core business. Establish a competitive advantage, a reason why customers should buy from you. Find the segment or niche in the market place which you can dominate. Concentrate all your resources hitting your market segment with your benefit and competitive advantage in your area of excellence. Many of the ideas in corporate strategy are similar to the goal-setting and goal-achieving ideas relating to individuals. This should not surprise us. Organisations do not have strategies. Only people have strategies. Set goals, learn what you need to know, and think positively.

1   WHAT IS STRATEGY?

Strategy gets you from where you are now to your ideal future. Where are you now? Where is your business now? Where is your business in terms of sales and net profit? What is your specialisation, your core business, your area of excellence? What benefit do you sell now? Why do people buy the benefit from you? Who buys the product or service? What resources are you using? What are your skills? What are your strengths, weaknesses, opportunities and threats (SWOT analysis)? It requires a good deal of self honesty, self analysis and courage to answer these questions.

What is your ideal future? Describe your ideal situation three years into the future, ten years into the future, twenty years into the future. What business will you be in three years from now? What will be the level of sales and net profit? Describe the perfect situation in terms of product, customers, suppliers, financing, employees, assets etc. What is your exit plan? Will you sell out for £1 million, £5 million? Will there be a management buy-out? Will you hand over the business to your children, float the company on the stock market? Will you die in the boardroom, or in the Seychelles? Most people do not set personal and business goals. They do not know what they want, and therefore cannot get what they want. They spend their lives drifting along with the breeze, probably working for somebody who does set goals. Millions of people drift along from one situation to the next, thinking that perhaps one day they might win the National Lottery. Remember that great line from business strategy, 'if you do not know where you are going, then any road will take you there.' Strategy is what takes you from where you are now to your ideal future.

Another way of looking at strategy is that strategy is the link between mission and net profit. The purpose of any business is to improve the lives of customers in some way. Our mission is to enrich the lives of our customers by providing a certain benefit, disguised as a product or service. We love our customers and we always do more than that for which we get paid. We are enthusiastic and excited about achieving the mission.

If we focus on our obsession with customer satisfaction, then there is always the possibility that we may operate at a profit. Profit is the result, profit is not the mission. Of course, we all understand that we wish to make a pile of money from the business. That is why we focus on the mission. Many people who become millionaires are not even aware that they are accumulating vast sums of money. They are so obsessed with enriching the lives of their customers, that they do not set aside time for counting the money. Strategy is the link between mission and profit.

For example, your mission is to enrich the lives of your customers by providing the best French restaurant in town. Your profit target is £150,000. Strategy gets you from the mission to the profit of £150,000. The benefit you provide – or your specialisation – is

French food. Your competitive advantage could be that you are the best quality in town. Your market segment/niche includes the people who want the best French food in town. Finally, you must concentrate all your resources hitting your market niche with your competitive advantage in your area of excellence. Your most important resources are your creativity, your strategic and marketing skills, your sales skills, your negotiation skills, your leadership and financial skills, and your ability to manage your time well.

If you do not know where you are going, any road will take you there.

2 WHY DO WE NEED STRATEGY?

There are at least six powerful reasons for implementing a winning strategy.

1 *Mission.* We need strategy to achieve the mission.
2 *Our ideal future.* We need strategy to get us from where we are now to our ideal future.
3 *Financial goals.* We need strategy to achieve the required financial result, measured in terms of return on equity, or return on total capital employed, or achieving the target market value of the company for sale.
4 *Repositioning the company.* We may need strategy to move the business from where it is now to where it needs to be to achieve the mission or required financial results.
5 *Strengths, weaknesses, opportunities and threats.* We need strategy to focus on our strengths and opportunities, and to either avoid or overcome our weaknesses and threats.
6 *To take action now.* Strategy must lead to action. Only action gets results. Do not confuse the mere existence of a strategic planning system with the actual implementation of a winning strategy. Strategy without action does not get results. Action without planning is a common cause of business failure.

3   WHO IS RESPONSIBLE FOR STRATEGY?

Strategy must come from the top. In large organisations the chief executive must be involved, together with his senior executives. All the key players in running the business should be involved. In smaller businesses, strategy must come from the proprietor, the partners, or the directors of a small limited company. We also strongly recommend that all businesses should use an outside consultant, somebody who understands the business, has considerable experience, and who can take the helicopter view. The consultant should have expertise in strategic planning, and should be a great help in eventually pulling together the strategic business plan. The most important decisions relating to mission, goal setting, and the ideal future can come only from the owners or directors. Remember, you cannot set goals for other people.

4   BASICS OF STRATEGY

Business strategy is often presented as a series of questions and statements. Where are we now? What business are we really in? Is it railroad or is it transport? Is it bungee jumps or excitement? Are we in journals or publishing? What business should we be in in the future? What are our strengths, weaknesses, opportunities and threats? Who is the competition? What can we learn from the competition? Can we benchmark ourselves against the competition? What is our history? What were our setbacks? What are our learning experiences? What are our areas of excellence? What is our ideal future? How can we get from where we are now to our ideal future? What is our mission? What is our net profit target? What is our exit plan? How can we get from our mission to our ideal financial outcome? Where is our market niche? Do we accept responsibility for results? Do we understand that professional advisors generally cannot manage? What is our target return on equity? What is our target return on total capital employed? What is our target profit as a percentage of sales? What is the target profit? How can we control our overheads?

We must start small. We must test everything on a small scale. We should not try to expand too quickly. We must never do anything that could bankrupt the business. We must develop a clear sense of mission. We must stick to the knitting and avoid conglomerate diversification. We must focus on results, not activities. We must love our bank manager, who will then love us. We must learn something new every day. We must go to work on positive mental attitude, bringing excitement and enthusiasm to the business. We must develop a set of priorities and a sense of urgency. We must commit ourselves to excellence. We must understand that hard work, dedication and drive are essential, but are not enough to guarantee success. Working hard at inappropriate tasks will not lead to success. We must work effectively in that we undertake those tasks which will lead to achieving the mission at a profit. We must implement a winning strategy.

'In strategy it is important to see distant things as if they were close and to take a distanced view of close things.'
– *Miyamoto Musashi, 1645*

WHAT BUSINESS ARE WE REALLY IN?
The only US railroad companies that survived were those that realised they were in transport.

Are you in ball bearings or engineering?
Are you in hairdressing or beauty care?
Are you a singer or an entertainer?

All businesses are the same. All businesses exist to improve the life of a customer, to help other people to be more, have more, do more. How does your business improve the life of your customer?

5   STRATEGY IS SPECIALISATION, DIFFERENTIATION, SEGMENTATION AND CONCENTRATION

Implementing a winning business strategy involves four key stages. Firstly, find the right product or service. Secondly, establish a reason why customers should buy the benefit from you, rather than the competition. Thirdly, find your customers. Fourthly, concentrate all your energy, creativity, people, financing etc. on bombarding your customers with your competitive advantage in your chosen area of excellence.

Specialisation

To which area of human improvement can you bring excitement and enthusiasm? What is it that you can do that improves the lives of others, which also makes you feel valuable and worthwhile? What is your area of excellence? What is your specialisation? What is your core business? For which product or service are you prepared to be a product or service champion? We are all in business for the same purpose, to improve the lives of our customers. The meaning of life is to improve the lives of others. The only reason anybody buys a product or a service is that they prefer the product or service to the money. It might look like a product or a service, but people buy improvements in their condition. What do you thoroughly enjoy doing for other people? What can you do for others that improves their lives?

Millions of people do not actually enjoy the jobs they do. They have not found their specialisation. You could ask yourself a few questions with a view to identifying your area of excellence. If you could do any job in any business, what would you enjoy doing the most? Which jobs have you done in the past which you thoroughly enjoyed? What have you achieved in your life to date that made you feel valuable and worthwhile? What is it that makes you feel important? What have you done that gave you a feeling of immense personal satisfaction, a strong feeling of self-worth? How much money would you like to be earning three years from now? How would you like to earn that

People buy benefits, improvements in their condition, enrichment of their lives.

money? If you knew you had ten years to live, how would you spend your time? Which challenge would you love to undertake if you knew you could not fail? If you focus and concentrate on answering these questions, it should eventually lead you to the business to which you should devote the rest of your life.

Differentiation (competitive advantage)

The law of cause and effect tells us that there is a reason for everything. There must be a reason why a customer buys a product or service from you. Remember we all sell benefits. It looks like a product or service, but the customer buys a benefit, an improvement in his or her condition. The customer buys from you because you are different in some way from the competition. The reason why the customer buys from you is your competitive advantage. A customer is somebody who is willing and able to pay for the benefit you offer. A customer buys from you because you are better, cheaper, faster or nicer than the competition. Your product or service could be better in that it is of a higher quality. There is always a market for top quality. The customer may buy from you because your product or service is cheaper than the competition. There is always a market for a cheaper product or service. In fact, the competitive advantage of most businesses is 'faster'. The competitive advantage of your local supermarket, local garage, local hairdresser, sandwich shop, etc. is that it is just down the road.

We have a strong tendency to do business with people whom we like. We prefer to do business with people who are caring, courteous and considerate. As customers, we tend to be lazy, ill-informed, selfish, greedy, disloyal, ruthless, impatient, irresponsible, unreliable and vain. To which of these human characteristics does your product appeal? We like to have the very best because we are vain creatures. We like the cheapest because we are selfish creatures. We like the fastest products because we are lazy, and we enjoy excellent service because we are lazy, vain, selfish *and* greedy.

Competitive strategy is one very important part of business strategy. Part of your marketing strategy is establishing competitive advantage, i.e. the reason why customers buy the product from you. We emphasise that there must be a reason why the customer buys a product from you. There is no such thing as an accidental sale. Finally, can you differentiate your benefit by establishing a brand name which stands for quality, reliability, value for money?

> ## COMPETITIVE ADVANTAGE
> There must be a reason why a customer buys from you, rather than a competitor.

Segmentation

Who cares that you are better, cheaper, faster or nicer? Where are your customers? What is their age, sex, and geographic area? What are their incomes? Which other products do they buy? If your competitive advantage is that you are faster, then your market segment could be simply the local community. If your competitive advantage is that you are a nice person, then you are probably selling to family and friends. If your competitive advantage is that you are cheaper, then this opens up a much wider range of possibilities. Finally, if you are the best in the business, then this enables you to identify a specific market segment. Is there some small, well-defined section of the market place which you could dominate? This could be your market niche. One useful rule of thumb is that you need to be at least 10 per cent better, 10 per cent cheaper, 10 per cent faster or 10 per cent more pleasant to persuade a customer to switch from the competition to you.

> ## SEGMENTATION
> Who cares that you are better, cheaper, faster or nicer?

NICHE
Is there some small section of the market which you can dominate?

Concentration

Are you concentrating all your resources, hitting your market segment with your competitive advantage in your area of excellence? Your resources include your creativity, your energy, your excitement and enthusiasm, your people, your advertising budget, your production capabilities, etc. 'Resource' does not simply refer to money. It is a popular myth that you need money to go into business. Many businesses, especially service businesses, are launched on a zero-cash basis. A great many businesses are launched with very little available funds. In business, learn to focus on the 20 per cent which usually brings in the 80 per cent. You will usually find that 20 per cent of your products bring in 80 per cent of sales and gross profit, 20 per cent of sales people account for 80 per cent of sales, 80 per cent of road accidents will involve 20 per cent of your drivers, 80 per cent of your employment costs will arise from 20 per cent of your employees, 80 per cent of enquiries will arise from 20 per cent of your advertising.

Learn how to focus and concentrate on the 20 per cent that brings in the 80 per cent. Focus on strengths and opportunities, rather than weaknesses and threats. Focus on results, rather than activities. Focus on the mission. Focus on exploiting opportunities available to you. Focus on proactive, rather than reactive management. Proactive management means making things happen. Focus on taking the necessary action which brings in the required result. Focus not on what you can do, but on what you can achieve. Maintain flexibility. Let go of investments which do not work. There is a great deal of emphasis on investment in business, rather than divestment. Avoid investments in managerial ego. Do not hang on to something just because it was your idea. Be patient. Never do anything that could bankrupt the business. Take high risks with your time, rather than high risks with your money. Learn how to delegate so that you can focus on the 20 per cent that brings in the 80 per cent. If you can learn how to focus, then you will make profits satisfying consumer wants in competitive markets by matching the resources of your organisation to the needs of the market place.

Adopt a zero-based approach to overheads. Start each planning period with a zero base. Keep asking the question: 'knowing what we know now, would we ...?' If the answer is negative, then cease that activity. If the question is: 'knowing what we know now, would we have launched that new product?', then if the answer is 'definitely not', then pull out of that product as quickly as possible. Close it down. Sell it to somebody else. Concentrate on learning the skills, acquiring the necessary knowledge. Focus and concentrate on adopting positive attitude, bringing excitement and enthusiasm to establishing your specialisation, establishing a sustainable competitive advantage, and finding your market segment or market niche. Concentrate all your energy, creativity, people, finance, productive assets etc. in hitting your market niche with your competitive advantage in your area of excellence.

Take high risks with your time, not your money.

Remember that small businesses have tremendous advantages over big businesses. Sole traders can react immediately to events. It often takes large companies several months and even years to change direction. Some large companies collapse because they cannot change. The sole trader can be available for twenty four hours each day. Many large organisations can only be contacted 9am–5pm, Monday–Friday. The sole trader can establish a very close relationship with members of his or her market niche. This is more difficult for the larger company with its constantly changing staff. The small business can dominate one small section of the market which larger companies choose to ignore. The large firm may even give away a small part of its operations which executives feel is too small to merit attention. The smaller firm should be less likely to suffer from overhead drift. Small firms can use larger firms to distribute their products, distribute their leaflets, even handle their cash collections.

RESOURCES
Your most important resources are
your creativity,
your ability to set clear goals,
implement a winning strategy,
get the marketing right,
be excellent at selling and negotiation,
give leadership,
manage your finances and time.

6 COMPETITIVE/INDUSTRY ANALYSIS

Ask your way to success. Who else is in the business? Discuss industry prospects with those who are already in the business. Which opportunities exist? Are there any gaps in the market? Make a close study of the industry, study the competition. What is the competitive advantage of the competition? Where is the market segment or the market niche for your competition? What are their strengths and weaknesses, opportunities and threats? What is their return on capital employed? What prices do they charge? What growth have they experienced? Where are their markets? How do they finance? Which people do they employ? Which technology do they use? What are their production capabilities? Who are the best performers in your industry? How can we creatively imitate the best in the business? How can we benchmark ourselves against the very best in our industry? Which are the most attractive market segments for our own business? What strategies do our competitors adopt for continuous improvement? How can we continuously improve our quality, customer care, customer satisfaction, advertising effectiveness, sales per sales person, return on investment, output per employee, etc.?

The process of asking questions can help you establish competitive advantage and find your market segment. You may even be persuaded not to enter an unprofitable market.

'Without competitors there would be no need for strategy.'
– *Kenichi O Hmae*

7   THE MISSION STATEMENT

Many organisations adopt a formal, written statement of mission. The statement should be qualitative, not quantitative. No mention is made of money. The statement must inspire and uplift. It gives meaning and purpose to work. It raises the self esteem of all members of the organisation. The statement can refer to excellence, to markets and even go as far as growth.

The statement identifies the way in which we intend to improve the life of our customers. It should read as follows: 'our mission is to enrich the lives of our customers by providing the highest quality ... best value for money ... most readily available ... most caring ... product/service ... in such-and-such a market.' The statement refers to the mission, the benefit we provide, our competitive advantage, the fact that we are the most excellent, highest quality, most readily available, etc. It refers to the excellence of our product/service, the high quality of our customer service, etc. It reflects our corporate values, beliefs and our culture.

Some organisations go beyond mission to vision. Our vision is our vivid concept of the future. It stimulates our energy, our commitment, trust and confidence in the future. Our vision might be 'I am recognised as the best in the business', 'I am providing affordable cars for the world', 'Our product sets the standard against which similar products are judged.' A vision statement would describe the ideal state of affairs existing at some time in the future.

> **VISION**
> I am recognised as ....
> We set the standard ....

'Without vision, the people perish.' – *Proverbs*

'The most pathetic person in the world is someone who has sight but has no vision.' – *Helen Keller* (who learnt to speak and write despite being blind and deaf)

MISSION
I am enriching the lives of my customers by ....

'A corporate mission is much more than good intentions and fine ideas. It represents the framework for the entire business, the values which drive the company and the belief that the company has in itself and what it can achieve.'
– *Colin Marshall*

8   CORPORATE VALUES AND BELIEFS

How would you like your friends and business associates to describe you? This is a very important question. It identifies your values and beliefs. What would you like members of your family to say about you? What would you like your friends to say about you? What would you like your bank manager, your suppliers, your employees, your customers, to say about you? How would you like the world to describe your business? Would the world testify as to your excellent products, the excellent levels of customer service, good payments record, respect for the individual?

We know that almost everything that happens to you is determined by your beliefs. Your beliefs are your reality. We recommend that you adopt the following beliefs which are associated with members of successful companies.

1   A belief that we are the very best in the business.
2   A belief in the importance of superior quality and excellent service.
3   A belief in the importance of growth in sales and profits.
4   A belief that most members of the organisation have a contribution to make towards creativity and innovation.
5   A belief in the importance of recognising people as individuals, and recognising that everybody has a contribution to make.
6   A belief that senior managers should be involved in the day-to-day activities, rather than trying to install systems of remote control. This is coupled with a belief in facilitate and empower, rather than command and control. Give people the skills to do the job, and then empower them to get on with it.
7   A belief in excellent communications, encouraged by informality between all levels of employees.

VALUES
What would you like other people to say about you?

'After I am dead I would rather have men ask why Cato has no monument than why he had one.' – *Cato the Elder*

---

9   CONSTANT CHANGE AND THE LEARNING ORGANISATION

Knowledge is being recognised as a key resource in most businesses.

Change is inevitable. Change equals opportunity. If you stay as you are, you stay where you are. The more you do of what you do, the more you get of what you have already got. You have to get rid of yesterday before you can go on to tomorrow. You have to be on the inside, before you become on the outside. The world belongs to those who are in love with the new. Of course, only people learn. When we refer to organisational learning, we are referring to the accumulated knowledge of the people in those organisations. The whole world is changing, and, if anything, the pace of change is accelerating. Such a world creates endless opportunities for all of us.

With a view to moving forwards, we must all learn more and be more positive in our attitudes. People who stay as they are, stay where they are. These people do not make any progress in life, because they refuse to change. Organisations which stand still are also subject to decline in a constantly changing world. Knowledge is replacing capital as the basic resource of commercial organisations. You have to believe that you are a £100,000 person on the inside, before you become a £100,000 person on the outside. Belief comes first.

We can use visualisation, emotionalisation and affirmation to change our beliefs. We can see ourselves in a certain position in life. We can imagine how good we feel once we have arrived. We can say to ourselves, 'I am excellent at marketing, I am excellent at selling, I am excellent at negotiation, I am a loving, caring father, etc.'.

Successful business people are flexible and adaptive. They love new ideas, suggestions for improvements, better quality, increased sales, increased profits, etc. Successful organisations believe in the personal development of everybody in the team. They believe in change, continuous improvement. In business only people get better. Buildings, plant and equipment, motor cars and computers all deteriorate, but people can be constantly improved. Improvement in the knowledge and skills of our people leads to better quality, higher levels of customer care, greater sales and greater profits.

Make a decision that you and your team will embark on a journey of continuous improvement, in both your knowledge and your attitude. Unfortunately, millions of people believe that education is something that you get at school, and ends when you leave school. Real education is equal to learning, and real learning is something which leads to a change in behaviour. Most people refuse to change their behaviour. They persist in justifying their existing behaviour. They refuse to change. They refuse to learn, they refuse to change their attitudes. By making a decision to stay as they are, these people make a decision to stay where they are. Learning is a process which should continue throughout our lives. We acquire programmed learning by attending courses, reading books, listening to educational tapes. Having acquired this additional knowledge, we are now ready to take action. Only action gets results. We use our knowledge, take action, and look at our results in increasing sales, lowering costs, increasing the quality of customer care, improving the quality of the product etc. We can now examine our results, and ask additional questions.

Once we ask additional questions we are now ready for more programmed learning, followed by more action, study of results, and asking more questions etc. This continuous improvement, continuous learning, should proceed throughout our lives. Never stop learning. If you stop learning, then you stop growing. Enjoy the learning process, enjoy the action, enjoy the results, enjoy more learning. Enjoy every minute. Enjoy setting goals, enjoy paying the price in terms of learning and adopting a more positive attitude, enjoy your results, enjoy asking questions, and enjoy more learning. Embark on a continuous programme of self development and develop your people.

If you stop learning, you stop growing. If you stay as you are, you stay where you are.

THE LEARNING ORGANISATION
More knowledge
More positive approach
People can be improved
Develop winning teams

'The secret of business is know something that nobody else knows.' – *Aristotle Onassis*

'Men of superior mind, busy themselves first in getting to the root of things; and when they have succeeded in this, the right course is open to them.' – *Confucius*

10   QUALITY

Quality is the extent to which a product matches the use to which it is put. Quality is the extent to which a service meets the service requirement of the customer. There are 20 ways of improving the quality of your product or service. There are 20 ways of improving the quality of your after-sales service. There are twenty ways of improving everything. In your search for continuous improvement, keep asking your customers what they want. We all tend to make the mistake of assuming that we know what customers want, rather than asking them. By making this assumption, we are helping our customer-focused competitors. Our competitive advantage can be that we make continuous improvements to the product in line with customer requirements. Where do you stand on the quality of your product or service? Where do you stand on the quality of associated services? Does everybody in your organisation know where you stand on quality? Do you communicate your quality strategy to everybody in the business? Do you use quality circles in your organisation to generate ideas for continuous improvement? Quality circles can meet on a regular basis, in groups of about seven, to ask focused questions relating to increasing sales, reducing costs, increasing the quality of customer care, improving advertising effectiveness, etc. For those who have doubts about the importance of quality, let us all be fully aware that there is a correlation in business between increasing quality and profitability.

11   THE BOSTON MATRIX

The Boston Matrix provides one very interesting way of thinking about your product or products. An individual product is described as a Question Mark, a Star, a Cash Cow or a Dog. Everything starts with ideas. There is no market for a good idea, because the skill in business is in taking the idea and turning it into a profitable business. Approximately 19 out of 20 new products, or new ideas, fail. Occasionally, a new idea comes along which turns out to be a success. It is developed into a Star. Sales rise very quickly, but the Star burns up a tremendous amount of resources. Eventually, the Star becomes a mature product. Sales growth is no longer maintainable. The product becomes a Cash Cow. It generates lots of cash. Finally, sales fall way as the Cash Cow becomes a Dog. Sales and profits decline and the Dog is finally sold or terminated.

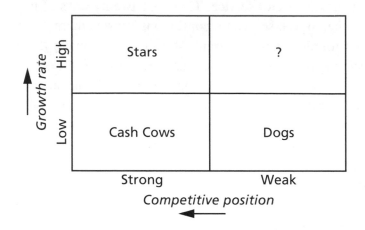

Question Marks and Stars are capable of rapid growth. Stars and Cash Cows have a strong competitive position. What kind of a product do you offer to customers? If you offer a range of products, which ones are the Stars, the Cash Cows, the Dogs? Are you generating enough new ideas in your organisation? Are you developing your Stars? Are you milking your Cash Cows? Is it time to part company with your Dogs? Can you acquire somebody else's brilliant Question Mark and sell it through your existing channels of distribution? Can you make a fortune by buying somebody else's Dog? Are you wasting time and effort promoting Dogs and Cash Cows? Are you enjoying the cash generated by your Cash Cows and Dogs, without devoting sufficient time and effort to Question Marks and Stars of the future? Do you have too many Stars in your organisation, burning up vast quantities of resources? Do you have too many dogs? Do you devote too much time and effort to developing new Question Marks, whilst ignoring possibilities for generating very high levels of positive cash flows from your Cash Cows?

12   GROWTH STRATEGIES

With a view to taking the business forward to its ideal future, you will almost certainly want the business to grow. There are essentially two growth strategies which can be adopted. We are here considering sales growth, which should be associated with growth in net profits. Of course, there could be growth in the number of employees, growth in the quantity of assets or capital employed, growth in market share, etc.

Organic Growth

This arises when the company increases its sales of existing products to existing customers and new customers. The business can also launch additional products to sell to existing customers and new customers.

Growth by acquisition

The second strategy for growth is to acquire other businesses. We can buy additional products to sell through our own distribution system to new and existing customers. We may acquire a customer base which provides additional outlets for new and existing products. This growth strategy can be effective and extremely successful. We encourage these acquisitions in our existing area of excellence, in our core business. We do not advise diversification into new industries where we do not have competitive advantage. Acquisitions for diversification have not been generally recommended. It is interesting that many conglomerates are now being disentangled.

Business history books show that the vast majority of acquisitions have not been economic successes, especially where acquisitions have been made in new areas, away from our core business, where we do not have competitive advantage and where we do not understand the corporate culture. We also recommend, that as a general rule, we should not buy the shares in target companies. On balance, we believe it makes more sense to acquire the assets, the customer base, the products, patents etc. This can avoid considerable arguments relating to outstanding legal matters, problems with patents and copyright, redundancy payments etc. We also advise extreme caution in the acquisition of other companies. As a general rule, people do not sell good businesses. Always look for the fatal flaw. You will be told that the seller has made so much money that she is ready to pass the business on to somebody else. You may also be told that she is so busy making a fortune running other businesses that she does not have the time to devote to this business.

It is generally found that the truth of the matter is that she is simply looking for somebody to take away her problem. If you do decide to acquire other companies, then make acquisitions in your own area of excellence. Buy into low technology businesses, or businesses which you understand. Buy companies where competition is difficult owing to barriers to entry. For example, there may be a shortage of skilled labour in a particular industry. Finally, acquire companies where there is evidence of overstaffing, so that all that is required is for you to reduce the fixed costs to make the business profitable.

13   THE STRATEGIC BUSINESS UNIT

At some stage in the development of the business you may find that you are producing and marketing a wide range of products. At this point, we would introduce the concept of the strategic business unit (Table 3.1).

Table 3.1   The strategic business unit: grouping of similar products. The matrix approach.

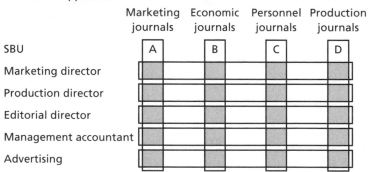

	Marketing journals	Economic journals	Personnel journals	Production journals
SBU	A	B	C	D
Marketing director				
Production director				
Editorial director				
Management accountant				
Advertising				

We were once involved in a company which produced and marketed a range of academic journals. By both organic growth and growth by acquisition, our number of journal titles increased to over thirty. We decided to introduce four strategic business units, A, B, C and D. We appointed a head of each division, one person for our group of marketing journals, a second for economic journals, a third for personnel journals and a fourth for production journals. Each strategic business unit has its own mission, sales targets, and profit targets. Our marketing director provides marketing services across all four strategic business units. He or she helps each manager of each SBU to establish competitive advantage and find the appropriate market niche. The marketing director offers support in the areas of product, price, place, promotion and people. The production director offers support in the printing of all journals across all of the four missions. The editorial director offers editorial support. The management accountant offers monthly accounting information. Our advertising executive offers advertising support across all four divisions, missions or strategic business units. We find this matrix approach works very well for small and medium-sized companies.

14 THE DRIVING FORCE

What is the driving force in your business? Most businesses are either product-driven or market-needs driven. People in product/-service-driven companies say, 'we make ball bearings and we sell as many ball bearings as we can.' People in market-needs driven organisations say, 'we offer every household item the housewife could reasonably expect to find in a supermarket.' Your company could be technology-driven in that you offer to produce any product which can be produced with your existing technology. You could be method-of-distribution driven in that you offer a range of cosmetics which your door-to-door salesforce is capable of distributing. You can also impose your own driving force on the business. We like the idea of a self-imposed organising principle for each year of the business. For example, this year our driving force is to increase sales by 25 per cent, this year our driving force is to increase the range of products from 25 to 35, this year the driving force is to earn a gross profit of 40 per cent on every contract, this year earnings per share will be increased from 40p to 55p. We find that this driving force, communicated to all members of staff, focuses all the resources of the business in achieving the one-year goal. It gives everybody a target at which they can aim. Everybody knows what is required. It makes decision-making very easy. The subconscious mind responds to clarity. Nothing could be more simple, more clear, than a one-year driving force.

15   ZERO-BASED THINKING

Do not make the mistake of thinking that overheads automatically must increase by 10 per cent or 20 per cent each year. It is true that overheads do tend to drift upwards. However, both overheads and variable costs can be reduced and even eliminated. You can 'outsource' production, advertising, production of monthly management accounting data etc. If you are an excellent marketing company, then perhaps production is not one of your areas of excellence. Can you 'outsource' your financial and management accounting, the sales function, advertising and promotion? In one of our businesses, we 'outsource' the invoicing of customers and cash collections. Zero-based thinking assumes a base of zero. You may well ask the question: 'what should that person's salary be next year?'

Here is a different question: 'knowing what we know now, should we continue to employ that person?'. If the answer to the question is 'no', then stop employing that person. Employing the wrong person is a very expensive mistake in business. Can you justify employing somebody to achieve that particular result? Are you employing the right person? Here are some additional questions:

- 'Knowing what we know now, should we be producing and marketing that particular product/service?' If the answer to the question is 'no', get out and get out quickly. What we are saying, in fact, is that it has all been a terrible mistake and we do not believe that it is going to get any better.

- 'Knowing what we know now, are we banking with the appropriate bank?' If the answer is 'no', then change your bank.
- 'Knowing what we know now, are we using the best suppliers?' If the answer to the question is 'no', change your suppliers.

Zero-based thinking helps us to avoid investment in managerial ego, overhead drift, employing inappropriate people, use of the wrong bank, use of inappropriate suppliers, use of inappropriate channels of distribution. By the way, 'knowing what you know now, are you married to the right person?'

16   CRISIS MANAGEMENT

In business, we do not wish to focus on problems, threats, or disasters. With positive mental attitude we focus on opportunities, challenges, success, the best possible outcome. At the same time, we appreciate that we must never do anything to bankrupt the business. If we take high risks, then we prefer to take high risks with our time, rather than money. We do not send out a mailing shot of 100,000 leaflets. We send out 500 leaflets, and await the response. If it works, we can send out 1000, then 5000 etc. If it does not work, then we can try a different approach. Sending out 100,000 leaflets could bankrupt the business.

Whilst not focusing on disaster, we do try to anticipate the worst possible outcome, and have a strategy for financial emergencies. We anticipate the occasional crisis by asking the question 'what if ...?'. What if our assumptions are incorrect? What happens if we find there is no market for this product? What if our advertising proves to be ineffective? What if we cannot find somebody to produce the product? What if the bank manager calls in the overdraft? What if our overheads drift upwards by 20 per cent next year? What if a key person leaves the business next month? What if the computer crashes? What if one of our important suppliers goes bust? What if our biggest customer does not pay at the end of the month? In business, just about every problem imaginable, plus a few extra which you cannot imagine, will be thrown at you. Be sure to have a strategy for coping with crises.

17   HOW TO GET RICH QUICKLY

Most people who get rich get rich slowly. Studies of all the millionaires around the world usually show that it takes about twenty years to make your first million pounds. These people find their area of excellence, their specialisation. They establish competitive advantage by differentiating their product from the competition in some way. They find their market segment or market niche, and concentrate all their resources bringing a particular benefit to their market niche within their area of core business or specialisation.

These people set personal and career goals. They resolve to pay the price in advance. They acquire the necessary knowledge, learn the necessary skills, and are excited and enthusiastic about achieving their goals, and doing whatever it takes to achieve their goals. In short, they adopt a very positive mental attitude. These people tend to have a vision of being recognised as the best in the business. Their mission is to enrich the lives of their customers in some way. They implement the necessary strategy which takes them from mission to net profit. They implement the necessary strategies to take them from where they are now to their ideal future.

The good news for those who do not want to take the slow road, is that about 20 per cent of millionaires make their first one million pounds in less than twenty years. It is possible to get rich quickly – legally! There are essentially three ways to get rich quickly:

1   the 10 per cent rule;
2   same product, different place;
3   buy a Dog.

The 10 per cent rule

Let us suppose that you decide to open a French restaurant. Where is the best place to open a French restaurant? Most people believe that the best place to open a French restaurant is somewhere where there is no French restaurant at the moment. This would entail a significant marketing exercise in that you would have to establish a competitive advantage and find a market niche. Why do you suppose there are so many Chinese restaurants in Gerrard Street in London? Do you think they like the competition? Why do you so often see one petrol station opposite another petrol station? Why do you often find several out-of-town electrical retail stores all on the same site?

In fact, the best place to open a French restaurant is across the street from another French restaurant which is totally and amazingly successful. All you have to do is open across the street and do it 10 per cent better, 10 per cent cheaper, 10 per cent faster or 10 per cent nicer. The existing French restauranteur has already done the marketing for you. They have established competitive advantage and a market niche.

Same product, different place

Next time you visit a different part of your own country, or travel overseas, make a note of those products and services which are selling extremely well. If a product is selling wonderfully well in London, Rome and Paris this week, then there is a very good chance that it will sell very well next week in Newcastle, Manchester or Liverpool. Read the business and trade magazines. Talk to people in successful businesses and successful industries. Ask your way to success. Never be afraid to make a telephone call asking somebody for an exclusive right to distribute or manufacture their successful product or service in your part of the world.

> We have an associate in Malaysia. He has made a fortune simply by marketing our management development programmes in a different market.

> An associate of ours came across some wonderful educational tapes in the USA. He has made a fortune marketing these tapes in Europe.

Buy a Dog

We have already noted that products and services can be classified as Question Marks, Stars, Cash Cows and Dogs. Larger companies tend to sell or close down their Dogs. Can you take a Dog off somebody's hands and turn it into a Cash Cow? Can you turn it into a Star? Many management buyouts can be perceived as the acquisition of a Dog from a large company.

> In the early 1970s we acquired a journal for the princely sum of £1 from a large publisher. The publisher no longer wanted to run an academic journal with only 600 subscribers. It was a Dog. We turned that journal into a Cash Cow, and used the cash to buy and launch many more titles. That particular business now has a market value in excess of £50 million.

If you wish to get rich quickly, then why not think about acquiring a Dog? A Dog may cost you nothing. In fact, the Dog may cost you less than nothing. We recently had dealings with a company which offered a cash balance of £200,000 to anybody who would take away its Dog. It is a popular myth that if you wish to succeed in business you need to come up with a new idea, a new product, a new service. New products are extremely dangerous.

The rule of thumb is that about 19 out of 20 new products fail. A second rule of thumb is that about 80 per cent of men going into business are out of business within five years. A further rule of thumb is that about 50 per cent of women going into business are out of business within five years. It is extremely dangerous to combine a man with a new product. If the man has a probability of success of .2, and the new product has a probability of success of .05, then the probability of a man succeeding in business with a new product is about 1 in 100. It is true that some men do successfully launch new products, but it is a rare event. These events often receive a great deal of media coverage, because they are rare events.

A second myth is that it is a good idea to buy somebody else's business. You simply put money in, and then money comes out. This is about 50 per cent true. In the case of most businesses, a great deal of money does go in, but unfortunately very little comes out the other end. In recent years many former executives have thrown their redundancy pay at business acquisitions. A great many of them will testify that buying a business is not a good idea. It is extremely difficult to establish competitive advantage when you have no special skills or experience in a particular industry. It can also prove extremely difficult to bring positive mental attitude to a business which is not your core business, your area of excellence, your specialisation. Simply throwing money at a business can not lead to success.

As a general rule people do not sell successful businesses. You must always look for the fatal flaw. If you do buy a business outside of your own area of specialisation, then look for a business in low technology, with barriers to entry, and preferably where there is gross overstaffing. You put yourself in a stronger position if you understand the business, if there are barriers preventing entry by competition, and where you can achieve profitability by reducing the fixed costs. If you do decide to try and get rich quickly by entering an area which is not your specialisation, then make a decision to get out after three or four years. There are millions of people around the world trying to be successful doing jobs which they do not particularly enjoy. They are working at jobs which do not make them feel valuable and worthwhile, jobs which do not raise their self-esteem, working in areas outside their areas of excellence, core business, specialisation, trying to sell products for which they are not really prepared to be product champions. These people are sometimes referred to as Type A people. They are aggressive and ambitious. They are always in a hurry. They tend to be impolite to subordinates. They are hypersensitive to criticism.

Do not make the mistake of working aggressively for long hours in an area outside your specialisation. It will kill you. You will suffer from burn-out. Type As die young. Type As can rise quickly in the early part of their careers, but they do not make it to the top. They make too many enemies. On the other hand, Type B people are more relaxed. They rise more slowly, but they rise to the top, and they live longer. They are patient. Type As often quit the organisation when in their late 40s they suddenly find themselves working for a Type B.

HOW TO GET RICH QUICKLY
1. Use the 10 per cent rule.
2. Same product, different market.
3. Buy a dog.

---

18   THE STRATEGIC BUSINESS PLAN

'Planning is one of the most complex and difficult intellectual activities in which man can engage. Not to do it well is not a sin, but to settle for doing it less than well is.'
– *Russell L. Ackoff*

The strategic business plan can be a substantial document, and is a powerful demonstration of your managerial competence. It should start with a vision or description of an ideal world perhaps 20 years into the future. It should contain a mission statement, a statement of corporate values and beliefs, our commitment to change and organisational learning, our strategy on quality, a complete industry and competitive analysis, a statement of our specialisation or core business, our competitive advantage, a description of our market segment or niche, a statement of resource requirements, our strategy for growth, a description of our strategic business units, the driving force, a statement of crisis anticipation, a strategy for financial emergencies, a comprehensive description of all the key players, forecasts of sales, costs and profits, and forecast financial statements for one year, three years, ten years and twenty years.

STRATEGIC BUSINESS PLAN

Vision

Mission

Values and beliefs

The learning organisation

Quality

Competitive analysis

Specialisation

Differentiation

Segmentation

Resource requirements

Growth strategy

Strategic business units

Driving force

Crisis anticipation

Strategy for financial emergencies

The key players

Forecast of sales, costs, profits

Forecast of cash flow

Forecast financial position

A list of key assumptions

'An objective without a plan is a dream.' – *Douglas McGregor*

19 MAJOR REASONS FOR BUSINESS FAILURE

There is one reason for all business failure – incorrect assumptions. Nobody goes into business with the intention of going bust. However, most businesses do go bust. Keep questioning your assumptions. What are our assumptions about the product? What are our assumptions about customers? What are our assumptions about credit periods? It is usually extremely difficult to say why a business went bust, because it is extremely difficult to measure the effect of taking certain actions and failure to take other actions. We produce a list below of the causes for business failure found in many surveys.

Specialisation

1 No mission, no clear goals, stated objective to make a pile of money.
2 Customer not perceived as a top priority.
3 Loss of momentum in sales, poor sales performance.
4 Impatience, trying to get rich quickly.
5 Operating outside own area of excellence, diversification into unassociated businesses.
6 Failure to focus on priorities, failure to focus on the 20 per cent that brings in the 80 per cent.

Differentiation

7 Failure to establish competitive advantage, failure to be better, cheaper, faster or nicer, trying to sell a commodity.
8 Product not suited to customer requirements.
9 Poor quality of product and support.

Segmentation

10 Failure to identify customers.
11 Reactive rather than proactive selling.
12 Incomplete marketing strategy, poor sales programme.

Concentration

13 Poor leadership, lack of integrity and competence of key staff, lack of commitment and persistence.

14 Mismanagement of working capital.

15 Failure to analyse and respond to trends, changes in the market place.

16 Failure to control overhead drift.

17 No business plan.

18 Inadequate financial records, poor budgeting, poor cash control.

19 Action without planning, failure to collect the relevant facts.

20 Paralysis by analysis, too much analysis, not enough action.

21 Poor relations with staff and employees, poor communications, command and control mentality.

In the early 1970s a university had a wonderful business school – excellent staff, excellent facilities, no competition. The university milked its cash cow to support its dogs. The good guys left, every other academic institution entered the market and in the late 1980s the economy entered recession. In the early 1990s the university decided to expand the business school. It was just too late. Twenty years too late, in a totally saturated market, at the bottom of a depression, they decided to go for growth.

There is always a 'too late'.

One publishing business with which we are associated has invested £1m in electronic publishing. 'The world is going electronic. Nobody wants paper any more.' In fact, people still like paper. Librarians like to see publications on library shelves. Perhaps in the future ...

There is always a 'too soon'.

20 MAJOR REASONS FOR BUSINESS SUCCESS

Specialisation

1 Clear mission, clear goals.
2 Customer is top priority.
3 Strong momentum in sales.
4 Patience, the ability to take the 20-year view.
5 Stick to the knitting, avoid pointless diversification.
6 The ability to focus on the 20 per cent that brings in the 80 per cent, ability to focus on priorities.

Differentiation

7 Clear competitive advantage, at least 10 per cent better, cheaper, faster or nicer than the rest.
8 Product suited to customer requirements.
9 Excellent quality of product and support.

Segmentation

10 Ability to locate customers, market niche.
11 Proactive as well as reactive selling.
12 Complete marketing strategy, excellent sales programme.

Concentration

13 Good leadership, integrity and competence of key staff, commitment and persistence.
14 Good working capital management.
15 Ability to analyse and respond to trends, changes in the marketplace.
16 Tight control on overheads.
17 Complete business plan.
18 Good accounting records, good budgeting, tight control of cash.

19 A focus on action which gets results.
20 Action follows decisions based on collection of relevant information.
21 Good relationships with staff and employees, excellent communications, facilitate and empower mentality.

21 CHARACTERISTICS OF EXCELLENT COMPANIES

Given all that we have said so far, it should not surprise us that the following are found to be some of the characteristics of excellent companies.

1 *A bias for action.* Only action gets results. Successful companies do it, try it, fix it. They are not obsessed with reports, committees, and meetings.
2 *Closeness to the customer.* Know your customer, love your customer, be passionate in relation to customer service. Listen to the wants and needs of your customers on quality and service, as do other excellent companies.
3 *Autonomy and entrepreneurship.* Top companies encourage innovation, find product champions, run the business as a set of innovative strategic business units.
4 *Productivity through people.* Excellent companies have respect for their employees. They continuously improve the quality of products and support by drawing upon the innovative talents of their employees. Employees are involved in the business.
5 *Hands-on, value-driven executives.* The senior executives in successful companies adopt a certain leadership style. They are involved in operations, they avoid hiding in ivory towers. They have face-to-face engagements. There is a strong corporate culture.
6 *Stick to the knitting.* Leading companies avoid conglomerate diversification. Stick to the knitting, stick to core business, areas of excellence, specialisation. Focus on strengths and opportunities.

7   *Simple form, lean staff.* Avoid unnecessary bureaucracy. Avoid complex staff structures, in line with other top companies. Reduce layers of management to the minimum requirement.

8   *Loose-tight properties.* Successful companies allow employees the flexibility to take initiatives within a strong corporate culture.

STRATEGY GETS YOU FROM WHERE YOU ARE NOW
TO YOUR IDEAL FUTURE.
STRATEGY WILL GET YOUR BACKSIDE
OUT OF THE GUTTER.
STRATEGY GETS YOU FROM MISSION TO PROFIT.
LEARN WHAT YOU NEED TO KNOW, BE VERY POSITIVE
IN YOUR ATTITUDE, ESTABLISH YOUR SPECIALISATION,
ESTABLISH COMPETITIVE ADVANTAGE, FIND YOUR MARKET
NICHE, THEN FOCUS ALL YOUR RESOURCES
SELLING YOUR BENEFIT WITH ITS COMPETITIVE ADVANTAGE
TO YOUR MARKET NICHE WITHIN YOUR AREA
OF EXCELLENCE.
IT WILL APPEAR TO OTHER PEOPLE
THAT YOU HAVE ALL THE LUCK IN THE WORLD.

Four

MARKETING IS THE KEY

How to implement a winning marketing strategy

Which orders would you like to win? The answer to this question is your marketing. How does your product or service improve the life of your customer? The answer to this question identifies the benefit you sell. Why should anybody buy this product or service from you? The answer to this question is your competitive advantage. Where are the customers for the product or service you offer? The answer to this question is your market segment or market niche.

1   MARKETING PHILOSOPHY

The meaning of life is to enrich the lives of others. The meaning or objective of all businesses is to improve the lives of others. Businesses exist to satisfy customers, to win and keep customers. If the market value of the firm's output is greater than its costs, costs which are usually paid for at market values, then the firm makes a profit. The emphasis has to be on improvements to the life of the customer, who will reciprocate by paying cash if the customer feels that the benefit or improvement received is worth at least the price paid.

In the competitive sector of the economy, customers decide who works and who does not work. Every time you spend your money, you decide who works and who does not work. Customers, not producers, decide what sells in the market place. A customer is somebody who is willing and able to pay for a product or service.

> A customer is someone who is willing and able to buy the benefit you offer.

A job is an opportunity to enrich the life of a customer. A job is not a position you are entitled to hold which is generally commensurate with your age, qualifications and experience. The marketing philosophy is that all the resources of a firm, i.e. its creativity, people, budgets, production facilities etc. are all directed to winning and keeping customers, directed towards customer satisfaction, customer care, relationship selling, a fanaticism for quality and service. Customer satisfaction is more important than profit. If you don't satisfy a need or a want for your customer, you cannot make a sale. No sales equals no salaries. No sales equals no profit. Providing benefits to customers, improving the lives of customers is the objective. Profit could be the result.

> A job is an opportunity to enrich the life of a customer.

MARKETING
Which orders would you like to win?
What benefit do you sell?
Why should a customer buy the benefit from you?
Where are your customers?

Many of our acquaintances work in the public sector. They hate to be told that they do not necessarily have jobs (a job is an opportunity to improve the life of a customer). They hate to be reminded that they get paid out of the taxpayers' pockets, not by customers (a customer is somebody who is *willing and able* to pay for the benefit you offer). Of course, they all justify their positions. They all claim that what they do has tremendous value. We then point out that if what they do has value, then obviously they would love to transfer to the private sector or have their departments privatised, so that they can be fully rewarded for the quality and quantity of what they do for other people.

They usually admit that they prefer to work in the public sector because there is no competition, they do not have to win business, they do not have to generate sales, they do not have to deal with customers, they get paid for their age, qualifications and experience, they get automatic pay rises, they don't get fired, they can come and go pretty much as they please, nobody measures what they do, they do not have to make profits, their job is to spend the budget, they are in the pension scheme, they can retire at 50 on an index-linked pension, they finish early on Fridays, they get great holidays, and they do not have to take work home with them.

Many of these people look enviously at successful people in the private sector. They want to be paid the same salaries as their 'counterparts' in the private sector. The fact of the matter is that there are no counterparts in the private sector. There is no basis for comparison. In the private sector, nobody has to buy anything. It's all voluntary. In the private sector, nobody has to pay for anything they do not want. Tax-payers are forced to pay for all public-sector expenditure, whether they like it or not. Tax-payers are forced to pay for 'services' even if they do not use them. For those people who really do wish to transfer from the public to the private sector, we offer the word TUPSY. A tupsy is a totally unemployable public sector yanker. Attitudes can be changed in seconds. Can you move from tupsy to a fanaticism for quality and service in a competitive world? Can you adopt the attitude, 'I love my customers and I always do more than that for which I get paid'?

2   DEFINITION OF MARKETING

Marketing answers the question: which orders would we like to win? Marketing is concerned with product, price, place, people and promotion. Which products/services do you wish to sell? At which price do you intend to sell your product? In which place do you intend to sell? To which people do you intend to sell? How do you intend to promote/advertise your product?

Marketing involves differentiating your product vis-à-vis the competition, i.e. establishing competitive advantage. Why should anybody buy the benefit from you? The answer to this question is your competitive advantage. Who cares? Where are the customers for your product or service? The answer to this question identifies your market segment, your market niche. Marketing includes the process of determining customer needs and matching the product or service to those needs. Marketing involves winning and retaining customers. Most people put making money at the top of their list. They state that the objective of the business is to make money, satisfying consumer wants, in competitive markets, by matching the resources of the organisation to the needs of the market place.

We place the emphasis on achieving the business mission by improving the life of the customer in some way. If firms focus on the benefit to the customer, then they are at least in with a chance of making a profit. Most people who go into business to make lots of money fail in business. Marketing is determining which orders you would like to win. Selling is getting out there and winning orders once you have decided which orders you would like to win. Marketing is a continuous process of creativity, research, testing, analysis, development and implementation. We must stay close to our customers. We must satisfy our customers' needs and anticipate their wants. We love our customers and we always do that little bit extra for which we do not get paid.

'The private sector is the part of the economy the Government controls and the public sector is that part that nobody controls.'
– *Sir James Goldsmith*

---

3   SPECIALISATION, DIFFERENTIATION, SEGMENTATION, CONCENTRATION

Specialisation is your area of excellence or core business. Differentiation is your competitive advantage, i.e. the reason why customers buy the product or service from you. Segmentation involves identifying your customers or market niche. Concentration means focusing all the resources of the business, hitting your market niche with your competitive advantage in your area of excellence. Many of us start out bclicving that busincss is about sclling rubbish products to idiots who don't really need or want them, but are still persuaded to buy them at prices they certainly cannot afford. Apparently, this is not the case. If we believe in the free-enterprise market system, then we believe, and a great deal of evidence suggests, that in order to run a successful business we must concentrate all our forces, hitting our market segment with our competitive advantage in our area of excellence.

4   SPECIALISATION

Which product or service would you like to produce and sell? In which area of human activity would you like to improve the lives of other people? To which area of human improvement can you bring excitement and enthusiasm? What is your area of excellence? What is your core business? For which product or service are you prepared to be a product champion? What would you love to do to improve the lives of others for 16 hours each day, even if you were to receive no financial reward? What is it that makes you feel valuable and worthwhile? Remember there is a strong relationship between high self-esteem and peak performance. The more you love doing something, the greater will be your success. All successful businesses specialise in their areas of excellence. Many unsuccessful people drift into areas where they do not have the excitement, enthusiasm, energy, knowledge etc. to establish competitive advantage and find their market segment.

What do you sell?
What is the benefit?
How does your product/service
improve the life of your customers?
Customers buy benefits!

'We act as though comfort and luxury were the chief requirements of life, when all that we need to make us happy is something to be enthusiastic about.' – *Charles Kingsley*

---

5 DIFFERENTIATION/COMPETITIVE ADVANTAGE

Perhaps the biggest question in any business is: why should anybody buy this product or service ... from me? This is in fact two questions. The first question is: why should anybody buy this product or service? What is the benefit? What is the improvement in the life of the customer? How is the customer's life enriched by acquisition of the product or service? If you cannot answer this question, then you do not know why a customer should buy the product or service. Remember the law of cause and effect. There is a reason for everything. There has to be a reason why your customer buys the product or service. There is no such thing as an accidental sale.

The second question is even more important. Why should anybody buy the benefit from me? Why should they buy the benefit from you? In competitive markets, the customer can always buy the benefit from another supplier. There has to be a reason why the customer buys from you. Fortunately, there are only four answers to the question. People and other businesses buy from you because you are better, cheaper, faster, or nicer than the competition.

Your product or service could be perceived by the customer as being better in some way. There is nearly always a market for a product which is cheaper. In fact, the competitive advantage of most businesses is 'faster'. The competitive advantage of your local service station, cinema, fish and chip shop, private school, shoe shop, supermarket, hairdresser, taxi service, is probably that it's just down the road. It may not be the best fish-and-chip shop, it may not be the cheapest fish-and-chip shop. However it is just down the road.

The fourth area of competitive advantage is that you could be a nicer person. We all have a very strong tendency to buy from people we like. We have a friend, Angela, who is a totally lovely and delightful person. We are unable to say 'no' to Angela. She runs a restaurant. She invites us along for the Italian Night, then the French Night, then the Indian Night, etc. We cannot refuse. It has to be said that the food is not 'better'. Her husband, Alan, is not much of a cook. It is not 'cheaper', costing £60 for a meal for two people. It takes Alan about three hours to serve the meal, and it is a 25-mile drive to the restaurant. The business fails on 'faster'. Angela's business thrives on the fact that she is such a wonderful person. Even if you do not have a wonderful product, even if the product is not cheap, even if you do not provide a speedy service, the business can thrive on you being a nice person. Many businesses thrive because they provide a very speedy and a very pleasant service.

'The bitterness of poor quality and service remains long after the sweetness of low price is forgotten.' – *John Ruskin*

If you are the best, you need not be the cheapest. Many of us start out believing that the quantity of sales is a function only of price. Price is only one factor. Why should anybody buy this product or service from you? Do they buy for the perceived quality? Do you offer the best value for money? Do they buy from you on price? Do they only buy from you because you are the local dealer? Do they buy from you because you are a nice person? You must be able to answer these questions to sell your product. If you cannot identify your competitive advantage, then ask your customers. Once you identify the benefit that you sell, and the reason why the customers buy the benefit from you, then you are ready to maximise your sales by identifying your market segment.

In a competitive world, you must be able to offset the competitive advantage of your competition. What is the competitive advantage of your competition? What benefit does your customer perceive from buying from your competitor? Why should a customer switch to you from the competitor? What is the advantage to the customer? For a customer to switch from your competitor to you, you must be at least 10 per cent better, 10 per cent cheaper, 10 per cent faster or 10 per cent nicer. Is there some unique way in which your product or service can be made superior to the competition? Can you establish a unique selling proposition for which there is an identifiable market niche? Can you establish a recognizable brand name which differentiates your product or service from the competition? Can you licence others to use the brand name?

Finally, do not be judgmental about the preferences of other people. We all buy products and services which are consistent with our self-concepts, our bundle of beliefs about ourselves. If you shop at Sainsbury's, you are a Sainsbury's person. If you shop at Asda, you are an Asda person. You choose the car consistent with your self-concept, clothing and hairstyle consistent with your self concept, etc. Where are the customers whose self-concepts are consistent with buying your product or services?

We cannot overstate the significance of competitive advantage. A company selling vodka found that customers bought the product, rather than some other form of alcohol, because vodka cannot be smelt on the breath of the drinker. Sales rocketed when their advertising announced: 'It takes your breath away', 'It leaves you breathless.' By identifying their competitive advantage, they identified their market segment – secret drinkers! Discovering the competitive advantage led to tremendous commercial success.

By contrast, a company produced hand-made bed frames and charged a premium for craftsmanship. Sales were not brilliant. A survey of customers revealed that generally people did not see any benefit in the craftsmanship. Once the mattress was thrown on the bed frame, nobody could appreciate that the bed was hand-made. Machine-made beds are just as good in the eyes of the customer.

Finally, a close friend of ours paid a large firm of UK accountants £30,000 to put together a business plan for an image-processing business. In a £100 million market it was assumed that sales would be £1 million in the first year. All projections were based on the £1 million sales assumption. We asked the questions: 'Why should anybody buy this product or service from you? Why should anybody drive past IBM to do business with you?'. Our friend could not answer the question, but insisted: 'It's only 1%.' We stressed that there has to be a competitive advantage – a reason why they buy it from you. Our friend chose to launch the business on the incorrect assumption that £1 million worth of sales would be accumulated within the first year. The business lost £1 million in the first year.

There is no such thing as an accidental sale. There has to be a reason why they buy a product or service from you. It always makes us wonder about the origin of human beings. If we really were designed by somebody, then that somebody must have had a great sense of humour. Everybody wants to be more, have more, and do more, and at the same time we are generally too lazy, ill informed, selfish, greedy, impatient, ruthless, disloyal, irresponsible, unreliable and vain, to actually achieve our desire to be more, have more, and do more!

COMPETITIVE ADVANTAGE
Why should anybody buy this product/service ... from me?

WHAT IS YOUR COMPETITIVE ADVANTAGE?
Are you better?
Are you cheaper?
Are you faster?
Are you nicer?

A company struggled to sell vodka. Market research found that secret drinkers prefer vodka because it leaves no smell on the drinker's breath. Once the company had discovered its competitive advantage, sales rocketed when they advertised the product on the basis that it leaves you breathless, it takes your breath away.

A company selling bed frames 'hand made by craftsmen' struggled in a competitive world. Market research revealed that the customer did not perceive 'hand made' bed frames as superior to machine-made frames. The company switched to much cheaper machine-made bed frames.

When businesses compete products and services get better, cheaper and faster. Suppliers get nicer. Competition gives customers choice. The customer is free to choose on quality, price, speed of delivery, or friendliness.

6   SEGMENTATION/MARKET NICHE

'The business of business is getting and keeping customers.'
– *Peter Drucker*

Who are your customers? Where are your customers? Who cares that you are the best? Who cares that you are the cheapest? Who cares that you are the local dealer? Who cares that you are such a nice person? The answers to these questions establish your market segmentation, or your market niche, i.e. a small segment of the market which you can dominate. If people buy from you because you are such a lovely person, then your market niche may well be your circle of friends and friends of your friends. If you own the village grocery store, then your customers are probably restricted to those living within a five-minute walk or two-minute drive, i.e. the local community. If yours is the best or cheapest product on the market, then this opens up huge opportunities.

Who is your customer? Who buys this product or service? Identify your market segment. Describe your customer: age, sex, income, occupation, education, other interests, area where he or she lives, type of family, other products he or she buys, etc. Where exactly is your customer? Identify the geographic concentration, understanding that 80 per cent of your customers will be within 20 per cent of your catchment area. How is your product normally distributed? How would you expect your customer to buy your product or service? To which customers does your competitive advantage make a big difference? Is there a small segment of the market which you could dominate?

Keep detailed records on every sale. Study the history of your company to identify those who have bought in the past. Make tremendous efforts to gain access to lists of people who have bought the product both from your business and from your competitors. Establish a database for repeat purchases.

SEGMENTATION
Who cares that you are better, cheaper, faster or nicer?

CUSTOMER CHARACTERISTICS
Everybody wants to:
be more
have more
do more.

---

7   CONCENTRATION

With a view to succeeding in business, we have to concentrate all our resources, hitting our market segment with our competitive advantage in our area of excellence. We have to concentrate our creativity, our marketing, our sales skills, leadership skills, finance, time, energy, excitement, enthusiasm, advertising and promotional efforts, production facilities, etc., all of these resources being concentrated in enriching the lives of our customers – at a profit.

Is the benefit we offer worth more to the customer than the price the customer is expected to pay? Can we provide the benefit at a cost which is lower than the customer is willing and able to pay? Can we provide the benefit at a profit? A manager's job is to get results. In business, the result we seek is a profit. The mission is to enrich the life of our customer in some way. We need people skills: leadership, delegation, supervision, and creativity. We need marketing skills: differentiation and segmentation. We need strategic skills: specialisation, differentiation, segmentation and concentration. We need financial skills: generate gross profit, control overhead, gross profit less overhead equals net profit.

Most businesses fail within five years. If we specialise, establish sustainable competitive advantage, strive to find our market niche, and concentrate all our resources, hitting our market segment with our competitive advantage in our area of specialisation, then we are at least in with a chance of making a profit.

An associate of ours decided to launch a business in image processing. He paid a firm of accountants £30,000 to put together a business plan. The financial forecasts were based on the assumption that the firm would earn £1m in revenue in the first year. We were told: 'It's only 1 per cent of the market.' Our associate could not answer the questions: 'Why should anybody buy this product/service from you? 'Why should they drive past IBM to come to you?'. He insisted: 'It's only 1 per cent.' The business lost £1m in the first year. We advised him to get out – quickly. This time he took our advice.

8   CUSTOMER CHARACTERISTICS

What are the basic characteristics of human beings? As customers we all tend to be lazy, ill-informed, selfish, greedy, impatient, disloyal, ruthless, irresponsible, unreliable and, despite having all these characteristics, we are incredibly vain.

People are lazy. Most of us have a strong tendency to do that which is unnecessary and easy, rather than that which is difficult but necessary. We drift into a comfort zone. We could cook our own food, make our own clothes, grow our own vegetables, but we can't be bothered. We prefer others to carry out these tasks for us. As a general rule, we would rather watch television or go to a public house.

People are ill-informed. Almost nobody knows how a television works, or how a car engine works. Most people simply like to watch the television and drive the car. Most people are extremely selfish. They think almost only of their own interests. They are greedy, in that they would rather have more for less. People are impatient. They want the benefit and they want it now. People are disloyal. After 15 years of dealing with one supplier, customers will switch, providing they can find another supplier who is 10 per cent better, cheaper, faster or nicer.

People are ruthless in that they take advantage of the weakness of others. We tend to be irresponsible creatures. We prefer to blame others for the conditions in our lives, rather than accept responsibility for ourselves. Most people are extremely unreliable, in that they are generally late for appointments, and that they do not hesitate to go back on their word. Despite all these characteristics, we are vain creatures. We love to be told that we are wonderful, admirable, exemplary individuals.

To be successful in life, to be successful in business and marketing, you have to develop the opposite of these characteristics. You need a tremendous amount of energy which is stimulated by your love for the customer, your excitement and enthusiasm in enriching the lives of others. You need to be well-informed. You need to be unselfish in that you offer good deals, which incidentally lead to repeat business. You do not take more than that to which you are entitled for the efforts you have made. You are extremely patient. Remember that it usually takes 20 years to make your first one million pounds. You are loyal to your customers, family, partners, suppliers, and even to your bank manager. You are a go-giver. You help other people. You accept responsibility for yourself and the results of the business. You are reliable in that you are never late for appointments. Your word is your bond, even if it costs you money. Finally, you are not vain. You are self-effacing. If other people wish to sing your praises, then so be it.

To which of the above human characteristics does your product or service appeal? Despite having these unattractive characteristics, people want to be more, have more and do more. How does your product help people to be more, do more or have more? People want to be more successful, more attractive, more healthy, more happy, etc. People want to have more paintings, more property, more money etc. People want to do more travel, more aerobics, etc. People want their lives to be enriched. People want their conditions to be improved. People want benefits.

9 BENEFITS

'It is thrifty to prepare today for the wants of tomorrow.'
– *Aesop*

Most of us want to improve our condition in many ways. We all came into the world uninhibited, unafraid, and with a success instinct. We all want to do more, have more and be more. In which ways does your product or service improve the life of your customer? What benefit do you sell? People buy benefits. It looks like a product or a service, but they actually buy the improvement, the benefit. Does your product satisfy the customer's ego needs, status needs, survival needs, or self-preservation needs? Does your product or service offer the customer greater peace of mind, improved relationships with others, greater financial freedom, the ability to pursue more worthy goals, greater self-knowledge, or greater self-fulfilment?

Is the benefit you offer greater safety, self-preservation, security, social status, recognition, prestige, admiration, more respect? If you are selling to business people, are you selling a higher level of sales, lower costs, or increased profits? Are you selling self-improvement, self-actualisation, excitement, popularity, self-expression, power, influence, better health, more success, more wealth, knowledge, companionship or higher self-esteem? Customers want excellent wine and food, better housing, furniture, paintings, gold taps in the bathroom, and gold hubcaps on their favourite motor cars. There seems to be no limit to the benefits people want.

In such a world, there is no such thing as unemployment. Clearly, there are many unemployable people, but as long as we all want to be more, have more, and do more, we must conclude that a very high level of employment is the natural state of affairs. Wealth is not a finite commodity. Our lives can be improved dramatically. This weekend you could decorate my dining room. I could teach your kids how to speak French. We could both be better off. We are all in the same business – to maximise the benefits we bring into the lives of other people, providing we are doing something which is legal, moral and ethical.

IS IT LEGAL, MORAL, ETHICAL?

Your social responsibility is to maximise the benefits
you bring into the lives of other people.
We all get rewarded for the quality and quantity
of what we do for other people.

One way or another, everybody is selling peace of mind,
improvements in the human condition, happiness.
After one of our courses we saw a sign on a van:
'We don't sell burglar alarms, we sell peace of mind.'

Is the benefit big enough? Is it big enough for people to actually buy it? How can you increase the value of the benefit? Can you put numbers on it? You should be able to state with confidence that spending £150,000 on a piece of equipment will result in savings of £250,000 per annum for four years. This is music to the customer's ears.

10 IDENTIFYING CUSTOMER NEEDS

Many businesses fail to identify their customers' needs. Many business people are ill-informed as to the benefit they provide and their own competitive advantage. Why not ask your customers? What benefit do they perceive? Why do they buy the benefit from you? Listen to customer complaints. Listen to your sales people, analyse customer service enquiries, organise discussions with focus groups, conduct customer clinics, arrange discussions with your individual customers, listen carefully to requests for additional products and services from your existing customers.

11 THE PRODUCT MIX

At any one time, you may have several products in your product portfolio. Everything starts with ideas. These ideas are your question marks. Some of these become Stars. They sell well, but require heavy expenditure on development, production, advertising, promotion and working capital tied up in stock and debtors. Eventually, these Stars, hopefully, become Cash Cows. They are well-established and generate high levels of positive cash flows. Sadly, these Cash Cows turn into Dogs. Competitors become well-established, sales fall away and we begin to think about closing down the product or selling it to somebody younger, perhaps with more energy.

Examine your product mix. Do you need to generate more ideas? Are you trying to finance too many Stars? Are your Cash Cows giving you a false feeling of security? When will they fade away into Dogs? Do you need to dispose of your favourite Dog? Can you redesign a Dog, and turn it back into a Star or Cash Cow? Do you have a well-balanced product portfolio which encourages the survival and growth of your business?

Stars	Question Marks
Cash Cows	Dogs

12   EXTENDING THE PRODUCT RANGE

Your best customers are your customers! Which products can you add to your existing product range? If your customers are already buying A, B and C from you, make the necessary effort to identify products D, E, F, G etc. Some years ago both authors were associated with a new business which bought one academic journal, one Dog of a journal, from a large quoted public company for the princely sum of £1. Shortly afterwards, a second journal was launched. It was decided to merge the two academic journals into one journal.

Your best customers are your customers. However, an examination of the subscription lists revealed that there was a very high overlap between subscribers. The managers of the business had a blinding flash of the obvious. They subsequently launched 160 journals and sold them to the same customer base, i.e. academic libraries throughout the world. Which additional customers exist for your existing products? Which additional products can you sell to your existing customers? Finding the answers to these questions has led to tremendous success for hundreds of businesses.

13   JOINT MARKETING

The authors of this book own six academic journals which are marketed throughout the world. We cannot afford world-wide marketing. However, large publishing companies can afford world-wide marketing. We have entered into an agreement with a much larger

publishing company whereby the larger company handles our sub-
scriptions and allows us to advertise and market our products
world-wide jointly with their products. This operation has proved
to be extremely successful for the smaller business, and we can only
assume quite satisfactory for the larger business.

Can you identify any larger companies with which you can negotiate joint mailings, joint marketing efforts, joint distribution? Can
you co-operate with a research institute, university, or a professional
institute? Can you co-operate with others in joint marketing? This
host-beneficiary relationship has proved to be extremely profitable
for many small businesses.

14   SHIFT THE RISK FROM THE BUYER TO THE SELLER

As customers, most of us are extremely risk-averse. We hate making
purchases which worsen our condition, in that the benefit is not
worth the price that we paid. Yet under law the rule is *caveat emptor*,
let the buyer beware. Your customers will be very impressed if you
shift the risk from them back to yourself, the seller. You could offer
30–120-days' free usage, guarantees for between twelve months and
three years, a guaranteed trade-in value after two or three years, a
100-per-cent money-back guarantee if the customer is not satisfied
in any way. If you sell oil paintings, imagine the effect on a customer
if you offer to buy back a painting at the full purchase price at any
time within the next three years!

Customers are extremely impressed when you take on the risk
which most business people assume should be accepted by the buyer.
The two authors of this book have purchased over two hundred
items of furniture from one dealer who guarantees that he will
always take back a piece of furniture at the price originally paid. We
have taken back nothing yet!

15   OPPORTUNITY GAP ANALYSIS

Is there an unfilled demand in your market for a superior product,
a cheaper product, a faster service, or a more pleasant dealer? Life

is full of opportunities. Opportunities are like buses. You need not worry if you miss one opportunity, because another one will come along in about 20 minutes. From our studies in creativity, we know that there are 20 solutions to every problem, 20 ways to rise to every challenge etc.

Which opportunities exist for you in the market place? Which gaps exist in the market place which you can fill? In which other ways could you sell your product or service? Have you considered direct mail, telesales, retail, auctions, office to office, wholesale, joint marketing with competitors, joint marketing with associated products? Which new customers exist for your existing product or service? There are 20 ways to increase the quality of your product. There are 20 ways in which you can market your product. There are 20 ways in which you can improve the quality of your customer care. How could you change your product or service to make it more attractive to your existing customers? How could you change your product to make it more attractive to new customers? In which ways can you make your product better, cheaper, faster, and in which ways can you be nicer to your customers? Which new products could you sell to your existing customers? Which new customers can you find for your existing products? How can you tackle market ignorance? Which non-customers could you approach? Which new products do your existing customers want? How do you distribute your product at the moment? Which new distribution channels exist for your products? Which additional products could you distribute through your existing channels of distribution? Can you develop new products for your existing channels? Which new markets exist for your existing products and services and your existing distribution systems? Which additional products could you manufacture with your existing facilities?

16   THE MAJOR OBSTACLE OR ROCK

What is the key obstacle or rock which stands between you and success in the market? Is it quality, advertising effectiveness, sales skills, the distribution system, finance, market ignorance, poor relationships with customers, inadequate competitive advantage, failure to find your market segment, failure to concentrate your resources, price, employing the wrong people, failure to train your existing people? If you could overcome these obstacles, which new opportunities would open up to you, which gaps in the market could you fill?

17   ADVERTISING

Billions of pounds are wasted every year on bad advertising. If you have no knowledge whatsoever of advertising then use AIDA and 'how to'. A is for attention, I stands for interest, D stands for desire and A is for action. Your advertisement must attract the attention of the reader. It must be interesting. It must arouse desire in your customer. The advertisement must tell the customer what action to take. The advertisement should focus on the benefit to the customer, and the reason why the customer should buy the benefit from you, i.e. your competitive advantage. Your headline must attract attention. Your headline or second headline could contain the words 'how to'. For example, 'how to get the job you want', 'how to acquire a four-bedroomed detached house in Tunbridge Wells for less than £200,000', 'how to get such and such a car for less than £10,000', 'how to lose fourteen pounds in less than two weeks'.

Bad advertising often starts with the name of the company, followed by a short history of the business ... Smith and Williams ... founded some 25 years ago in 1975, Smith and Williams have vast experience ... You have already lost the attention of the reader. The headline must catch the attention of the customer: Affordable yachts; live close to your work; 50% off school fees; how to win friends and influence people; how to make your first £1 million in business; do you make these mistakes in English?; beautiful hands ... or your money back; original oil paintings ... for less than £500; choose three best sellers for only £1; learn any language ... in 2 weeks; do you suffer from stress?; is your home picture-poor?; how much is stress costing your company?; if you were given £150,000, isn't this the kind of home you would build for yourself? Change the above headlines to suit your business.

Having attracted the reader's attention, disclose something interesting about your product or service. 'You may have recently read that ...', 'Research shows that ...'. Then stimulate the desire of your reader. 'You could benefit ... you could increase your sales, reduce costs, increase profits ... you really could afford ...'. Finally, ask for action ... 'Ring this number, fax me ... etc.'.

With an initial advertising budget of £1,000 how can you spend £10,000 on advertising? The answer is that you direct say 50% of new sales income back into advertising. The advertising budget does not benefit from repeat business, only from new sales income. This focuses minds on winning new business and provides a continuous flow of funds into the advertising budget.

18   OVERCOMING MARKET IGNORANCE

Your main competition in the market place may not be your competitors. Your biggest rock could be market ignorance. People do not even know that you exist. You can overcome market ignorance by using good advertising, gaining access to good lists for your mailing shots, and by good public relations. You can gain access to free publicity on the radio and even television if you can come up with interesting stories which are of genuine interest to listeners and viewers. Similarly, newspapers are always looking for items of interest to their readers.

19   INDUSTRIAL MARKETING

Most businesses sell to other businesses. When you are dealing with other businesses, just as when you are dealing with end users, focus on the benefit to the customer. Do not focus on the product or service as you see it. Remember that other businesses are primarily interested in increasing sales, reducing costs and increasing profits. You may well be offering to increase the quality, to add value to the product of your customer. Your customer knows that increasing the quality will increase sales which should result in increased profits. If you are dealing with the marketing/sales people, focus on increasing sales. If you are holding discussions with the Production Manager and Management Accountant, then focus on reducing costs. If you are in discussion with the Chief Executive and other Board Members then focus on increasing profits. Try to put numbers on the financial benefit to your customer.

> ## INDUSTRIAL MARKETING
> If you deal with other businesses,
> then you are really selling:
> increased sales
> reduced costs
> increased profits.

20 MARKETING COMMODITIES

You may be in the unfortunate position of not having a competitive advantage. One ton of steel appears to be pretty much the same as another ton of steel. A gallon of petrol from one petroleum company is pretty much the same as a gallon of petrol from some other petroleum company. These are tough markets. In these commodity markets, products are sold on price, pressure and promotion. Price is extremely important. You can develop relationships by providing tickets to rugby matches, the opera, by organising golfing events etc. You can promote your company by financing amateur sports, financing professional sports, supporting good causes. You can try to differentiate your product by giving it a recognisable brand name. These can be very difficult markets.

Our advice is that you try to establish competitive advantage, some unique selling proposition which differentiates you from the rest. If you can't be better, then maybe you can provide a faster service, or maybe you can be a very, very pleasant person. Otherwise, it's price, price, price, pressure and promotion!

We have worked with a steel company for many years. Attempts have been made to differentiate the product, but a ton of steel is still a commodity which can be acquired from several sources. Price is extremely important. The company's sales people provide lots of tickets for events, they establish relationships with customers based on friendship and nationalism, and they sponsor sports events. Yes, with commodities it's price, price, price, pressure and promotion. Do try to differentiate your product. Do try to establish a competitive advantage. Make every effort to be faster and nicer.

> ## COMMODITIES: TOUGH MARKETS
> A commodity can usually only be sold
> on price, price, price, pressure and promotion.
> You could be faster and nicer.

21 MARKETING NEW PRODUCTS

A useful rule of thumb is that 19 out of every 20 new products fail. The world is full of wonderful new ideas. The vast majority of new businesses fail within five years. If you start a new business with a new product, then the probability of success is extremely low. Nevertheless, some businesses do succeed. Some new products do succeed.

Is this new product within your area of specialisation, your area of excellence? Is it at least 10 per cent better, or 10 per cent cheaper, or 10 per cent faster than its competition? Is the same product available elsewhere? If it is, you can only sell it on price, pressure and promotion. What is the benefit? Which desire does it satisfy? Which fear does it allay? Would you buy it? Is it consistent with human characteristics? Have you studied the market for this product in newspaper articles, academic articles, advertisements, trade-show statistics, trade magazines, import/export figures? Have you read the appropriate journals on success, fortune, venture capital, money, entrepreneurship and business trends? Have you had lengthy discussions with people in that business, in that industry? Have you sought out the negative opinions of your family, friends, business associates and especially your bank manager, as well as customers, and the competition?

Have you tested the market? Do you have a demonstration model or a photograph? Have you discussed prices and delivery dates with distributors? Have you discussed the product with professional buyers and prospective customers? Have you carried out a detailed analysis of your product versus the competition? Have you attended trade shows? Have you carried out the one store test or the one customer test? Have you carried out a mailing shot of the most likely 100 customers? Do not make the mistake of making an initial mailing shot of 100,000. This in itself could bankrupt your business. Test everything that you do in business – on a very small scale at first. If you do this, failure may not turn out to be defeat.

If you are thinking of buying somebody else's business, then please be very careful. Always look for the fatal flaw. In general, nobody sells a good business. You will be told that the seller is making so much money running some other business that she does not have time to devote to this particular business. What this means is that this business is losing so much money it is likely to bring down every business in which she is involved. Alternatively, you may be told that she has made so much money in this business that she is now considering passing it on to let somebody else have their turn.

Remember, nobody ever sells a good business. If the business is that good, then the existing employees/managers would want to buy the business. When considering the acquisition of a business, take the twenty year view. How would you like to run this business for the next twenty years? Do your homework. Discuss the prospects with people in that industry, with your bank manager, with your family, friends and business acquaintances as outlined above.

THE MOST SUCCESSFUL BUSINESS PEOPLE ARE
THOSE WHO CAN IDENTIFY THE BENEFIT THAT THEY SELL,
THEIR COMPETITIVE ADVANTAGE,
AND THEIR MARKET SEGMENT.
THEY CONSISTENTLY ASK, THEY CONSISTENTLY FOCUS
AND CONCENTRATE ON THE QUESTIONS
APPEARING IN THIS CHAPTER.
SEEK AND YE SHALL FIND.

'Chance favours the prepared mind.' – *Louis Pasteur*

Five

SALES SKILLS WILL MAKE YOUR FORTUNE

How to be excellent at selling

No sales equals no salaries. Everything gets paid out of sales income. Improve your nine basic sales skills. Lead a winning sales team. Use your creativity to generate 20 ideas for improving all aspects of selling. This one skill can make your fortune. You can take your selling skills anywhere.

'Everyone lives by selling something.'
– *Robert Louis Stephenson*

1   RELATIONSHIP SELLING

In the old model of selling, 70 per cent of time and effort was devoted to making a presentation to the customer and closing the deal. Building trust and identifying the needs of the customer accounted for only 30 per cent of time and effort. In the new model of selling, only 30 per cent of time and effort is devoted to presenting and closing the sale, whereas 70 per cent is devoted to building trust and identifying the needs of the potential customer. The new model is relationship selling. Most businesses depend upon repeat purchasing by clients. Repeat purchasing depends upon building excellent relationships with our customers. We tend to buy from people we like. We tend to buy from people who are caring, courteous and considerate. Simply focusing upon the customer, building trust, identifying needs, and being caring, courteous and considerate, can make a dramatic difference to success in selling. We love our customers and we always do that little bit extra for which we do not get paid.

> Your best customers are your customers.
> Most business is repeat business.
> Establish a database for repeat business.

A building society employed people to sell financial services including pensions, life insurance, building insurance, savings accounts etc. Sales people were given lists of customers who already had mortgages with the building society. Given this database, sales people made more commission every month than the managers of top building society branches were paid in salary. The sales people were so successful that building society managers insisted that lists of customers with mortgages with the building society should no longer be made available to the sales people.

> We love our customers and we always do that little bit extra for which we do not get paid.

Help people. Compliment people. Remember people's names. They will like you. They will buy from you.

2   IMPROVE YOUR NINE BASIC SKILLS

In the vast majority of businesses, we find the Pareto principle prevails, in that 80 per cent of sales are made by 20 per cent of the sales people. We also find that within the top 20 per cent, the top 20 per cent of the top 20 per cent account for 80 per cent of the sales of the top 20 per cent. This means that top sales people earn many times in commissions the amounts earned by the average of the bottom 80 per cent. These top sales people are usually selling exactly the same products, to exactly the same audience, in exactly the same market segment, at exactly the same price. How can we account for the wide variations in sales? Why are some people so much more successful than others at selling? With everything else held constant, it can only be the difference in the people!

Successful sales people have learned the nine basic skills required for excellence in selling. They tend to be a little bit better at the basics. They are not many times better, but they are just that little bit better on the basics that makes all the difference. This is the winning edge concept. You only need to be marginally better at selling to be many times more effective, many times more successful in sales. Very dramatic results can be achieved with only a small increase in learning the nine basic skills. These nine basic skills are: be very positive in your attitude towards selling, manage sales activities effectively, know your product and its competitive advantage, identify your customers, identify customer needs, make excellent presentations, handle objections, close that deal, and be sure to follow up.

80 per cent of sales are made by
20 per cent of sales people.
Why? Same product, same price, same customers.
It's the sales person!
Improve your nine basic sales skills.

3 BE POSITIVE IN ATTITUDE, LOVE SELLING (BASIC SALES SKILL NUMBER ONE)

Many people bring negative emotions to selling: fear of failure, hate, blame. Many people suffer from the self-limiting belief that they could never sell anything. In many businesses, successful selling is the rock that stands between the present situation and the success desired. We have had many conversations along the following lines when visiting clients for the first time:

Consultants: 'Well, what lovely premises. We are impressed.'
Client: 'No problem, it's on a 100 per cent mortgage.'
Consultants: 'We like those expensive cars in the car park.'
Client: 'No problem, we can get fantastic leasing deals these days.'
Consultants: '... And what beautifully equipped offices.'
Client: '... All on loans of one kind or another.'
Consultants: '... And all these people must cost you a fortune?'
Client: '... But we are still well within our overdraft limit.'
Consultants: 'Well how are you doing on sales?'
Client: 'Funny you should mention sales. That's exactly what we wanted to talk to you about!'

Make a decision to enjoy selling. It is fun. If necessary, change your attitude. It is widely accepted that the excitement and enthusiasm of the sales person accounts for around 50 per cent of success in selling. In a world in which everything counts, the excitement and enthusiasm of the sales person affects the customer's response.

Good sales people have high self-esteem, in that they practise the affirmation 'I am a valuable and worthwhile person.' Selling is absolutely critical to the survival of the business. No sales equals no salaries. Everything gets paid for out of sales income, not only salaries and other costs, but also bank loans, leases on cars, mortgages, the bank overdraft, etc. Beliefs have a strong effect on expectations. Expectations have a strong effect on attitudes.

Successful people have high expectations of themselves and others. Successful sales people have the beliefs of successful people. Practise the affirmations, 'I am brilliant at selling', 'I love my customers', 'I confidently expect that my customer will buy', etc. In addition to these affirmations, use visualisation and emotionalisation.

See yourself being excellent at selling. Imagine how marvellous you feel being recognised as the best sales person in the business. As well as using positive self-imagery, put yourself on a positive mental diet. Read books relating to excellence in selling. Read books relating to successful sales people. Listen to educational tapes relating to excellence in selling. Attend at least four sales courses per annum. Spend time with the people you admire for their excellence. Form a mastermind alliance, whereby you spend time with other people who are brilliant at selling. Design a personal development plan for improving your ability to make sales.

Love selling. Attitude is about 50 per cent of success.

Make selling your area of excellence, your specialisation, the activity which makes you feel valuable and worthwhile. You will only become brilliant at doing something which you love doing, and which makes you feel that you are a valuable and worthwhile person.

'Remember that a man's name is to him the sweetest and most important sound in the English language. Successful sales people never forget it.' – *Dale Carnegie*

---

4 MANAGE YOUR SALES ACTIVITIES EFFECTIVELY (BASIC SALES SKILL NUMBER TWO)

Most people think of sales income as Units × Price = Sales. This is correct. We then focus on increasing the number of units sold or increasing the price. This is perfectly satisfactory, but you have probably already put a great deal of effort into this. Here is another way of thinking about sales income:

Sales activities lead to sales. Manage the activities and you manage the sales.

*No of customers × Average sale × Frequency of purchase/visit
= Sales income*

If, at the present time, you have 20 customers making an average purchase of £1000, visiting your premises two times each year, then your sales are £40,000 per annum, 20 × £1000 × 2 = £40,000. If you can double the overall level of business activity, increasing your number of customers to forty, the average sale to £2000 and the frequency of purchase to four, then sales increase to £320,000, i.e. 40 × £2000 × 4 = £320,000. In fact, doubling the overall level of activity increases sales eight times. There are 20 ways of increasing your customer base. There are 20 ways of increasing the average sale. There are 20 ways of increasing the frequency of purchase. Focus and concentrate on the 20 ideas which will generate much higher levels of sales income.

> No. of customers × average sale × frequency of order = sales.
>
> 20 × £1000 × 2 = £40,000
> 40 × £2000 × 4 = £320,000
> There are 20 ways to increase your customer base.
> There are 20 ways to increase the average sale.
> There are 20 ways to increase the frequency of order.
> 20 × 20 × 20 = 8000
> There are 8000 routes you can take to increasing sales.

As a sales person, you are responsible for results. You can achieve the required result by setting it as a goal, and then resolving to pay the price that must be paid to achieve the goal. You need to establish clear sales goals. The subconscious mind responds to clarity. Having established the sales goals, it is necessary to determine the actions or activities which must be undertaken to achieve those goals.

Information is important. We need information to make decisions. Decisions should lead to action. Only action gets results. Your sales activities lead to your sales results. What is the price you have to pay to achieve the desired result? The price you have to pay is that you have to undertake the necessary activities. We all need clear sales activity goals relating to presentations, mailing shots, 'thank you' letters, cold calls, approaches to new customers, approaches to old customers etc.

Controlling and monitoring activities is essential. Activities lead to sales. Sales is a numbers game. If your presentations to customers have a 40 per cent success rate, then ten presentations lead to four sales. One hundred presentations lead to forty sales. One thousand presentations lead to four hundred sales, etc. Make a careful study of the activities you undertake for comparison with sales achieved. Use the 80/20 rule to set priorities. You will probably find that 80 per cent of sales arises from 20 per cent of your activities. Focus on the 20 per cent which brings in 80 per cent of sales. Develop a sense of urgency, a do-it-now mentality. Focus and concentrate on the desired result, the desired level of sales. Focus not on what you can do, but on what you can achieve. We undertake activities to achieve results. Become totally results orientated, rather than activity oriented.

In a world in which sales people are notorious for starting late, make a decision to make your first sales call early in the morning. Again, sales is a numbers game. The more contacts you make with potential customers, the higher level of sales you achieve. Failure to sell at the first attempt, does not mean that you should not make another attempt. You are not defeated just because you lost, you are only defeated when you give up. Make the second effort, go the extra mile. You can always open a negotiation with new information.

Finally, look after your health and appearance. Look as though you expect to sell successfully. We all tend to judge others on a first impression. You never get a second chance to make a good first impression. Your appearance and the way in which you conduct yourself must be consistent with achieving the success you confidently expect.

An excellent sales person can give the company competitive advantage by being faster and nicer.

Sales really is a numbers game. We have so often seen people earning tremendous incomes simply by following the formula. In a recent company visit, sales people were required to make sixty telephone calls per day, which should lead to six enquries, which should lead to one order. Using these numbers, many people were earning over £100,000 per annum.

Remember these very important numbers. A mailing shot will probably achieve less than one per cent success in sales. Three mailing shots to the same people followed by a telephone call should improve your success rate to around three per cent. A successful telephone call which leads to a face-to-face discussion should have a thirty per cent success rate. There is no substiture for belly-to-belly discussion. Learn what the success numbers are in your business, and for yourself. Do the numbers! You will make sales! Sales is a numbers game!

'The way to succeed is to double your failure rate.'
– *Thomas J. Watson* (founder of IBM)

'The man who makes no mistakes does not usually make anything.' – *William Connor Magee*

---

5   KNOW YOUR PRODUCT, ITS BENEFIT AND COMPETITIVE ADVANTAGE (BASIC SALES SKILL NUMBER THREE)

Why does your customer buy the product or service? What benefit do you sell? It might look like a haircut, but it's probably admiration.

It looks like a motorcar, but it's probably status. It might be called a bungee jump, but it's probably excitement. If you're selling to other companies, the benefit is probably increased sales, lower costs or higher profits. In which way is your product different from the competition? Do you have a unique selling proposition? What is your competitive advantage? Why should anybody buy the product or service from you? Is your product perceived by the customer as being better in some way? Is it cheaper? Is it faster? Does the customer buy because you are an extremely pleasant person? Who is your competition? Why do some customers buy from the competition? What is the competitive advantage of your competitor? In which areas are your competitors superior? In which ways are they inferior? How can you creatively imitate your competitor?

Most important of all, how can you offset the competitive advantage of your competition? If the competitor is cheaper, then you have to be better in some way, faster in some way or more pleasant to deal with in some way. You must be able to point out to your customer that although the competitor is better, he or she is far more expensive, slow on delivery or unpleasant in some way.

If there is no reason why the customer should buy from you, then the customer will buy from the competition. There is a reason for everything. There has to be a reason why the customer buys a product or service from you. A most important point to remember is that good sales people can give the company competitive advantage simply by being faster and very pleasant. Remember that customers are impatient creatures. They want the benefit now, and they have a strong tendency to buy from attractive, pleasant people.

> You must be prepared to offset the competitive advantage of your competitor.

6 IDENTIFY YOUR CUSTOMERS/PROSPECTING (BASIC SALES SKILL NUMBER FOUR)

Why should anybody buy your product or service? What is the benefit or improvement in their condition? Whose life will be enriched?

Who will get the greatest improvement from your product or service? With which customers does your competitive advantage make a difference? With which customers does your competitive advantage make the biggest difference?

Customers want to be more, have more, do more. People buy for ego needs, status needs, self-actualisation needs etc. People buy for safety, security, admiration, social status, recognition, prestige, respect, to increase sales, lower costs, increase profits, self-improvement, excitement, popularity, greater health, self expression, influence, power, financial success, more knowledge, greater skills, companionship, self-esteem, fear of loss, desire for gain.

Where are your customers? Where do they buy the benefit at the present time? How do they buy? When do they buy? How do they pay? Which complementary products do they buy? Are they listed in the Yellow Pages? Can you gain access to competitors' lists? Can you gain access to the lists of purchasers of complementary products? Who will save time, money and effort by buying the product?

Again, remember that good sales people can give the business competitive advantage by being fast and pleasant. Being friendly is one way in which you can be better. Being fast is another way in which you can be perceived as better, bearing in mind that customers are impatient creatures. Acting quickly could save your customer money.

Focus on the 20 per cent of customers who account for 80 per cent of sales. Focus on your active customers, followed by your inactive customers. Focus on the active customers of your competitors, followed by the inactive customers of your competitors. Focus on the right approach for each type of customer – telephone calls, mailing shots, cold calls, presentations, 'thank you' cards, social meetings, meetings at sporting and musical events, etc. Given that your customer is buying improvements in his/her life, your responsibility is to maximise sales, providing you are behaving legally, morally, and ethically.

In one property deal, we took an 'unsaleable' property in part exchange. It was a Victorian terraced house without a garden in the most run-down part of town surrounded by dereliction, unattractive factories and busy roads. The estate agents had had no 'luck' in two years. We asked the question 'who is the customer for this property?'. We interviewed the neighbours. It was found that the people who live in this area work in the nearby factories. Our advertisement 'live close to your work' was displayed in the canteens of six factories. The house sold within two weeks. Did your estate agent do this for you?

Who is your customer?
Where is your market niche?

Who will get the greatest benefit?
Who will save time, money and effort?

7 IDENTIFYING CUSTOMER NEEDS (BASIC SALES SKILL NUMBER FIVE)

Do not focus on trying to sell the product which you produce. Warehouses throughout the country are full of products nobody wants to buy. Ask questions, ask questions, ask questions! Find out what benefit your customer desires. Talk to your customers. You will be surprised how often price is not the priority. They may be looking for a local supplier, excellent service, a guarantee, any risk of loss to be assumed by the supplier, immediate delivery, staged payments.

If you know your customer, then you have a far greater chance of forming a lasting relationship which should lead to permanent relationship selling. If you listen very carefully, you may well find the hot button which enables you to make the sale. If you have to start the ball rolling, then start strongly with an interesting question: 'Would you like to see an idea that can increase your sales by 30 per cent over the next six months?' 'Would you be interested in reducing your factory heating costs by 15 per cent?', 'Would you be interested in making one of the most exciting journeys you have ever made in your life?'. Focus all your attention on the prospective customer. We are curious creatures. Try to stimulate the curiosity of your customer. Ask more questions. Find the benefit your customer seeks. Keep talking about the benefit. Don't talk about the money, the price, how much it is going to cost. Focus on the benefit to the customer.

Remember the customer's favourite radio station is WIIFM – What's In It For Me? Keep collecting information. You must come away from the initial discussion knowing exactly what your prospective customer wants. You do not have to make a sale on the first call. You can always come back with new ideas, additional information, additional proposals. People love to be asked questions. If you want to be interesting, be interested. If you show interest in the customer, the customer will find you interesting. The customer will want to reciprocate, perhaps by buying the benefit you offer.

Make notes after every discussion with a customer. What did you do well? In which areas can you improve? What was the hot button? What would you do differently if you could start once again at the beginning? Did the customer like you, trust you, believe in you? Customers buy from people they believe, trust and like. Are you a go-giver? Did you offer the customer something extra, something for nothing? Did you provide the customer with information relating to a good restaurant, the quickest route to a destination, the best hotel at a resort, etc.?

If you did, the customer wants to reciprocate. Did you provide social proof, testimonials, reference to those who have already bought the product and gained tremendous satisfaction? Did you offer mega credibility? After listening intently to the prospective customer, did you make reference to the biggest users of your product or service, the most regular users, stories of totally satisfied customers, written testimonials, etc.? One final important detail, if you meet a prospective customer over lunch, then discuss the proposition during the meal and afterwards, but not before the

Ask questions.
If you want to be
interesting, be
interested.

meal. Discussion before the meal leads the customer to believe that the meal is conditional upon agreeing to the purchase.

WINNING NEW BUSINESS

Is there any way in which your present supplier could improve the price, the credit terms, the quality, the delivery period, the reliability, the financing?

'She/he who asks a question is a fool for a moment, she/he who never asks a question is a fool for life.' – *Confucius*

---

8   MAKE EXCELLENT PRESENTATIONS (BASIC SALES SKILL NUMBER SIX)

Focus on the
benefit (not the
cost).
Find the hot
button.

Giving a presentation is one of the most feared events in Western society. In surveys of people's fears, death is usually ranked around number six. Giving a presentation is usually number one. To be excellent at selling, you have to give presentations. Start out by giving a brief presentation to your friends, stating your name and address. Follow this with a brief five-minute presentation on your life and interests. Make a habit of giving brief presentations. Despite all the discomfort, you will gradually get into the swing of it. Face that which you fear, and eventually the fear is removed.

When making a presentation to customers, focus on the benefit. Do not mention the cost. Can you imagine trying to sell management development programmes for groups of executives in the same company at £100,000 per annum? The cost is too high. The £100,000 is too much for the budget. We have tried management development in the past and it did not work! The simple fact is that nobody has got £100,000 to spend on management development. Therefore, do not talk about the cost. Focus on the benefit. The skills acquired by executives during the programme will lead to greater sales, lower costs and greater profits, i.e. greater managerial ability for the foreseeable future. In fact, the programme guarantees an increase in profit of £1 million in the first year of the programme. If you focus on the benefits of increased managerial skills, and the £1 million added to the bottom line, then the £100,000 cost of the programme does not seem excessive. By the time we have focused on the benefit, then the £100,000 is mentioned at the end of the presentation as a mere detail.

Whenever you mention the price always keep talking and move on to another subject immediately. Make a few additional points. Ask the potential customer a question. It is critical to get away from the price without discussion. If you can achieve this then there is a good chance that the customer has subconsciously accepted the price. Keep using expressions along the lines 'what this means to you is ...', 'what this means to you is that sales will be increased by 20 per cent, what this means to you is that costs will be reduced by 20 per cent, what this means to you is that you will have the holiday of a lifetime, etc.'. Your prospective customer is permanently tuned into his or her favourite radio station, WIIFM – What's In It For Me? Listen carefully for feedback. Look for benefit as perceived by your customer. You cannot set goals for other people, but you can use the powers of love and suggestion on other people. The customer must feel that you are acting in his or her best interests. You can suggest to your customer that certain benefits work to their advantage.

Be positive. Be excited and enthusiastic about your product or service. Speak confidently. Dress for success. Be sure to present your product or service in its best light. Use mega credibility – who has already used the product successfully, offer recommendations from other customers, present lists of clients, stories of satisfied customers, and independent verification from other companies, research institutes, universities. You cannot offer too much credibility. Nobody wants to be the first sucker to give it a try! Use your judgement to offer trial closes as follows: 'is this the kind of thing you had in mind?', 'is this the kind of idea that could be of interest to you?', 'is this what you were looking for?', 'does that make sense to you?'

If you can get the prospective customer to nod or agree in any other way to one of these questions, then you are well on the way to making a sale. As well as appealing to your prospective customer's desires, you could also use a little bit of fear. You could mention the fact that your customer's competitors have already done it! Next, be prepared to handle all possible objections.

A STRUCTURED SALES PRESENTATION

Prepare a structured sales presentation for your product/service. What is the benefit? Put numbers on it. What is the hot button? What is its competitive advantage? Who is using it with great success, fantastic results. Can you get the customer involved in doing something, trying it out, making some simple calculations? If this increased your sales by 20 per cent, reduced your costs by 20 per cent, increased your profits by 20 per cent, how much would that be worth to you this year?

'Language is the dress of thought.' – *Samuel Johnson*

'Whatever you teach, be brief, that your readers' minds may readily comprehend and faithfully retain your words.' – *Horace*

9   HANDLE OBJECTIONS (BASIC SALES SKILL NUMBER SEVEN)

'We don't want it, we can't afford it, we don't believe you, we've tried it before and it didn't work, we are perfectly happy with our present supplier and it's not in the budget.' Your initial reaction could be that you are not going to make the sale. This is incorrect. You have to understand that an objection is a request for more information.

As long as the customer is objecting, you are selling. Only when the customer disappears have you possibly lost the sale.

Most objections are simply requests for more information. 'We don't want it' simply means 'tell me more about the benefit.' 'We can't afford it' means 'can you do something about the price or arrange financing?'. 'We don't believe you' means 'give me more information, convince me.' 'We have tried it before and it didn't work' means 'explain the improvements you have made'. 'We are perfectly happy with our present supplier' means 'can you explain your competitive advantage, the reason why we should switch from our present supplier to you?'. 'It's not in the budget' means 'can you invoice me at a later date?'.

Familiarise yourself with the objections that customers usually make. Rehearse your replies. Compliment your customer for the objection along the lines 'that's an excellent question ... that's an interesting observation ...'. Handle the objection along the following lines: 'many people felt that way at first, but this is what they found ... that's exactly what some of my biggest customers suggested at first, but this is what they found ...'. Then, produce the evidence, produce the proof, handle the objection.

For free tuition in handling objections, talk to any car sales person. You stand there admiring the car. The sales person approaches and says 'nice car?'. 'Yes, but I can't afford it', you say. You think that will get rid of him. It does not work. You have made an objection. The sales person can tweak the price, ask you about a possible trade-in, suggest two years' finance, three years' finance, **Objections** five years' finance, leasing, contract hire, etc. The sales **equal sales.** person knows that if he or she can overcome your objection, the sale is possible. You tell the sales person that the car has a reputation for poor reliability. 'Yes, that was true of the old model. However, if you read such and such a car magazine, you will see that this is now the most reliable car in its class.' Alternatively, you tell the salesman that you work for a company and that the budget has been spent for this year. 'That's all right', says the sales person, 'You can pay a small deposit now and the balance in the next budget period.'

As long as you are objecting, the sales person knows that a sale is possible. Only when you walk away is the sale probably lost.

10   CLOSE THAT DEAL
(BASIC SALES SKILL NUMBER EIGHT)

A customer is someone who is willing and able to purchase the benefit you offer. In a successful sales presentation, you eventually reach the point when it is time to ask for action, time to close that deal. You may or may not have already tried one or two trial closes. It is now time to make the final close. You could try an invitational close: 'should we complete the paperwork? ... should we arrange delivery? ... should we give it a try...?'. You could try an assumptive close: 'let's arrange the delivery ... let's complete the paperwork.'

Perhaps the most popular approach is the alternative close: 'will you be paying by cash, cheque or credit card ... the blue one or the red one ... the deluxe or standard ... were you thinking of holding the programme before or after Christmas?'. Another approach to the alternative close is the minor point or secondary close: 'will you take it with you now or would you like us to deliver? ... did you want it with the hardback or the softback?'.

It is extremely important to note that once the customer is considering the answers to these questions, the purchasing decision has already been made. You have made the sale. We are now discussing mere details. On occasion you will be able to identify a hot button close where the customer has got to buy the product because it's red in colour, and it's the only red one he or she has seen in two months. On occasion the customer makes it perfectly clear that he or she must have that armchair because it is the exact same colour as the curtains and the carpet in the living room. Given the chance, go for the hot button close. Identify the most attractive feature to the customer and keep talking about that feature. Finally, congratulate the client on making such an excellent selection. Then make an additional sale to the same customer.

> Use the alternative close:
> Cash, cheque or credit card?
> Before or after Christmas?
> Take it with you or have it delivered?

11   FOLLOW UP, MAKE THE SECOND EFFORT (BASIC SALES SKILL NUMBER NINE)

You may not sell on the first visit or first occasion. Make a decision to go the extra mile, make the second effort, follow up your initial approach. Contact the prospective customer once again within three days. You can always reopen a negotiation with new information, new price, new terms, a better offer following discussions with your boss, partner etc. Keep your customer informed. Educate your customer to appreciate the benefit you offer and your competitive advantage.

Ask for referrals. Create a golden chain.

After making a sale, contact the customer within four weeks with a view to making the next sale. Follow up direct mail with a telephone call. Follow a presentation, visit or discussion with a note, small gift or a 'thank you' card. Many businesses have been completely turned around by the simple technique of getting each sales person to send out a number of thank you cards every Friday afternoon.

Remember that it is activities which lead to sales. Ensure that your final contact with the customer is always positive. The customer must appreciate that you are caring, courteous and considerate. Do not be afraid to ask for referrals. Referrals alone can guarantee a successful business. Every customer should be able to recommend you to two additional prospective customers. Use your existing customers to create a golden chain. Ask your satisfied customers to provide you with a reference, an endorsement of your product, something on paper which you can use to give you mega credibility with prospective customers. Everybody knows six people who will give an excellent recommendation!

Sometimes you have to educate your customer.

12   WINNING SALES TEAMS

The sales function is often carried out by a team. The sales manager is the manager of the team. Every team depends upon excellent performance from each team member. In recent years many studies have been carried out on winning teams. There appears to be some consensus that winning teams have the following six characteristics, which we suggest you introduce into your own sales team (and any other team) for maximum effectiveness.

1   *Clear leadership.* Winning teams have effective leaders. Team members know who the boss is. The leader sets the standards, calls the tune, measures performance, gives clear coaching, and is the leader on merit.

2   *Clear strategy and planning.* Winning teams know what they must do to get from where they are now to the ideal future. Team members know what must be done, they have clear activity assignments. Winning teams focus on being brilliant on the basics. They understand that 20 per cent of activities leads to 80 per cent of results/sales. Winning teams focus on the 20 per cent which brings in the 80 per cent. Time is set aside for planning, discussing changes, introducing improvements, continuous improvement.

3   *People-development focus.* Winning teams focus on reading, listening to educational tapes, attending courses, and spending time with those who are excellent at selling. Continuous learning, continuous attention to greater enthusiasm and excitement leads to better results. Only people get better, only people improve. Property, plant and equipment and motor vehicles all depreciate, but people can be continuously improved.

4   *Commitment to excellence.* Winning teams understand that only excellence motivates. Neither failure nor mediocrity motivates. Winning teams are led by high-expectations bosses. Effective leaders are good listeners, they set clear goals, and they expect excellent results.

5   *Selective player assignments.* Winning teams play to their strengths. Each member carries out those activities to which he or she is best suited, which lead to the greatest contribution in sales, and eventually profits. Winning teams also focus on those products and services which result in higher sales and higher profits.

6   *Good communications.* Winning teams have open communications, free access to information, the sharing of information, no politics, no hidden agendas, no cliques. Team members have the information, resources, support, coaching to achieve desired results. Team philosophy is built on facilitate and empower, rather than command and control.

13   CLEAR OUTPUT RESPONSIBILITIES FOR TEAM MEMBERS

Each team member needs clear sales targets and clear activity targets. Every sales person needs the output responsibilities of the job defined in terms of sales and volume. Activities lead to sales. The sales manager cannot control the level of sales, but the sales manager can control the activities, the actions taken by sales people. These output responsibilities must be defined in terms of numbers of calls, numbers of letters sent out, number of leads followed, contacts with old customers, contacts with new customers, presentations, interviews, sales orders completed, 'thank you' cards sent out at the end of each period.

Sales people need clarity. The subconscious responds to clarity. Sales people do not like uncertainty, they do not like having too much or too little to do. Sales achieved and activities undertaken must be checked daily, weekly and monthly. Remember the golden rule of delegation: what gets measured gets done. If you do not measure it, then they will not do it. You must inspect what you expect. Use the powers of love and suggestion on your sales people. Let them know that you like them, and that you confidently expect that they will achieve their sales targets and undertake the necessary activities. Suggest to them that they can achieve their targets, that they can be excellent at selling. Confidently expect that sales and activity targets will be achieved. Remember the law of expectations: we all get what we confidently expect.

CLEAR ACTIVITY TARGETS	
Personal visits	Catalogues
Leads	Telephone calls
New customers	Leaflets
Interviews	Referrals
Thank you cards	Old customers
Letters	Presentations

14   GOOD COUNSELLING AND REVIEW FOR TEAM MEMBERS

What gets measured gets done. What gets rewarded gets repeated. Team members need a regular review of their performance in relation to sales and sales activities. The review is not an aggressive occasion. The performance review is in the best interests of the team member as well as the sales team and the business. The team leader should ask questions: 'what did you do correctly?, what have you learned?, what would you do differently?'.

The objective is to improve the performance of the team member. You are a high-expectations boss. You listen carefully. You offer good counselling and good review. You are there to encourage the team member, to bring excitement and enthusiasm to the sales function, to raise the expectations of the team member, to raise the self-esteem of the team member. Which changes are necessary? Does the team member need more information, a higher level of skills, a more positive attitude? What can we do to change the behaviour of the team member?

Learning is a change in behaviour. Recommend courses, books, tapes, a role model to the team member. Bombard the mind of the team member with information, experiences, situations, and people which are consistent with high achievement. Remember how people learn. We collect information, take action, review our results against the knowledge we have acquired, and then ask questions. Once we ask questions, we are ready to experience more programmed learning. As the team leader, will you accompany team members on sales presentations? Will the leader make the first sale for the beginner?

You must inspect what you expect.

15   REWARD STRUCTURE FOR TEAM MOTIVATION

Sales people love to be rewarded for their successes. Sales people love to achieve sales, love financial rewards, love status, recognition, attention and promotion.

1   *Achievement.* Excellence is the great motivator. Sales people are motivated by success. Sales people love the achievement of making sales.

2   *Financial rewards.* Sales people love to be rewarded financially for achieving results. Commission is the great financial motivator in sales. We recommend financial rewards related to sales, rather than fixed salary. Commission motivates.

3   *Status.* Sales people love to strive for a better car, for an expensive trip, for rewards which raise them above the average sales person.

4   *Recognition.* Sales people love prizes, best sales person of the month, medals, wall plaques, certificates, etc.

5   *Attention.* Sales people love the recognition of time spent with the sales manager, lunch with the sales manager, a place at the table with the board of directors, etc.

6   *Promotion.* Sales people love to be promoted to sales manager, deputy sales manager, leader of a section of the sales team, etc.

16   CONTINUOUS IMPROVEMENT/TRAINING FOR TEAM MEMBERS

The sales manager is responsible for continuous training of each member of the team. Team members need sales training, regular review, reinforcement of their excellent abilities, encouragement to love selling, continuous reminding of the required activities, greater knowledge of benefits and competitive advantage, identifying customer needs, identifying customers/prospecting, making excellent presentations, handling objections, closing deals, making the second effort, reference to books, courses, tapes, people who can help, courses in telephone skills, listening skills, etc.

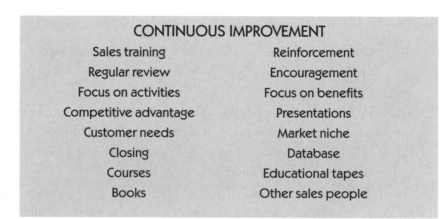

CONTINUOUS IMPROVEMENT

Sales training	Reinforcement
Regular review	Encouragement
Focus on activities	Focus on benefits
Competitive advantage	Presentations
Customer needs	Market niche
Closing	Database
Courses	Educational tapes
Books	Other sales people

17   BASIC NEEDS OF TEAM MEMBERS

Sales people need autonomy. They need the empowerment to work as individuals, achieving sales targets and undertaking sales activities. At the same time, sales people need dependency on the group. They need to be part of a successful team. Sales people need information from regular sales-team meetings. They need training for motivation and raising of self-esteem. They need recognition for their achievements. The sales manager praises in public, punishes in private. He spends time on a one-to-one basis with excellent performers. He deals with the average sales people in groups. The sales manager must try to raise the self-concept of each sales person. The sales manager raises the self-concept level of income of the team members. He raises the individual's self-concept of his or her ability to sell. The sales manager makes team members feel important by praise, reward, acknowledging success, good feedback, approval, recognition, encouragement and acceptance as a member of the team. The sales manager provides a rock on which volatile sales people can rely for support, encouragement, good counselling and review. The sales manager offers a role model as the best in the business.

18   TWENTY-FIVE WAYS TO INCREASE YOUR SALES INCOME (WHICH YOU HAVE PROBABLY ALREADY CONSIDERED)

1   *Sell more units/increase the price.* With a view to increasing sales income, we can either increase the units sold or/and the price.

$$Units \times Price = Sales\ income$$

There are 20 ways to increase the number of units sold. There are 20 ways in which we can justify a price increase. Focus, concentrate and dwell upon the ways in which you can increase units sold and the selling price. No doubt, you have already considered these factors.

2   *Commitment to excellence.* Make a 100% commitment to excellence. Only excellence motivates. There is a strong relationship between quality and sales. Make a decision to be the best in the business.

3   *Love of the customer.* We have a passion for excellence. We love our customers and we always do that little bit extra for which we do not get paid. There are always 20 ways in which we can improve the service we offer to our customers.

4   *Fanaticism for service and quality.* Make a decision that everybody in the business is a service and quality fanatic. Focus and dwell upon the 20 ways in which you can increase your service and quality.

5 *Caring, courteous and considerate.* We are always caring, courteous and considerate when dealing with our customers. There are 20 ways in which we can be more caring, more courteous and more considerate.

6 *Relationship selling.* The old model of selling focused on giving presentations and closing the deal. The new model of selling focuses on building trust with a client, and identifying the needs of the client. The new model of selling is relationship selling for repeat business. Build life-long relationships with your customers.

7 *Sustainable competitive advantage.* There must be a reason why a customer buys your product or service from you. Make a decision to establish a reason, or discover the reason if you are not sure what it is. Ask your customers!

8 *Unique selling proposition.* Make a decision to try and establish some unique reason why a customer should buy the product or service from you. Can you establish a brand name which is recognized as the market leader in quality, price, value for money, quick service, excellent service, reliability, friendliness?

9 *Better.* Make a decision to improve the quality, to establish yourself as the best in the business. There are 20 ways in which you can be better than the competition.

10 *Cheaper.* There are 20 ways in which you can provide better value to your customer.

11 *Faster.* There are 20 ways in which you can improve the speed and ease with which your customer can acquire the benefit you offer. Do they really have to fill in that form?

12 *Nicer.* There are 20 ways in which you can increase the quality of your customer care.

13 *Market segmentation.* Who cares? There are 20 ways in which you can improve your success rate in finding your customer. Remember, you have to be at least 10 per cent better, cheaper, faster or nicer for a customer to switch from your competitor to you.

14 *Market niche.* Is there some small section of the market which you can dominate?

15 *Mega credibility.* Make a decision to accumulate 20 sources of additional credibility for your product or service.

16 *Use the 80/20 rule.* Focus on the 20 per cent of product which yields 80 per cent of sales. Focus on the 20 per cent of customers who account for 80 per cent of sales income. Focus on the 20 per cent of geographic area, the 20 per cent of advertising that works, the 20 per cent of sales people who account for 80 per cent of sales, etc.

17 *Overcome market ignorance.* Provide interesting stories for radio, newspapers and television which should help you to overcome market ignorance. Use direct mail, direct sales, telesales, etc. to overcome market ignorance.

18 *Make ordering and buying easy.* There are 20 ways in which you can make it easier for your customer to order and buy your product or service. Remove the difficulties. Do not ask a customer to complete an eight-page questionnaire. Do not ask a customer to come back next week or after lunch, etc. Never ask a customer to fill in a form. We have been flogging ourselves to death for years telling this to banks. Will they ever listen? Ask the customer the questions, but fill in the form yourself. Then ask the customer to sign the form, and possibly return it in the stamped addressed envelope. You have probably noticed that everytime you enter the public sector, they ask you to fill in a form. Imagine the joy throughout this nation, if tax returns were scrapped! We make it easy for the customer to buy fuel. Instead of the customer having to ring up and order, we offer to check the storage tank every four weeks and top us as necessary. Sales have increased from zero to £5.25 million in three years in a commodity market, where we have established a competitive advantage by making it easier (faster/nicer) for the customer.

19 *Creatively imitate your competition.* What is the competitive advantage of your competitor? What can you learn from your competitor? How can we creatively imitate our competition to increase sales income?

20 *Practise price discrimination.* Different customers have different self-concepts of expenditure on the same product or service. Identify different prices for different customers. Sales and profits should be much higher when you discriminate on price.

21 *More pressure.* Commodities are difficult. Try putting your customer under more pressure.

22 *More promotion.* Commodities are difficult. Try greater promotion.

23 *Educate your customer.* Make sure that your customer understands fully the benefit you offer, the reason why the product or service should be bought from you, and just how easy it is to order and purchase your benefit. Your customer should understand why it is such a good deal!

24 *Communicate with your customer.* Communicate frequently with your customer. Use bulletins, news of new ideas, new product developments, new prices, etc.

25 *Ask for referrals.* In the early stages of the business, you must ask each customer for referrals. Use your customers to create a golden chain. Every customer should lead you to two new customers. With repeat purchases, the business should grow in sales and profits.

19 TWENTY-FIVE WAYS TO INCREASE YOUR SALES INCOME (WHICH YOU MAY HAVE ALREADY CONSIDERED)

1 *Attitude.* Be more positive, more excited, more enthusiastic about selling.

2 *Manage the activities.* Activities lead to sales. Make a decision to send out so many mailing shots per week. Do a certain number of presentations, send out a certain number of 'thank you' cards every Friday, etc. These activities will lead to additional sales income.

3 *Increase knowledge of competitive advantage.* Make sure you understand your own competitive advantage. Be fully aware of the competitive advantage of the competition. You must be able to offset the competitive advantage of the competition.

4 *Prospecting for new customers.* There are 20 ways in which you can seek out new business.

5 *Identify the needs of your customer.* There are 20 ways in which you can increase your skills in listening to customers.

6 *Improve your Presentation.* There are 20 ways in which you can improve your presentation skills.

7 *Learn how to handle objections.* There are 20 ways in which you can improve your ability to handle objections.

8 *Close that deal.* There are 20 ways in which you can improve your ability to close a deal.

9 *Follow up.* There are 20 ways in which you can improve your skills in making the second effort.

10 *Sales training.* Many businesses have become extremely successful following a simple decision to improve the quality of sales training for all those involved in selling. Make a decision to invest time, if not money, in sales training.

11 *Develop a winning sales team.* Implement and develop the attributes of winning sales teams in your business.

12 *Establish clear standards of performance.* Ensure that everybody involved in sales is fully aware of the standards expected.

13 *Check the outputs of your sales people.* Count the number of calls, letters, presentations, mailing shots, telesales, 'thank you' cards, approaches to existing customers, approaches to new customers, approaches to other people's customers, cold calls, etc. Sales is a numbers game. Count the activities. It is the activities which lead to sales.

14 *Reward structure for motivation.* Sales people love to be rewarded. Implement a reward structure which motivates your sales people.

15 *Outsource the sales function.* If neither you nor anybody in your organisation can sell, then buy in an excellent sales person, or consider outsourcing the selling function to some person or some organisation which can generate sales.

16 *A useful formula for thinking about sales.* Earlier we recognised that units x price = sales. Consider the following formula:

Number of customers × average purchase × number of orders/visits = sales

There are 20 ways in which you can increase your customer base. There are 20 ways in which you can increase the average purchase. There are 20 ways in which you can encourage customers to order/visit your premises.

17 *Test different prices.* Some prices are far more attractive to customers than other prices. Test your prices on small samples of customers. A higher attractive price will lead to greater sales income than a lower, unattractive price. Carry out tests on small numbers of customers to identify high attractive prices.

18 *Test everything.* Send out 50 brochures, 50 mailing shots, make 50 telephone calls, send out 50 letters, hold face to face discussions with 50 customers. Organise a conference for 50 customers. Do everything on a small scale. Do not ever send out 10,000 of anything, until you have tested, tested and tested again!

19 *More effective advertising.* There are 20 ways in which you can make your advertising more effective.

20 *Public relations.* Gain free publicity and free advertising by providing interesting stories for newspapers, radio and television.

21 *Send Christmas cards to your products.* Many companies send Christmas cards to their customers. Have you considered sending a Christmas card to the piece of furniture you sold to your customer, to a painting, to your customer's pet poodle?

22 *Reactivate old customers.* Stimulate your inactive customers by communication.

23 *Stimulate your competitors' inactive customers.* Can you arrange a swap with your competitors on a one-for-one basis whereby you can stimulate your competitors' inactive customers, and your competitors can stimulate your inactive customers?

24 *Separate the price from the terms.* Price can be a major obstacle to making a sale. Make it easy for your customer to avoid paying the full price at the time of sale. Have you considered instalment payments without interest?

25 *Offer credit.* There is one way in which you can always accumulate almost infinite quantities of sales. All you have to do is offer infinite credit. Naturally, infinite credit would very quickly lead to insolvency. However, you can stimulate sales by arranging the finance from banks, finance houses, higher purchase agreements, leasing etc. Have you ever considered winning an endorsement from your bank whereby you sell the product and your bank provides the finance?

20   TWENTY-FIVE WAYS TO INCREASE YOUR SALES INCOME (WHICH YOU MAY NOT HAVE CONSIDERED)

1 *Free samples.* Have you considered free samples for new customers? Have you considered free samples for big spenders? Have you considered free samples for the biggest customers of your competitors?

2 *First year free.* Would you switch to an accountant, dentist or hairdresser who offered you the first year free? Can you use this idea in your business?

3 *Quantity discounts.* Have you considered offering big discounts to existing customers, new customers, and selected individuals, possibly for attending at your showroom, an exhibition, a conference?

4 *30-day free trial.* Have you considered a 30-, 60-, 120-day free trial?

5 *Free offer to lock-in sales in advance.* Have you considered making an initial free offer on condition that the customer spends a specified amount with you in the future? Can you learn anything from mail-order book companies?

6 *The one-off irresistible offer.* 'We have overstocked. As one of our most highly-valued customers, we are making this one-off 40 per cent reduction ...'. There are 20 ways in which you can use the irresistible offer to increase sales income.

7 *Reduction off next purchase.* Have you considered offering a coupon, £5 off the next meal, £5 off the next visit to the hairdresser? Having made the initial sale to a new customer, have

you considered offering 30 per cent off the next purchase? Have you considered offering a 30 per cent discount on all purchases made in the following 12 months?

8 *100 per cent money-back guarantee.* Have you considered offering the 100 per cent money-back guarantee on books, tapes, records, videos, management development programmes?

9 *Guaranteed trade-in price on goods sold.* Have you considered offering a 75 per cent guaranteed trade-in on replacement of the product sold to your customer? This helps to allay the fear of loss to the customer.

10 *Extended guarantees.* Have you considered guaranteeing the quality of your product? Can you offer two years' free maintenance?

11 *Endorsements.* Can you sell the products of other customers with your product? Can you get others to sell your product with their product?

12 *Complementary products.* If you sell golf clubs, can you also sell golf clothing? If you sell furniture, can you sell furniture wax? If you sell yachts, can you also sell sailing jackets, contracts for maintenance? Make a list of 20 products which complement your existing products!

13 *Your best customers are your customers.* If your customers buy A, B and C from you, identify products D, E, F, G, H etc. If they buy marketing journals from you, will they also buy finance journals? If they buy art books from you, will they also buy books on furniture? Many businesses have enjoyed tremendous success by the simple technique of extending the product range. Twenty-five years ago we purchased our first academic journal for £1. When we launched the second journal we found that both journals had the same customer base – academic libraries throughout the world. The business now sells more than 100 journals to the same customer base, and in 1997 the business generated a cash flow of £8.5 million.

14 *Commission-only sales.* Have you considered taking on self-employed sales people on a commission-only basis?

15 *Networking.* Have you considered organising a network of several businesses which trade together for mutual advantage? Networking enables you to sell, purchase and finance. Your network allows you to help others to sell, purchase and finance. It's relationship selling, relationship purchasing, relationship financing, relationship distributing etc. Our telephones keep ringing from members of our network established days ago, months ago and even 25 years ago. Are you accumulating a network?

16 *Use a big distributor.* Rather than distribute your own product, have you considered using a nation-wide or international distributor? Many pop groups make excellent recordings, but do not make the necessary efforts to find a nation-wide or international distributor. Does your product need a major distributor?

17 *Franchising.* Have you considered franchising out the production and distribution of your product? Can you put a brand name on your product/service and then sell other people the right to use the brand name? We are franchising our management development programmes. How many academics/trainers have the same opportunity of selling others the right to use the teaching materials they have spent years in developing? Have you considered franchising in the excellent products of other businesses?

18 *Upsell.* Have you considered selling higher-quality and higher-priced items to your existing customers?

19 *Cross sell.* Have you considered selling additional products of your own or additional products of other businesses to your existing customers, usually at the point of sale?

20 *Licensing.* Have you considered licensing the selling or manufacture of your product to others? Have you considered obtaining a licence to market or manufacture the products of other businesses?

21 *Sell and sell again.* Make it a matter of routine that you contact every customer within two–four weeks after making a sale.

22 *Point of sale sales.* At the point of sale, offer an excellent deal on an additional purchase.

23 *Telesales.* Make a habit of selling over the telephone. It will often be the case that the initial call will be followed by literature, a meeting, presentation and possibly a successful sale.

24 *Telephone after mailing shot.* A dramatic improvement in results is often the case when an initial mailing shot is followed by a telephone call.

25 *Joint ventures.* Have you considered joint ventures with other businesses, to sell your product by direct mail, trade shows, auctions, national advertising, etc.? Our own tiny academic-journal publishing business undertakes joint world-wide advertising with a much larger publisher. We achieve world-wide promotion at a small cost. The larger publisher receives a contribution towards its promotional efforts.

21   TWENTY-FIVE WAYS TO INCREASE YOUR SALES INCOME (WHICH YOU HAVE PROBABLY NOT CONSIDERED)

1 *Use your competitor.* If a customer chooses the competitive advantage of your competitor, then earn a commission from your competitor by referring the customer to your competition. Have you considered an exchange of customer lists with your competitor on a one-for-one basis? Have you considered a joint effort to reactivate the dormant customers of your competitor on a one-for-one basis? Have you considered a joint mailing shot with your competitor?

2 *Competitive product lists.* Can you obtain lists of customers who have bought competitive products?

3 *Complementary product lists.* Can you obtain lists of customers for complementary products?

4 *Other businesses' inactive customer lists.* Can you obtain lists of inactive customers from other businesses in the same industry?

5 *Profit on bankruptcy/liquidation.* Can you approach the liquidator and acquire lists of past and present customers of businesses in liquidation?

6 *Profit on bankruptcy/liquidation.* Can you take over the existing contracts and other existing customers for insolvent companies?

7 *Switch the risk from the customer to yourself.* Customers are risk-averse. How can you switch the risk of loss from your customer to yourself?

8 *Bring customers together.* People come together for money and circus. Can you bring your customers together for a fortune telling, a sixties' night, a barbecue, boat trip, casino night?

9 *Special sales occasions.* Can you organise special sales weekends for lawyers, doctors, chief executives? Such lists can be compiled from trade directories and the Yellow Pages.

10 *Organise a conference.* Can you organise a Think Tank on the future of your industry? Can you organise a trade show, a conference, an exhibition?

11 *Invitation to the board.* Can you invite a customer to join the editorial board, to be a consultant to your company, to be a non-executive director, a full director? Can you win the support of your customer, suppliers, your bank manager? We noticed that in the case of one academic journal, the editorial board members were also subscribers. We invited more people to join the editorial board. Should we have a large editorial board, one for North America, one for Europe, and one for the Far East? Can you use this idea in your business? Can you invite a customer, supplier, financier, distributor to join your business as a non-executive director, advisory partner, consultant?

12 *Exclusivity.* What would be the effect on your potential customers of a referrals-only policy? Can you place an advertisement in your local newspaper which states that, owing to pressure of demand from customers, that new customers will only be accepted in the future on the basis of a referral from an existing customer/client? In the publishing world, we have established a literati club for authors with annual awards for best

contributions. This gives the publisher access to 30,000 authors. It ensures adequate copy for our publications, and encourages publications of high quality. It also helps the publishing business sell its products to its contributors.

13 *Strategic alliances.* Can you form a strategic alliance with a university, research institute, professional association or large company? This could amount to mega-credibility in the eyes of your customer. Our own small publishing business has a strategic alliance with a much larger publisher. We use their logo, their prices, their distribution system, and even their cash collection procedures. They keep 10 per cent of our revenues, we receive a monthly cheque for the 90 per cent balance.

14 *Sell to other people's customers.* Make a list of 20 other businesses whose clientele is probably very similar to your target audience. List 20 ways in which you could co-operate with that business for mutual advantage.

15 *One store test.* Make the necessary effort to approach at least one major store or other major distributor with the idea of testing your product with that one organisation. This gives tremendous feedback both to you and the store.

16 *Acquire somebody else's dog.* Larger companies either sell their Dogs or cease production and sales. Thousands of companies have prospered by acquiring Dogs from larger companies and turning them into Cash Cows, or even Stars. Make a list of 20 larger companies in your industry which you can approach with a view to acquiring their Dogs.

17 *Use the 10 per cent rule.* The best place to open a restaurant is opposite a very successful restaurant. The best place to open a petrol station is opposite an extremely successful petrol station. The existing business has established a market in that area. If you are 10 per cent better, 10 per cent cheaper, 10 per cent faster or at least 10 per cent nicer, then you can win sales in that area.

18 *Same product/new market.* If it is successful in the capital city this week, then it could well be successful in the provinces next week. When you are away from your business area, take a good look

at products which are succeeding. You can take that idea, you can take that product or service, and you can sell it in your own area.

19 *Use your suppliers and bank manager.* Your suppliers and your bank manager have a vested interest in your success. Ask your suppliers and your bank manager for leads.

20 *The Internet.* Collect the facts. Some companies are already winning sales on the Internet. Many people are using the Internet to reach customers, suppliers etc. Some are finding that the Internet creates an intensely competitive world in which your competitive advantage can be matched quickly by the competition.

Your website is your shop window with potential availability to the world. It is probably not a competitive advantage in itself, although it could make you faster than the rest. Customers still make their decisions on the basis of better, cheaper, faster, nicer.

21 *Database marketing.* Organise lists of active and inactive customers, other companies' active and inactive customers, purchasers of complementary products, liquidators' lists. Ask for referrals. Milk that golden chain. Shift the risk from customer to supplier. Extend the product range etc. Our first journal acquisition for £1 gave us a list of customers. We have developed, extended, nurtured this customer base for twenty five years. A friend of ours was in the business of concrete repair. When a rival business went into liquidation, he gained access to the sales ledger for £1000. This gave him a wonderful list of new customers, who had recently lost their regular supplier. Can you use this idea in your business?

22 *Fail, fail, fail.* Nobody has a 100 per cent success rate in selling. Sales is a numbers game. The more you fail, the more you succeed. Keep testing and failing.

23 *Ask your way to success.* Talk to the most successful sales people in your industry. How do they succeed? Creatively imitate the best!

24 *Proactive selling.* Many companies are totally reactive in their selling. If the telephone rings, they usually refer the call to the

'sales' person. The company simply takes orders. Make a decision to be proactive in sales in that you make sales happen, you set activity goals, learn sales skills, lead a winning team, seek out 20 additional ways to increase sales etc.

25 *Focus and concentration.* Use your creativity to generate 20 ways in which you can increase sales income. Make the necessary efforts. The good book does not say that ye shall find whether or not ye seeketh. It says: 'Seek and ye shall find.'

BECOME EXCELLENT AT SELLING.
LEAD A WINNING SALES TEAM.
STUDY THE ABOVE LISTS OF THE 100 WAYS
IN WHICH YOU CAN INCREASE YOUR SALES INCOME.
KEEP ABREAST OF CURRENT EVENTS
SO THAT YOU CAN ADD TO THE LIST.
CONTINUOUS LEARNING CAN MAKE THE DIFFERENCE
BETWEEN SUCCESS AND FAILURE.

Six

EVERYTHING IS NEGOTIABLE

How to negotiate better deals

Planning is 80 per cent of success in negotiation. Learn how to make a friendly opening, make statements of starting positions, bargain, and make a final agreement. If you refuse to negotiate you probably will not get what you want.

'Let us never negotiate out of fear, but let us never fear to negotiate.' – *John F. Kennedy*

1   DEFINITION OF NEGOTIATION

Serious negotiation begins when two parties are prepared to make an exchange for mutual advantage. Company A has something to offer Company B which Company B values more than Company A. Likewise, Company B has something to offer Company A which Company A values more than Company B. Reciprocation is possible. A successful negotiation can lead to the improvement in the conditions of both parties. There are usually five phases in any negotiation.

Preparation accounts for 80 per cent of your success in negotiation.

1   *Planning.* This takes place before the meeting and usually accounts for 80 per cent of success.

'If I had nine hours to cut down a tree, I would spend six hours sharpening my axe!' – *Abraham Lincoln*

---

2   *Creating a Friendly Environment.* This takes place at the meeting, presentation, negotiation.
3   *Making Statements of Opening Position.* Both parties state what they want from the negotiation.
4   *Bargaining.* Both parties trade concessions with a view to reconciliation.
5   *Agreement.* Both parties agree to a settlement, and perhaps future co-operation.

2   OBJECTIVE OF A NEGOTIATION

The objective of a negotiation is to reach agreement. Both parties should be satisfied. A settlement is reached in their mutual interests. Both parties feel that their respective conditions have been improved. This is a constructive, rather than a competitive negotiation. Some people enter a negotiation with the intention of screwing the other guy. In a constructive negotiation, both parties accept the settlement willingly, and leave the negotiation intending to fulfil their

People who refuse to negotiate do not usually get what they want.

commitments, and enter into further negotiations, additional deals. A constructive negotiation is simply part of relationship selling. As you read through this chapter, you will notice that many negotiation skills are similar to selling skills.

3   OUTCOMES OF NEGOTIATION

There are six possible outcomes to a negotiation:

1   No deal takes place, no settlement is reached, the negotiation collapses.
2   You win, the other person loses.
3   The other side wins, you lose.
4   Both sides lose.
5   You both reach a compromise.
6   Both sides win, both sides improve their condition, both parties leave the negotiation very satisfied.

In most negotiations, we are looking for win-win solutions, just as we would in any sales negotiation. Both sides leave the negotiation feeling that their conditions have been improved. At worst, go for the compromise, whereby both parties leave the negotiation feeling that they have to some extent improved their positions. Sometimes there has to be a winner and a loser, as in many court cases. There are many lose-lose negotiations in which both parties spend a fortune, and neither side achieves anything positive. Unfortunately, the most common situation in life is that people simply will not enter into a negotiation of any kind, and no deal takes place.

4   CHARACTERISTICS OF SUCCESSFUL NEGOTIATORS

The deal has to make sense for both parties.

Most people refuse to negotiate. They take a 'take it or leave it' approach to any negotiation. These people do not go into business, or they fail in business. They do not acquire the houses and cars they would like to own. They simply refuse to do deals, unless they get the ultimate price, the ultimate terms, unless they can dictate the outcome of a deal.

> We were surprised in a recent £50 million deal that the other side would not negotiate. They issued ultimatums. They walked away and we arranged a better deal elsewhere at £55 million.

Good negotiators are adaptive and flexible. They enjoy doing deals. They accept that negotiation is a process which exists throughout life. They are willing to change, they avoid taking fixed positions. They take a co-operative, understanding approach to dealing with others, rather than a dictatorial and belligerent approach. They take a co-operative approach towards creating a satisfactory deal, rather than competing with the opposition for the ultimate deal.

Good negotiators do not try to manipulate or trick other people into making unsatisfactory arrangements. They are well prepared for the negotiation, they seek win-win solutions, and they do not use the phrase 'generous offer'. Good negotiators simply take a positive and constructive view of the situation. They understand that a deal has to make good sense for both parties. Good negotiators ask questions. Good negotiators discover the hot button.

> We were recently involved in the sale of a business to a major newspaper organisation. We thought we were selling titles of journals and books. When we asked the simple question: 'Why are you interested in buying this company?', the other side explained that they wanted to use our products as a database for 30,000 distance-learning students. They helped us considerably by explaining why the business was worth far more money to them than to anybody else.

5   PREPARATION: DEFINE THE PERFECT OUTCOME

Develop clear ideas as to the perfect outcome, but be prepared to be flexible. Visualise the perfect outcome. Make notes. Plan the perfect outcome on paper. Define the price, quantity, quality, delivery, terms etc. What is the highest or very best you can achieve? What is acceptable? What is your lowest or ultimate fall-back position? Make a decision to define your highest defensible position. At the same time, define with great clarity the minimum you are prepared to accept.

In negotiation, clarity will always defeat vagueness. The person who is well prepared tends to get the better deal. What is negotiable? What is not negotiable? What is your walk-away position? Anticipate the areas of conflict. What is your starting position? When you make your opening statement of your position, what exactly will you say? Whether this is a formal negotiation, a sales presentation, or just a discussion, make sure that the people with you at the meeting know exactly what they can and cannot discuss. What are your priorities? What do you think will be the priorities of the other side? How can you maintain goodwill and reach a settlement at the same time?

Ask for what you want. Ask for the best deal you can justify. Then be flexible.

Having fully prepared for the negotiation, go back to the beginning and ask the questions: what is the subject matter of the negotiation, what are our goals, what is the perfect outcome? Remember that 80 per cent of your success in negotiating depends upon the quality of your preparation. Poor negotiators are unprepared.

'Before everything else, getting ready is the secret of success.'
– *Henry Ford*

'When schemes are laid in advance, it is surprising how often circumstances fit in with them.' – *Sir William Osler*

---

6   PREPARATION: THE FOUR STAGES IN THE ACTUAL NEGOTIATION

Organise your planning around the following four stages of the negotiation, which take place once you are in the presence of the other side.

1   Establishing a friendly relationship.
2   Each negotiator states his or her opening position.
3   The negotiators negotiate by trading concessions.
4   A settlement is reached.

7   PLANNING: EVERYTHING IS NEGOTIABLE

Everything starts with ideas. Planning starts with ideas, lists of the possible issues, concentrated thinking on the substance. Eventually we pull out the key issues for negotiation. Terms are not carved in stone by The Almighty. Prices are made by somebody and can be revised by somebody. Delivery dates are negotiable, credit terms are negotiable, quantity discounts are negotiable. Do not be afraid to ask for a better deal. Every deal can be improved in some way. The product can be better, it can be made more cheaply, and it can be delivered more quickly, by much more pleasant people.

Take a positive, adaptive, flexible approach to the negotiation. Be prepared to change. A rejection of your idea is not a rejection of you. Do not take it personally, do not suffer from identification. Do not keep justifying your position. Do not make personal remarks about the other side. If the other party says something which you don't like, then simply say: 'thank you for being so frank'. Stay positive, keep smiling. Remember that negotiation is excellent fun, it's just a game. The outcome is not going to kill you or the other party.

> Everything is negotiable.
> Quality – price – terms.
> Delivery – financing – discounts.

8 PLANNING: DEVELOP OPTIONS

Use your creativity to develop a range of options for yourself, and the other party. Separate the price from the terms. If they wish to dictate the price, then you can dictate the terms. You can agree to a ridiculous price, provided the other side agrees to equal instalments over 20 years without interest!

Separate the price from the terms.

> We have made excellent deals on property by separating the price from the terms. A property valued at £140,000 was sold for £160,000. We agreed an initial payment of £140,000 with the balance to be paid, interest free, in equal instalments over 5 years.

9 PLANNING: POWER IN NEGOTIATION

Your power is your perceived power, not necessarily your actual power. Your perceived power is increased by your tremendous knowledge of the subject, your financial strength, the fact that you are in no rush to do a deal, you are not desperate, you have other interested parties, you have an alternative source of supply, an alternative customer, you own a scarce resource, you are indifferent to the deal, you have tremendous authority, you have tremendous courage, and commitment to success. Your power is also increased if you are aware of the lack of knowledge of the other party, financial distress of the other party, the desperate need of the opposition to do a deal, the inability of the opposition to do a deal elsewhere etc.

Your power is considerably increased when the opposition understands that you have the ability to reward and punish. Serious negotiation begins when the other side believes that you have the power to offer them or deprive them of something they desire. Your power is also increased dramatically when you know that the other side has made a tremendous investment of time, money and effort in the negotiation. Focus and concentrate on how you can increase your perceived power.

> **POWER**
> Your perceived power is increased by:
> tremendous knowledge – financial strength
> patience – other interested parties
> ownership of a scarce resource
> authority – courage
> positive attitude.

10   PLANNING: SITUATION REVERSAL

Reverse the argument. Argue the case from the position of the other side. This gives tremendous insight into the negotiation. If only lawyers would practise this technique. We once asked our lawyer what would be the outcome of a court case. He replied: 'How should I know? We turn up and state our position. The other side states their position, and then the judge makes a decision.' We asked the lawyer: 'Can you imagine Napoleon turning up at Waterloo with that attitude?'. On the eve of the Battle of Waterloo, if Napoleon were to be asked what would be the outcome, would you expect Napoleon to say: 'How should I know? We turn up with a hundred thousand troops, they turn up with a hundred thousand troops, and at the end of the day somebody will win and somebody will lose.' Make a habit of arguing the case for the opposition. This will lead to a far more successful negotiation for you.

11   PLANNING: USE THE POWERS OF LOVE AND SUGGESTION

Be positive. Be patient, be supportive of the other party. Let the other party know that the deal must make sense for them as well as you. Meet in comfortable surroundings, with good lighting, clean air and access to satisfactory refreshments. Create a relaxed, rather than a hurried pace. Use friendly body language, i.e. open hands rather than clenched fists. Position yourselves around a round table, and try to avoid adversarial positions. If you sit opposite somebody, there is a tendency to engage in battle. It is difficult to argue with the person sitting next to you. Finally, arrange the meeting on your home ground or on neutral ground. Try not to attend negotiations at the other party's home ground.

12   ESTABLISH A FRIENDLY RELATIONSHIP

Start with a firm handshake. Try to establish friendship. Try to establish a cordial climate, a breaking of the ice. Try to establish a good first impression. Talk about the weather, football, admire the scenery, admire the photograph of the family, discuss a painting on the wall. Make a decision to be co-operative as well as businesslike. Do not rush into the deal. Do not go too far, too quickly. Eventually, address the questions: why are we here, what do we do, and how long have we got? Acknowledge that both parties will have done some preparation, and make an agreement to keep things moving. Make a decision to discuss an agenda, a procedure, a plan for moving forward. Make a conscious decision to avoid mistrust, agitation, wariness. Make decisions as to how long the meeting will last, the procedure you will follow, and make a decision to arrive at a satisfactory outcome. This helps to remove the uncertainty. At last, you agree an agenda, how long the meeting will last, and one party agrees to start the ball rolling by making a statement of his or her opening position.

'Industrial relations are like sexual relations. It's better between two consenting parties.' – *Lord Vic Feather*

'Watch out for a man whose stomach doesn't move when he laughs.' – *Ancient Chinese proverb*

---

13 STATEMENTS OF OPENING POSITION

Both parties have now established good first impressions, and agreed to proceed in a cordial and co-operative atmosphere. One party now outlines his or her position. At the planning stage, you have already decided to make the highest defensible bid. You have positive expectations. You have decided what to bid, how to put the bid, and how to respond to the bid of the other side. You ask for clarification. You make the other party justify the bid. You leave room for manoeuvre. You ask questions. You ask for more information. You try to establish common ground. You see things the other person cannot see. The other person can see things that you cannot see. There are some aspects of the negotiation that nobody expected. Telling and listening leads to understanding.

Eventually, the second party makes his or her statement of opening position. Both parties achieve fresh insights. The independent exposition by both parties raises questions, insights, and understanding. You do not argue with each other. You do not contradict. There are no rights and wrongs. Both sides collect information, search for hot buttons, find out what is important, what is of less importance. Occasionally, you restate something which the other party has said, something which is now agreed. Both sides ask for agreement on matters which are commercially defensible.

You discuss price, quantity, quality, length of contract, delivery dates, payment terms etc. You continue to agree on everything on which you can agree. You ask questions about constraints, boundaries, the essentials, maxima and minima, possible concessions, the way forward. You may have already thought of chipping away at the deal as proposed by the other party. You may have already considered making counter-offers, or even concessions.

At this point, it may be convenient to have a 15-minute recess for both sides to consider their positions in private, or in discussions with other colleagues.

'Asking a question is like sharpening a pencil: each apt question … whittles down the problem.' – *Gerald I. Nierenberg*

'When a man tells me he is going to put all his cards on the table, I always look up his sleeve.' – *Lord Leslie-Hore-Belisha*

14   BARGAINING: INCORRECT ASSUMPTIONS

After any break, use the restart as an opportunity to state clearly what has been agreed so far. Having collected a tremendous amount of information from the other party, you are now prepared to bargain, trading concessions with the other side with a view to reaching a settlement. Incorrect assumptions are the reasons for most failure. What are your assumptions? What are your assumptions about the other side? Were your original assumptions incorrect? What is the ideal outcome for the other side? Ask the other side. What are the critical issues for yourself? What are the critical issues for the other side?

Be patient and persistent. Keep searching. Don't rush into any settlement. Try to avoid fixed positions. Do not let the other side lose face. Always offer a concession in exchange for a concession. Surrender something which is unimportant for something which is important to you. If you hit a snag, move on to something else. Keep agreeing on everything on which you can agree. Look for indications, search out priorities, be prepared to make counter offers. Again, do not rush into a settlement.

'Speak when you are angry and you will make the best speech you will ever regret.' – *Ambrose Bierce*

15   BARGAINING: AVOID EMOTION

We are emotional creatures. Unfortunately, if you bring emotion to the bargaining situation, you will probably arrive at an unsatisfactory settlement. Avoid greed, fear, outbursts of anger. Avoid showing your desire, your ruthlessness, your selfishness, your self-pity. Practise detachment, i.e. step aside from the situation, do not take it personally. Avoid identification. Stop justifying your position. Be flexible, adaptive. Be prepared to let the deal collapse. It is not the only deal in the world. You may find that you must bring strong emotion to the situation in that you must buy that car. Under these circumstances, get somebody else to conduct the negotiation for you. A third party brings no emotion to the situation. A friend or colleague can offer £11,000 for the £15,000 car. An independent negotiator can offer £11,500, £12,000, and walk away from the showroom having left a walk away price of £12,500. The sales person eventually agrees a price of £12,600. You probably could not have negotiated this deal, because the salesman knows that you must have that car, you really want it, and you will pay the price.

'If you are patient in one moment of anger, you will escape a hundred days of sorrow.' – *Chinese proverb*

---

16   BARGAINING: TIME IS ON YOUR SIDE

Any sign of impatience or urgency weakens your hand. If the other side is anxious for something which you have the power to give them, then this gives you tremendous strength. Remember the old proverb: delay is the cruellest form of denial. If you are aware that the opposition must get a deal by 5 p.m. this afternoon, then make sure that all the important issues are left for the last few minutes. You will negotiate an excellent deal for yourself.

17   BARGAINING: SAVE THE IMPORTANT ISSUES FOR THE END

In negotiation we find the 80/20 rule usually applies in that 80 per cent of the substance is agreed in the final 20 per cent of the time. Make a habit of saving the most important issues for the last few minutes. During the negotiation you have focused on the benefits for the other side. You have left the agreement on price for settlement in the last few minutes.

18   BARGAINING: PERSUASION, RECIPROCATION AND SOCIAL PROOF

You are a go-giver. At the start of the negotiation, you let the other side know that you are concerned about their interests as well as your own. You wish to arrive at a settlement, an agreement which is as acceptable to them as it is to you. You reciprocate in that you trade concessions on a tit-for-tat basis. You agree on everything on which you can agree. If you hit problems, these are put aside for discussion later in the negotiation. Your fairness encourages co-operation. You use mega-credibility to illustrate your position. You quote facts, you offer lists of satisfied clients, you produce references from those who have accepted the same deal. Any deal accepted by so many other negotiators, must be a fair deal for the other side.

19   BARGAINING: IT'S TIME TO AGREE THE PRICE

If you are the seller, you must set a minimum price below which you will not sell. Anything above that is a bonus. Usually, people are extremely anxious to learn how to get the price down. Here are a few tactics which will save you a lot of money.

1   *Pull a face.* Whenever anybody mentions a price to you, always pull a face to demonstrate the price is totally unacceptable. This should get you a 10 per cent reduction.
2   *Do your homework.* Whatever the price, make the statement: 'I can get it cheaper elsewhere'. You must come up with an alternative source. If you can provide the evidence, the vendor will reduce the price.

3 *Ask tough questions.* You must have the courage to ask the following questions: 'Have you ever sold this product for less?', 'Is that the very best price you can offer?', 'What is your walk-away price?'. Once you have established a walk-away price, walk out of the shop, walk away from the deal. If you do not get a further reduction, then you can always return later and make the purchase. Shopkeepers know that very few people return to the shop after leaving.

4 *Low ball.* Offer a ridiculously low price. If you see a painting which you like for £800, then tell the dealer 'I like it, but I never pay more than £200 for a painting', or 'I like it, but I'm on a strict budget of £200.' Ask the dealer just how close he or she can get to £200. You can offer cash rather than cheque or credit card. You will be amazed how many times you get the deal you never thought would happen.

5 *The big order.* If you intend to buy a car, then negotiate the best price you can. After that, surprise the salesperson by informing him/her that in fact you want twelve of these vehicles for the salesforce in your business. Ask again: what is the best price the salesperson can offer? You will get a large discount. You then tell the salesperson 'Thank you very much. I'll take just one for the time being, and come back for the rest in a few months' time.' You may not get the deal you wanted, but at least you can go to another showroom and state with all honesty: 'They quoted me such-and-such a price at such-and-such a showroom.'

6 *Delegate price negotiation.* If you have an emotional involvement in that you must have that car, then get somebody else to negotiate the deal on your behalf. Finally, as part of your sales training, you should know that in any negotiation you focus on the benefits. By the time you have finished talking about the £1 million benefit, the customer should not care about the £100,000 cost. At the end of a good sales presentation, the price should be a mere detail.

> **PRICE**
> If you are the buyer:
> 1 Always pull a face
> 2 Do your homework on the competition
> 3 Ask tough questions
> 4 Offer a very low price
> 5 Ask for a quote for a large order
> 6 Delegate price negotiaton.

20 AGREEMENT

You finalise the deal, arrive at a settlement. Perhaps you needed a second break before finalising the negotiation. The end usually arrives very quickly. Seize on the agreement as soon as it is completed. State what the agreement is. Some writers suggest that you should argue at length on one final detail, at last conceding the point to the other side, letting the other guy go away believing that he has got a great deal. Finally, congratulate the other side on the excellent deal they have negotiated.

If the deal fails, if the negotiation fails, be prepared to make the second effort. You can always start a new negotiation on the basis of new information, new orders from Head Office, new price opportunities etc. If you have to renegotiate, then renegotiate on the basis of benefits to the other side. You are prepared to trade more concessions to get the deal. Be extremely careful at the end of a negotiation, since a skilled negotiator might claw a major concession from you just after the deal is completed. You could use the same tactic on the other side.

We do not advocate tricks in negotiation, since you are usually looking to enter into further business arrangements with the other side in the future. It is not worth jeopardising your relationship with your customer for the sake of one advantage in one deal.

'Build your adversary a golden bridge to retreat across.'
– *Sun Tzu*

---

21 PRACTICE

Your negotiating skills, like your selling skills, will improve with practice. Collect the facts, plan for the negotiation, separate the people from the situation, identify the needs of both sides, ask for what you want, develop options, seek win-win solutions, trade concessions, and arrive at a settlement. The more you practise, the luckier you get!

> PRACTISE YOUR NEGOTIATION SKILLS
> THROUGHOUT THE REST OF YOUR LIFE.
> LEARN HOW TO NEGOTIATE BETTER DEALS.
> YOU CAN NEGOTIATE BETTER BUSINESS DEALS,
> OWN THE HOUSE AND THE CAR YOU WANT,
> AND BOTH MAKE AND SAVE YOURSELF A FORTUNE.

Seven

WE ALL NEED LEADERSHIP

How to lead a winning team

Adopt the characteristics of leaders; do what leaders do, and you become a leader. Leaders set clear goals. They think positively. Their excitement and enthusiasm has an effect on others. Everything counts.

1   DEFINITION OF LEADERSHIP

Leadership is the ability to motivate people to strive to achieve common goals. Leadership is the ability to draw extraordinary performance from ordinary people. Leadership is about making things happen, getting results. Transactional leaders are those men and women of action who have the ability to motivate others to get things done. Transformational leaders are those men and women of vision who inspire others to high levels of achievement. In short, leaders make things happen and encourage and motivate others to make things happen. Leadership is about getting results. A manager's job is to get results. Leadership is one important business skill which can be learned.

LEADERS
draw extraordinary performance from ordinary people
motivate people to strive towards common goals.

2   THE BASIC SKILLS OF LEADERSHIP

'In the simplest terms, a leader is one who knows where he/she wants to go, and gets up, and goes.' – *John Erskine*

Three of the fundamental attributes of leadership are:

1   Leaders set goals.
2   Leaders have high expectations of themselves and others.
3   Leaders are good listeners.

Most people do not know what they want. Most people need leadership. If you set goals, then you become a leader. Leaders have a vision, a sense of mission which inspires the leader and others. Leaders understand that goals can unite people in a common cause.

People who do not set goals are probably destined to spend the rest of their lives working for people who do. People love working for high-expectations bosses. High-expectations bosses raise the self-esteem of their followers.

Leaders are good listeners. When the leader listens to the follower, it makes the follower feel more valuable and worthwhile, as well as raising the self-esteem of the leader. A fourth basic attribute of leaders mentioned here is that leaders have positive mental attitudes. Leaders are excited and enthusiastic about achieving the mission. They bring love and joy to the process of achieving the mission and vision. They have high expectations of themselves and others. They believe that the mission will be achieved. They attract into their lives the people, circumstances, and information necessary to achieve their goals.

Leaders understand that leadership is an acquired skill. All leaders are readers. They study other leaders. They understand that all leaders were once followers. Leaders avoid negative **Only excellence** emotions. They do not blame others for the situation, they **motivates.** do not suffer from self-pity, they do not envy others their successes, they do not hate others, they do not suffer from self-doubt, fear of failure or fear of rejection. Leaders focus on the mission, not a profit.

3   CHARACTERISTICS OF LEADERS (1)

Vision, mission, clear goals

Leaders have a vision of some ideal future. They have a **Leaders have a** sense of mission in that they wish to improve the lives of **clear vision of** others in some way, to be the best in the business, to be **the future.** the most excellent, to be acknowledged leaders in that industry. Leaders set clear personal and family goals, clear business goals, and clear goals for self-development.

'Someone once described a bureaucracy as a group of people who are brought together for a purpose but very quickly forget the purpose for which they are there.' – *Edward de Bono*

'The lowest form of thinking is the bare recognition of the object. The highest, the comprehensive intuition of the man who sees all things as part of a system.' – *Plato*

4 CHARACTERISTICS OF LEADERS (2)

High expectations, commitment to winning

Leaders have high expectations of themselves, and members of the team. They focus and concentrate on success, they have a 100 per cent commitment to winning. They want to be the best, highest quality, to be recognised for their excellence. They understand that a failure is just a setback. They are only defeated when they give up. A setback can be a valuable lesson. Leaders understand that only excellence motivates. They focus on achieving the mission, at a profit. In business, net profit is equal to victory. If the firm makes a profit, we have successfully concentrated all our resources, hitting our market segment, with our competitive advantage, in our area of excellence.

> We all suffer setbacks.
> You are not defeated just because you lost.
> You are only defeated when you give up.

'Some people have greatness thrust upon them. Very few have excellence thrust upon them. They achieve it.' – *John Gardner*

'Only mediocrity is always at its best.' – *Max Beerbohm*

5   CHARACTERISTICS OF LEADERS (3)

Listening skills

Leaders are good listeners. They learn from others. They raise their own self-esteem and the self-esteem of others by listening carefully. Leaders are attentive towards others. They do not interrupt. They give others undivided attention. They are excellent at the one-to-one discussion with no telephone interruptions, in private, with the door closed.

'Tell me, I may listen. Teach me, I may remember. Involve me, I will do it.' – *Chinese proverb*

'Let thy speech be better than silence or be silent.'
– *Dionysius the Elder*

'The deepest principle in human nature is the craving to be appreciated.' – *Dale Carnegie*

'There are some people that if they don't know, you can't tell 'em.' – *Louis Armstrong*

---

6   CHARACTERISTICS OF LEADERS (4)

Action

'Leadership is action, not position.' – *Donald H. McGannon*

Leaders take action. They understand that only action gets results. Information is necessary, decision-making is necessary, but it is only the action we take which gets results. Leaders say: 'Let's do it, let's fix it, let's give it a try'. Leaders live in the future, think about the future, are fascinated by innovation and entrepreneurship. Leaders do not suffer from fear of failure. They understand that failure equals succeeding. It is not a failure, it is a setback, it is a valuable learning experience, it is a rock which has to be overcome before we achieve the success which we shall inevitably achieve in the future. Leaders work hard and, by their example, encourage others to work hard. In a world in which everything counts, the behaviour of the leader affects followers.

'We have to understand that the world can only be grasped by action, not by contemplation …' – *Jacob Bronowski* (author of *The Ascent of Man*)

'Above all, leaders are doers.' – *Peter F. Drucker*

---

7   CHARACTERISTICS OF LEADERS (5)

Courage

Leaders have the courage to take action in an uncertain world. They understand that if you face that which you fear, then the fear will soon be removed. If you act with courage, unexpected forces will automatically come to your assistance. Your persistence is your measure of your belief in yourself. Leaders have the courage to be patient, to stay the course. Leaders initiate action, they go onto the attack. They understand that the world belongs to those who are in love with the new. Leaders are not afraid to ask the question: in this situation, what would Winston Churchill do, what would Napoleon do, what would Jesus Christ do, what would Richard Branson do? Go forward with confidence in the direction of your dreams! I love uncertainty. I am thriving on chaos. He or she who controls uncertainty has power.

Face that which you fear and the fear is removed.
Unexpected forces will come to your aid.
Fear is **F**antasised **E**xperiences **A**ppearing **R**eal.

'Don't be afraid to take a big step if one is indicated. You can't cross a chasm in two small jumps.' – *David Lloyd George*

'Whatever you can do or dream you can do, begin it. Boldness has genius, power and magic in it.' – *Goethe*

8   CHARACTERISTICS OF LEADERS (6)

Planning

Leaders think strategically. They think in terms of mission, specialisation, differentiation, segmentation and concentration. How can we get from where we are now to our ideal future? Given the mission, what is the strategy that will get us to our profit target? How do we specialise? What is our competitive advantage? Where is our market segment? Which resources are required to achieve our goals?

A business leader tries to see the big picture, focuses on the strengths of our business, focuses on the weaknesses of our competitors, focuses on ways in which we can respond to the competition, focuses on our ability to react quickly to the opposition, does not dwell upon the past, understands that the rest of our business lives will be spent in the future. Business leaders focus and concentrate on the future of the economy, the future of our industry within the economy, and the future of our business within the industry.

Leaders implement winning strategies.

9 CHARACTERISTICS OF LEADERS (7)

Results orientation

Leaders focus on results, rather than activities. They focus on the 20 per cent which brings in 80 per cent of the desired result. Leaders accept responsibility for results. They understand that they cannot blame others. They set priorities, and carry out action plans to completion. Leaders understand the winning-edge concept, in that just being a little better in key areas can lead to significantly better results. Leaders are proactive, rather than reactive. They make things happen, rather than reacting to events.

10 CHARACTERISTICS OF LEADERS (8)

Enjoyment of leading

Leaders want to lead. They enjoy it. Leadership is entirely consistent with their self-concepts. They believe that they are controlling the information, the circumstances, and contact with others, which will lead them to achievement of the mission. Leadership is entirely consistent with their self-concepts. They believe that they are leaders. We all behave in a manner consistent with what we believe.

11 CHARACTERISTICS OF LEADERS (9)

High self-esteem

Leaders, either consciously or subconsciously, use the affirmation: I am a valuable and worthwhile person. Leaders have high self-esteem. They do not believe that they are superior to other people, but they certainly do not believe that they are inferior to other people. They have the courage to be honest with themselves. They understand their own strengths and weaknesses, they are prepared to make the necessary efforts to focus on their strengths and to either overcome their weaknesses, or compensate for their weakness in some way, possibly by employing the required skills of some other person or some other organisation. They are prepared to consider the advice of others. They are prepared to make use of the specialisation of some other business.

'The elusive half-step between middle management and true leadership is grace under pressure.' – *John F. Kennedy*

---

12   CHARACTERISTICS OF LEADERS (10)

Self-motivation

Leaders do not depend upon others for motivation. They are internally driven by their own vision, mission and goals. They are internally driven to higher levels of achievement. Leaders are able to get commitment to the achievement of their goals from others. Leaders are not lazy, ill-informed, selfish, greedy, impatient, ruthless, disloyal, irresponsible, unreliable, or vain. Leaders tend to be full of energy, extremely well informed, unselfish, not greedy, patient, generous, loyal, responsible, reliable, and self-effacing.

13   CHARACTERISTICS OF LEADERS (11)

Continuous learning

Leaders have a thirst for knowledge, a need for continuous improvement. They attend the courses, conferences, exhibitions, and seminars. They read books, listen to tapes, and spend time with other leaders. All leaders are readers. Leaders understand that they can ask their way to success. Leaders build on their strengths, and learn how to compensate for their weaknesses. They are prepared to change. They understand that change is inevitable, and that change equals opportunity. They understand that the world belongs to those who are in love with new ideas. Leaders understand that knowledge is becoming the basic resource of most businesses.

14   CHARACTERISTICS OF LEADERS (12)

Integrity

Leaders have high integrity. Their word is their bond, even if it costs money. You can trust leaders. Leaders have credibility. If they err, then they err on the side of fairness. Leaders insist that the other party to a negotiation is satisfied with the deal. *My word is my* Leaders have a fanaticism for quality and service. Their *bond – even if it* actions are consistent with their words. *costs money.*

'Men occasionally stumble over the truth but most of them pick themselves up and hurry off as if nothing had happened.'
– Sir Winston Churchill

'One must have a good memory to be able to keep the promises one makes.' *– Friedrich W. Nietzsche*

---

15   WHAT DO LEADERS DO? (1)

Leaders inspire and motivate others

Leaders inspire trust, confidence and loyalty from other people. Their excitement and enthusiasm affects others. Leaders empower others. The 100-per-cent commitment to excellence and success of the leader is an inspiration to other members of the team. Leaders are visible people. They do not hide behind closed doors or bureaucratic rules. They manage by MBWA, management by walking around. They inspire and motivate through excellence. They inspire by being high expectations bosses. They delegate to others. This gives them time to take high risks, not necessarily with money, but with time. Leaders are always available to allocate their time to the 20 per cent that brings in the 80 per cent, to learning, attending conferences, being seen. Leaders focus their attention on critical areas of the business, those areas which guarantee the future. They continue to learn. They understand that knowledge could be the competitive advantage of the business. Followers look up to the leader as a role model.

16   WHAT DO LEADERS DO? (2)

Leaders put meaning and purpose into work

For millions of people, work is a necessary evil, just a chore, another day, another dollar. Leaders put meaning and purpose into work. They set demanding goals, have a commitment to excellence, inspire and motivate others. People love working for a high-expectations boss. Leaders understand that other people wish to improve their conditions, to become more, have more and do more. Leaders raise the expectations of followers. They facilitate and empower. They give people the skills, the motivation, the tools to carry out their tasks, and then empower people to learn, make mistakes, become more successful.

Many modern leaders empower people to accept responsibility, to take control of their activities, to achieve personal and family goals by achieving the goals of the organisation. Leaders encourage people to strive for peak performance. Leaders make the customer the central focus of the organisation. They are obsessed with customer care and customer satisfaction. This is the worthy goal of the business. Achieving goals makes followers feel valuable and worthwhile. It raises the self-esteem of the employee. The leader encourages by example, training, coaching, good counselling and review.

'Men will die for medals.' – *Napoleon*

---

17 WHAT DO LEADERS DO? (3)

Leaders communicate well

Leaders tend to be excellent communicators. They listen attentively and are extremely effective in one-to-one discussions, they run effective meetings, they give excellent presentations, and write short, excellent reports. Leaders agree clear goals with followers. People know exactly what is expected of them. They know that it will be measured. They understand that they will receive excellent feedback, counselling and review. They understand why the contribution they make is so important. Leaders make other people feel important. Leaders are excellent at selling. They are excellent at win-win negotiating. Leaders know where to find their audience.

Leaders make people feel important.

GOOD COMMUNICATIONS
the one-to-one discussion
meetings
presentations
reports.

18 WHAT DO LEADERS DO? (4)

Leaders build winning teams

A great deal of work is done by teams. Given that we do not all have the same contribution to make, the leader needs to build a balanced team. The leader is the linker, he or she brings together the talents of team members to form a winning team. Human beings are vaguely classified as being creators/innovators, explorers/promoters, assessors/developers, thrusters/organisers, concluders/producers, controllers/inspectors, upholders/maintainers, and reporters/advisers. We need people to come up with ideas and explore possibilities. Others can organise and make things happen. We need controllers to keep the operation running effectively, and we need specialist advisers. The effective leader leads a winning team by drawing upon the different talents of team members.

Leaders build winning teams.   The leader selects SMART people. S stands for smart in that the prospective employee has an attractive appearance and appears to be generally on the ball. M is for motivation, highly-motivated people being prepared to set goals and pay the price to achieve those goals. A is for attitude, in that we employ people for their excitement and their enthusiasm, rather than their paper qualifications, age or experience. R is for results orientation, whereby we employ people who are prepared to accept responsibility for results. T stands for trust, in that we employ people we feel we can trust. As a general guide, we recommend that you interview at least three people for any position, and that you interview these people at least three times and in three different situations. Employing the wrong people is extremely expensive. The characteristics of winning teams are:

1   *Clear leadership.* Winning teams have effective leaders. Team members know who the leader is.
2   *Clear strategy and planning.* Winning teams know precisely what they must do to get from where they are now to the ideal future.
3   *People-development focus.* Winning teams focus on courses, educational tapes, reading, and spending time with the mastermind alliance. Continuous learning is part of the group philosophy.
4   *Commitment to excellence.* Only excellence motivates. Winning teams are committed to excellence.
5   *Selective player assignments.* Each member of the team is allocated those activities to which he or she is best suited, where the greatest contribution is made to achieving goals.
6   *Good communications.* Winning teams have open communications, free access to information, no hidden agendas, no cliques.

LEADERS EMPLOY SMART PEOPLE

S	Smart
M	Motivated
A	Attitude
R	Results
T	Trust

The leader establishes clear output responsibilities for team members. He or she provides good counselling and review on a regular basis for team members. The leader measures the outputs of team members. What gets measured gets done. What gets rewarded gets repeated. The leader establishes clear reward structures for maximum team motivation. Team members are rewarded by recognition for their achievements, financial rewards, status rewards, attention from the leader, and promotion. Team members are encouraged to undertake continuous improvement.

> What gets measured gets done.

The leader empowers and facilitates. The leader delegates everything possible to team members. This frees the leader to focus on the 20 per cent which brings in the 80 per cent. Delegation enables the leader to take high risks with his or her time. Our advice is: delegate everything that it is possible to delegate!

For leaders of small businesses, one piece of advice we always give is that they should not train people on the job. It is simply too labour intensive. Buy in the skills you need. The leader should focus on what can be achieved, not what can be done. One final point on delegation is that delegation is not abdication. The leader is still responsible for the results of the team.

> What gets rewarded gets repeated.

'By asking the impossible we obtain the best possible.'
– *Italian proverb*

---

19   LEADERSHIP STYLES

There are essentially three leadership styles:

1   *Leadership by command.* The leader makes all the decisions. Everybody else does exactly what they are told, or else!
2   *Leadership by consultation.* The leader makes the decisions, after discussion with team members.
3   *Leadership by consensus.* The team decides.

In this chapter we are generally recommending leadership by consensus. Maximum motivation is aroused where team members feel that they own the objectives. It is their company, their mission, their goal etc. Participative decision-making tends to be the most effective kind of decision making. However, we all have to recognise that there are some very effective leaders who lead by command, or by consultation. There are some circumstances in which only leadership by command, or leadership by consultation can be effective.

> **WHAT IS YOUR LEADERSHIP STYLE?**
> Command and control; or
> Facilitate and empower.

20   HOW TO BECOME A LEADER

If you set goals, become a high-expectations boss, and a good listener, then you are well on the way to becoming a leader. You become a far more effective leader if you develop a vision, develop a sense of mission, become action-oriented, have courage, think strategically, plan, become results-oriented, enjoy leading, develop high self-esteem, be self-motivated, learn continuously, have high integrity, inspire and motivate others, give work meaning and purpose, communicate well, build a winning team, delegate, supervise, and give good counsel and review.

Study leadership and practise leadership. Set it as a goal, and resolve to pay the price in advance. Visualise, emotionalise and affirm. See yourself as a leader. Imagine how you would feel as a leader, and use the affirmation: 'I am a leader'. Be persistent in your attempts to be a leader. Your persistence is your measure of your belief in yourself. Never give up. Never, never give up. Take high risks with your time. Avoid the comfort zone. Face that which you fear and unexpected forces will come to your aid.

21 CHARACTERISTICS OF SUCCESSFUL ENTREPRENEURS

An entrepreneur is someone who is determined to improve the life of a customer in a competitive world. A customer is someone who is willing and able to purchase the benefit you offer in a competitive world.

The vast majority of people cannot be entrepreneurs. They choose to work for a state monopoly. They expect to be rewarded for their time, for their qualifications, and their experience. They refuse to set goals, they refuse to pay the price in advance, they fail to establish their specialisation, they do not want to make the necessary effort to establish a competitive advantage, they do not wish to address the uncertainty of a customer, and they are not prepared to focus and concentrate on hitting their market segment with their competitive advantage in their area of excellence.

They are doomed to be followers. They are doomed to £23,000 per annum or less. People in the public sector cannot be entrepreneurs. There is no scope for business in the public sector. People in the public sector do not have customers. People in the public sector self-select themselves to spend their lives spending the budget. They self-select themselves not to compete in a competitive world.

When businesses compete, products/services get better, cheaper, faster, nicer. Businesses differentiate themselves on the basis of quality, price, speed, niceness. The customer is free to choose. The customer is free to choose whether he or she wants the benefit, whether the benefit should be bought on quality, price, speed, or niceness, and the customer does not have to spend a single penny on any product or service unless the customer desires that product or service. It does not work that way in the public sector. There is no opt-out from the National Health Service, you cannot opt out from paying your taxes for state schooling, the fire service, the police, or anything else.

If you have read this chapter carefully, then it will come as no surprise to you that the following have been found to be the general characteristics of successful entrepreneurs.

1. *A sense of mission.* Successful entrepreneurs set out to improve the lives of their customers. They do not simply set out to make a pile of money. They are completely absorbed in their work. Being a workaholic is perfectly healthy, provided you are working hard at something you love doing. Focus and concentrate on your area of excellence.
2. *Self-belief.* They believe that they will be successful. They expect to be successful. Even when bankrupt, they still believe that one day they will be successful.
3. *Resolution to pay the price.* Entrepreneurs understand the price that must be paid to achieve their goals, and they resolve to pay the necessary price.
4. *Acceptance of responsibility.* Successful entrepreneurs are found to accept responsibility for themselves, and not to blame others.
5. *Commitment to success.* Successful entrepreneurs have a 100-percent commitment to becoming successful. They focus and concentrate on their area of excellence.
6. *Judgement.* They are not necessarily clever with words, arithmetic, music, art, or mechanics. However, they have developed social skills intelligence and judgement. We often remind students on MBA programmes that they are on the course to learn judgement.
7. *The helicopter view.* Entrepreneurs can see the big picture, anticipate trends. They have foresight in that they always look to the future, understanding that the rest of our business lives will be spent in the future.

8 *Leadership skills.* They set goals, have high expectations of themselves and others, and listen carefully. They have the ability to draw extraordinary performance from ordinary people.

9 *Excellence in selling.* Entrepreneurs generally are excellent at selling. They focus on benefits to the customer, satisfying customer desires, allaying customer fears. They make excellent presentations, and show the product or service in its best light.

10 *Excellent communications.* Successful entrepreneurs tend to be excellent in private discussion, conducting meetings, giving presentations, and submitting reports.

11 *Managing time effectively.* They develop the ability to focus on the 20 per cent that brings in the 80 per cent of success, and delegate the 80 per cent to others.

12 *Persistence.* Successful entrepreneurs persist. They understand that it usually takes 20 years to make the first £1 million. They are prepared to go the extra mile, and do that little bit extra for which they do not get paid.

'Victory belongs to the most persevering.' – *Napoleon*

SET CLEAR GOALS.
BE A HIGH EXPECTATIONS PERSON, AND LISTEN TO
OTHERS. COMMUNICATE WELL, BUILD A WINNING TEAM,
AND YOU WILL GIVE MEANING AND PURPOSE TO
THE WORK OF OTHERS.
YOU WILL INSPIRE AND MOTIVATE.
YOU WILL DRAW EXTRAORDINARY PERFORMANCE
FROM ORDINARY PEOPLE.

Eight

EVERYTHING YOU DO AFFECTS SALES, COSTS AND PROFITS

How to understand the financial implications

If we strive to achieve the mission by implementing a winning strategy, then there is the possibility the business might make a profit. Profit is the result. We all need to understand that sales value less the cost of sales equals gross profit or gross margin. Gross profit less overheads equals net profit. Net profit is victory. Just about everything you do in business has an effect on sales, costs and net profit. Keep your eyes on gross profit, overhead, net profit and cash flow. Focus on these four key numbers.

1   NET PROFIT

Profit is an improvement in the human condition. Customers buy products and services because they prefer the benefit received to the money sacrificed. The business person makes a profit by providing goods and services to customers which are worth more to the customer than the cost of providing the benefit. Business people make profits by concentrating all their resources, hitting their market segment with their competitive advantage in their areas of excellence. Profit is net income. Profit is the amount a person can consume during the year and still be as well off at the end of the year as at the beginning of the year. Profit is an increase in wealth. This is all very well, but for our present purposes we must emphasise that in business, accountants define and measure profit as follows:

Net profit = invoiced sales less invoiced cost of sales, wages, overheads and depreciation.

Profit is based on invoices, not cash. If a car dealer buys a car for £2000 on credit and sells it for £3000 on credit, then the profit is £1000, i.e. invoiced sales of £3000 less invoiced cost of sales, £2000, gives a gross profit of £1000. No cash has changed hands but the gross profit is £1000. The dealer then deducts expenses or overheads. These are the cost of rent, telephone, printing and stationery, accounting fees, depreciation of office equipment, etc. These amount to £600. The net profit in business is gross profit of £1000 less the overheads or expenses of £600 equals £400 net profit. In measuring profit we do not take into account whether invoices for sales, cost of sales, and overheads have actually been paid. Profit is based on invoices. Depreciation is charged as an expense against profit although it does not involve an annual cash payment. We pay in cash when we purchase office equipment, plant and equipment etc. The cost is then written off against profits over the estimated useful life of the asset.

2   GROSS PROFIT

Gross profit or gross margin is the profit made on a sale, i.e. the difference between an invoiced sale and the invoiced cost of that sale. Gross margin is critical in business. Making sales is extremely hard work and in itself does not make the business successful, not unless sales yield gross profit. We need gross margin to make a contribution towards overheads and net profit. We are eternally grateful to the senior manager of a major British car producer who, on a management-development programme, gave us the immortal quotation: 'we lose money on every item we sell, but we make it up on the volume'. Needless to say, the business subsequently crashed.

3   OVERHEADS

Overheads are those expenses which cannot be directly charged against a product, division or an invoiced sale. Overheads would normally include office salaries, rent and accommodation costs, printing and stationery, telephone costs, depreciation, head-office costs, personnel costs, general advertising and promotion costs, accounting department costs, etc. Overhead drift is a major cause of business failure. Overheads always drift upwards. If the overheads are greater than the gross profit, then the firm does not make a net profit.

We encourage managers to think in terms of zero-based budgeting. Start every planning session with a base of zero for overheads. Everything above zero must be justified. Do not begin your financial planning with the assumption that overheads must increase by 10 per cent, 15 per cent or 20 per cent each year. With a view to reducing overheads, keep asking the question: 'knowing what we know now, would we incur such and such a cost?'. Eliminate those costs which cannot be justified in terms of increasing sales, gross margin and net profit.

A former MBA student of ours had a brilliant idea. He decided to make paper bags for takeaway food restaurants. He took out a ten-year lease on premises, bought a machine, and employed three people to make paper bags. They produced vast quantities of bags. When they finally struggled to get in and out of the building, someone had a brilliant idea: 'let's sell some of these paper bags.' Unfortunately when they went out into the market place, they found that somebody had come up with an even better idea – plastic bags. The MBA student lost his life's savings.

Do your marketing first.
Do not buy if you can lease (short periods).
Do not lease if you can rent (short periods).
Run it from home.
Do not lead with your overheads.

4   CASH FLOW

We have already noted that profit flows are based on invoices. Cash flow is not based on invoices. Cash flow is real money coming in, less real money going out. Everybody with a purse or a trouser pocket understands cash flow, until they discuss cash flow with their accountants. We advise business people not to discuss cash flow with accountants.

Remember that cash flow is money in less money out, and that you do understand it. If you compare the amount of cash in the business at the beginning of the year with the amount of cash in the business at the end of the year, then the difference is the total cash flow of the business for the year. Total inflows less total outflows equals the change in the cash and bank balances for the year.

The total cash flow of the business can be broken down into operational cash flows and non-operational cash flows. Non-operational cash flows include loans made and received, interest received and paid, dividends, issue of shares for cash, directors loans, introduction of cash by the partners etc. Operational cash flows are the cash flows which arise from the running of the business. The operational cash flow plus the non-operational cash flow equals the total cash flow for the year.

Profit is extremely difficult to measure. We have already defined net profit as invoiced sales less invoiced cost of sales, wages, overheads and depreciation. How should we depreciate motor vehicles, plant and equipment, computers? Should we write them off over two years, five years or ten years? Our decision will affect the reported net profit, but it will have no effect on cash flow. Should we write off research and development over two years, five years or ten years? Our decision will affect the net profit, but will have no effect on cash flow. Should we make a general provision for bad debts? This again would affect the net profit, but have no effect on cash flow. How should we value closing stock? This again will affect the net profit, but it will not affect the cash balance.

Several accountants preparing the accounts for the same business would arrive at several different measurements of net profit. They should all have the same measure of cash flow. Profit is an opinion, but cash flow is factual. There are many other reasons why profit flow and cash flow will be different. Invoiced sales appear in the profit and loss account, but only cash received from customers will affect cash flow. Invoiced costs appear in the profit and loss account, but only cash payments to suppliers will affect cash flow. Capital expenditure affects cash flow when we acquire fixed assets, or sell fixed assets. This capital expenditure has no effect on reported profits until we write off these assets in the profit and loss account under the heading 'depreciation'.

At the end of an accounting period the amount of invoices outstanding or debtors will be included in sales, although the cash balance will not be affected until our debtors pay us in cash. At the end of each accounting period the amount of creditors for supplies will be charged in the profit and loss account as an expense, although cash flow is not affected until we actually pay our creditors. During a trading period we may burn up a tremendous amount of cash building up stocks. This will affect the cash balance but the net profit will not be affected until we write off our stock as a cost of sale.

As already discussed, depreciation is charged as an expense against profits, but has no effect on cash flow. Cash flow is affected when we purchase capital items.

Successful cash flow management is critical to the success of your business. The day you find that you cannot pay your suppliers roughly corresponds to the day on which your suppliers refuse to give extra trade credit. The day you stop paying the wages of employees roughly corresponds to the day employees stop working for you. The day your bank manager realises that you will never be able to repay loans and overdrafts roughly corresponds to the day on which your bank manager calls in your loans and overdrafts.

Do not run out of cash! Conserve cash, conserve cash, conserve cash! Chase your debtors for cash, negotiate longer credit periods with your suppliers, cut back on production, sell assets, borrow, put more of your own cash into the business, issue additional shares for cash, sell your car for cash and acquire another one on hire purchase, acquire another business which has substantial cash balances ... but never run out of cash!

'Words pay no debts.' – *William Shakespeare*

Annual income twenty pounds, annual expenditure nineteen pounds nineteen and six, result happiness. Annual income twenty pounds, annual expenditure twenty pounds ought and six, result misery.' – *Charles Dickens*

A close friend of ours wanted to go into oil delivery. He asked us for £250,000 to launch the business, £150,000 for a delivery wagon, and £100,000 for one month's stock of oil. After we had negotiated 10 days' rolling credit from three oil companies and purchased another company's surplus vehicle for £10,000 on a three-year bank loan, we found that by operating the business from home, no initial financing was required for the business.

There are 20 ways of launching your business without capital. Do not buy anything new. Do not buy anything if you can lease it. Avoid long leases. Do not lease anything if you can rent it. Do not rent anything for more than three months. Do everything on a small sample basis. Ask for 100 per cent or 50 per cent cash with order. Many people still pay cash on delivery. Ask for credit. Offer deals as a percentage of sales. If you cannot do it yourself, outsource it to somebody else. Go for zero fixed costs. Do not lead with your overheads.

5   PROFIT AND LOSS ACCOUNT

We have now introduced some of the key numbers in accounting and finance – sales, gross profit, overhead and net profit. Invoiced sales less invoiced cost of sales equals gross profit. Gross profit less overhead equals net profit (victory). These numbers appear, usually annually, in your firm's profit and loss account, a statement designed to show that sales less total costs equals net profit.

PROFIT AND LOSS ACCOUNT

Invoiced sales	180,000
Less cost of sales	144,000
Gross profit	36,000
Less overheads	28,600
Net profit	7,400

6   BALANCE SHEET

A balance sheet is a list of all the 'things' a firm owns, and a note where the funds came from to finance those assets. The 'things' a firm owns are called assets. They appear on one side of the balance sheet under the heading 'investments' or 'employment of capital'. Fixed assets are for permanent use in the business, i.e. property, plant and equipment, motor vehicles, office equipment. Fixed assets may also include brand names, investments in associated companies, and goodwill. Goodwill is the amount paid for an asset, such as another company, over and above the book value of the net assets of that company. Current assets include stock, debtors and cash at bank. These assets are sometimes called the circulating assets or working assets. Cash at bank and debtors are the 'liquid' assets. Cash is used to produce or purchase stock, stock is sold to customers who become our debtors, and debtors eventually pay us in cash. This is the working capital cycle. Fixed assets plus current assets equal total assets, or total investment.

The other side of the balance sheet is simply a list of the sources of capital, a note of the sources of funds to acquire all the assets. Businesses are financed with equity, loans and the use of trade credit. 'Creditors' represents the amount of invoices unpaid for stock, telephone, stationery etc. Loans are from various lenders, usually banks. The equity is made up of share capital and 'reserves'. The share capital represents the amount of cash paid into the business by shareholders for their shares. The amount 'reserves' is often referred to as the balance on profit and loss account, retained earnings or the

BALANCE SHEET

Sources of capital		Investments (Employment of capital)	
Share capital	100,000	Fixed assets	103,520
'Reserves'	54,900		
Shareholders' funds/equity	154,900		
Current liabilities:		**Current assets:**	
Creditors	23,000	Cash at bank	-
Bank overdraft (loan)	10,620	Stock	40,000
		Debtors	45,000
Total capital =	188,520	Total investment =	188,520
A note of the sources of capital		A list of assets owned by the company	

ploughed-back profits. If the firm makes a profit, then dividends and tax payments may be charged against profit, any surplus increasing the 'reserves' of the company.

Many people assume that there is cash in a financial reserve. Unfortunately, this is not true. There is no cash in 'reserves'. This figure is a note that the company has a positive balance for retained earnings. There is no money in share capital, reserves, creditors, loans or overdrafts. These are notes of where the funds came from to acquire the assets. If we wish to know how much cash a company has, then we must look under the heading 'cash and bank balances' on the investment side of the balance sheet. This company has no cash. It has a negative cash balance called a bank overdraft on the other side of the balance sheet. The balance sheet balances. Total capital equals total investment.

The balance sheet must always balance because all the assets of the business must be financed using somebody's capital. There are no free fixed or current assets. If the company uses cash to purchase stock, then the cash balance decreases and the amount of stock increases. When the company sells stock at a profit, then stock decreases, and debtors increase by an amount greater than the stock. The balance is the profit on the deal which is added to reserves on the other side of the balance sheet, thereby making the balance sheet balance once again.

When we acquire fixed assets, cash reduces, fixed assets increase. When we reduce the book value of the fixed assets by depreciation, then the book value of the fixed assets in the balance sheet falls, and since depreciation is charged as an expense against profits, then the amount 'reserves' falls by the same amount. When we pay our creditors, cash and creditors are reduced by the same amount. If we borrow money, then loans and the cash balance are increased by the same amount. If we issue new shares for cash, then cash increases by the same amount as the share capital. If we make a bonus issue, which does not involve any cash, then the share capital increases and reserves are reduced. If we acquire another company which has net assets of £50,000, for which we pay £60,000, then the cash balance falls by £60,000 with the assets increasing by only £50,000. Clearly, the balance sheet would not balance. In order to correct the situation we have to introduce the asset 'goodwill' in the sum of £10,000 on the assets side of the balance sheet. Finally, the balance sheet is not a statement of value. Assets are generally recorded at cost less estimated depreciation.

7   GEARING (LEVERAGE)

Gearing is the use of low-cost debt. Many business people are tempted to rush out and borrow funds to finance the business. Low-cost borrowings can be used to gear up or lever up the returns to the owners of the business, i.e. the equity. Borrowing money from the bank at 6 per cent and investing in projects which are expected to yield over 20 per cent often appears to be a good idea. The problem/challenge is the risk. Interest on loans has to be repaid together with the loan.

On the other hand, all businesses are risky. The outcome of business activity is extremely uncertain, returns are extremely volatile. The activity which is expected to yield 20 per cent may yield 35 per cent, 15 per cent, 5 per cent or perhaps even a negative return of 10 per cent or 20 per cent. If the cash flows generated from the business investment are inadequate to make interest and loan repayments, then the business could be in serious trouble. The business could fail. Extensive borrowing often appears to be the cause of business failure. In fact, the real cause of business failure is the collapse of the firm's investment schedule which fails to generate adequate cash flow. So how much should a firm borrow?

One rule of thumb is that in low risk/low volatility businesses such as the letting of property, firms can borrow up to 70 per cent of permanent capital (loans plus equity), whereas in high risk/high volatility businesses such as an engineering jobbing shop, managers should borrow up to 30 per cent of permanent capital. Interestingly, in the real world we find a wide range of debt-equity ratios in the same industry. It appears that the key determinant of gearing/leverage is the attitude of the person controlling the business. We encourage business people to remember that firms with the highest levels of borrowings are usually the first to go bust when there is an economic downturn. Leverage is a two-edged sword. It can lever up returns to shareholders, and it can hasten the death of your business. We also encourage managers to examine carefully the terms attached to loan agreements. Pay careful attention to those 'restrictive covenants' which limit your freedom to manage the business as you would wish.

8   VALUE ADDED

A manager's job is to get results. If we implement a winning strategy to achieve the mission of enriching our customers' lives in some way, then there is a chance that we may make a profit. Net profit is usually regarded as the result. A different measure of the firm's result is given by value added. If we take our invoiced sales and deduct the cost of bought-in materials and services, this tells us the amount of value we have added to our bought-in materials and services through our own efforts. What is the value we have added to our bought-in materials and services? Value added equals sales less external costs (bought-in materials and services).

Alternatively, we can start at the bottom of our profit and loss account by taking the figure for retained profits and adding back dividends, tax payments, interest and lease payments, hire charges, depreciation, wages and salaries. If we take our retained profits and then add back appropriations of profit such as dividends and tax payments, and also add back 'internal' charges such as depreciation, wages and salaries, then this figure also tells us the amount of value we have added during the accounting period.

9   RATIOS

Consider the following:

$$\frac{\text{Profit}}{\text{Sales}} \times \frac{\text{Sales}}{\text{Capital employed}} = \frac{\text{Profit}}{\text{Capital employed}}$$

Given a net profit of £100, sales £1000 and capital employed £500, then:

$$\frac{100}{1000} \quad \times \quad \frac{1000}{500} \quad = \quad \frac{100}{500}$$

or   10%   ×   2   =   20%

The company earns 10 per cent on its sales (one measure of trading success), turns over its capital employed twice (one measure of efficiency) and therefore earns 20 per cent on its capital employed (one measure of firm performance). Return on capital employed can be increased by either making more profit on sales or turning over capital employed more times, i.e. using less capital (on one side of the balance sheet) or another way of expressing it, for any given level of sales using a lower level of investment in fixed and current assets (on the other side of the balance sheet).

We can use our creativity to generate hundreds of business statistics. Here are 21 statistics we expect could be of interest in your business.

1 Gross profit on sales (%) = $\dfrac{\text{gross profit}}{\text{sales}}$

2 Net profit on sales (%) = $\dfrac{\text{net profit}}{\text{sales}}$

3 Earnings per share (EPS)(£) = $\dfrac{\text{net profit for shareholders}}{\text{number of shares}}$

4 Stock turnover (times) = $\dfrac{\text{sales}}{\text{stock}}$

 (preferably at selling prices)
 How many times are we turning over our stock? Twice implies 6 months' stock on hand.

5 Debtors turnover (times) = $\dfrac{\text{sales}}{\text{debtors}}$

 How many times are we turning over debtors? Four times implies 3 months' credit.

6 Return on total assets = $\dfrac{\text{net profit}}{\text{total assets (total investment) (or total capital)}}$
(return on total capital)(%)

7 Return on equity (%) = $\dfrac{\text{net profit for shareholders}}{\text{shareholders' funds (equity)}}$

8 Value added per employee (£) = $\dfrac{\text{value added}}{\text{number of employees}}$

9 Investment per employee (£) = $\dfrac{\text{investment}}{\text{number of employees}}$

10 Sales per employee (£) = $\dfrac{\text{sales}}{\text{number of employees}}$

11 Sales growth (%) = $\dfrac{\text{this year's sales} - \text{last year's sales}}{\text{last year's sales}}$

12 Growth in gross profit (%) = $\dfrac{\text{this year's gross profit} - \text{last year's gross profit}}{\text{last year's gross profit}}$

13 Growth in net profit (%) = $\dfrac{\text{this year's net profit} - \text{last year's net profit}}{\text{last year's net profit}}$

14 Balance sheet gearing (%) = $\dfrac{\text{long term debt}}{\text{long term debt} + \text{equity}}$

15 Income gearing (times) = $\dfrac{\text{net profit before interest (fixed financial charges)}}{\text{fixed financial charges}}$

16 Income gearing (times) = $\dfrac{\text{operational cash flow before interest (fixed financial charges)}}{\text{interest (fixed financial charges)}}$

17 Percentage balance sheets.
Express all the fixed and current assets as percentages of total assets (100 per cent). On the other side of the balance sheet, express all sources of capital as a percentage of total capital (100 per cent).

18 Percentage profit and loss accounts.
Express all expenses in the profit and loss account as a percentage of sales (100 per cent).

19 Current ratio (times) = $\dfrac{\text{current assets}}{\text{current liabilities}}$

Is the company in a position to pay its immediate creditors?

20 Acid test, quick ratio, liquidity ratio, or solvency ratio (times) = $\dfrac{\text{cash + debtors (liquid assets)}}{\text{current liabilities}}$

Are the company's liquid assets sufficient to cover immediate creditors?

21 Market value relative to balance sheet value of equity (times) = $\dfrac{\text{(estimated market value of the equity)}}{\text{balance sheet/book value of the equity}}$

This is a measure of our estimated or actual market value of the company against the historic level of investment by shareholders.

Absolutely fascinating, but what do we do with these numbers?

1 *Trend analysis.* If we plot these numbers over time, say over five years, some indication will be given as to where we have been, together with some possible indication as to the direction in which we are travelling.

2 *Inter-firm comparison (IFC).* We can compare our performance with other firms in the same industry. We can 'benchmark' ourselves against the best in the business.

3 *Actual performance* v *target performance.* At the end of each period we can compare our actual performance with planned performance.

4 *Aid to forecasting.* Once we have gone through the process of making our decisions for next year, we can use financial ratios as an aid to forecasting future profit and loss accounts, balance sheets, and cash flow statements.

10   PROFIT PLANNING (MARGINAL COSTING)

In business some costs are volume-related in that they fluctuate with the level of activity measured by either output or sales. These are called variable costs and usually include expenses relating to the cost of sales such as material costs, piece-work labour, power consumption, and commissions. Other costs are non-volume related in that they do not generally fluctuate with small changes in output or sales. These are called the fixed costs and generally include rent, office salaries, the cost of running the personnel department, accounts department, security costs and building maintenance. When planning for profit we need to identify fixed and variable costs. If, in the first instance, we deduct the variable costs from invoiced sales, this gives us a number called 'contribution'. This is the contribution towards fixed costs and profit. Contribution less the fixed cost equals the net profit. Contribution is often very similar to gross profit, although sometimes gross profit may be arrived at after deducting some fixed costs included in cost of sales. Furthermore, overhead may not be exactly the same as fixed costs, because some overheads can resemble variable costs. Nevertheless, in many businesses contribution is very similar to gross profit, and overhead is very similar to fixed costs.

Mrs Pettman buys snibbods for £20 and sells them at £25. Before selling anything she has to meet fixed expenditures for typing, advertising, and general office costs amounting to £95. In her first trading period she sells 20 snibbods. What is her profit? If unit sales double, what will be her profit? How many snibbods must she sell for break-even (no profit or loss)?

	Now	**Sales double**	**Break-even**
Units	20	40	19
Sales	500	1000	475
Less variable costs (80%)	400	800	380
Contribution (20%)	100	200	95
Fixed costs	95	95	95
Profit	5	105	-

Sales – variable costs = contribution
Contribution – fixed costs = profit

In the first trading period sales are 20 × £25 = £500, and variable costs are 20 × £20 = £400. The contribution is £100. The contribution is 20 per cent of sales value or alternatively the contribution is £5 per unit. This means that each unit of sales gives a £5 contribution towards the fixed costs and profit. In the first period the profit is £5. If sales double to 40 units, then the contribution doubles to £200. The fixed costs remain the same at £95 and the profit is therefore £105. Doubling the sales does not double the profits, given that we have some fixed costs. In fact, doubling the unit sales increases profit 21 times from £5 to £105. For break-even, we need a contribution of £95 to cover the fixed costs. At £5 per unit we need to sell 19 units for break-even. Once we have some idea of our fixed and variable costs, this allows us to plan for profit. For any profit target we know how many units we must sell. Given the number of units to be sold at £25 we can estimate the net profit.

11   PRODUCT PROFITABILITY ANALYSIS

Many businesses produce/sell more than one product. Many businesses have several operating units. Consider the Dobbman organisation which has three products, A, B and C, or three operating units, A, B and C. Sales are known for each product or division. Variable costs such as materials and wages are also known. Head-office costs amount to £100. In the first instance these costs are charged against each product or division as a proportion of wages. This is called absorption or total costing, all the fixed costs being charged on some basis against individual products or operating units. After allocating the fixed costs as a percentage of wages, product A shows a profit of £30, B £25 and C a loss of £5.

If we were to jump to hasty conclusions, we may consider terminating product or operating division C. In fact, product or operating division C makes a positive contribution towards the fixed costs and profit. The variable costs associated with C are £75 for materials and £15 for wages, a total of £90 for variable costs. When these are deducted from the sales of £100 we arrive at a positive contribution of £10. If we terminate C, then we lose a contribution of £10 and the profit for the Dobbman organisation will fall from £50 to £40. We are assuming that we lose sales of £100 and save variable costs of £90, and that production cannot be moved to A or B. Rather than allocating fixed costs as a percentage of wages, we could allocate these costs on the basis of materials, materials plus wages, sales, contribution, headcount, or even floorspace. If we base our decisions on absorption costing, then these different methods of allocating fixed costs could lead to different decisions.

The Dobbman Organisation

	Total	A	B	C
Sales	500	200	200	100
Materials	250	100	75	75
Wages	100	35	50	15
Fixed costs (100% of wages)	100	35	50	15
Total costs	450	170	175	105
Profit (loss)	50	30	25	(5)

We suggest that managers use marginal costing rather than total or absorption costing. If we deduct the variable costs from the sales income then we arrive at a contribution of £65 for A, £75 for B and £10 for C. Product or division A makes a contribution of 32.5 per cent, B 37.5 per cent and C 10 per cent. If these are three similar operating units, then we prefer to allocate a £1000 contract to operating unit B, as this appears to promise a contribution of £375, compared with £325 for A, and only £100 for B. If A, B and C are three different products then we can use the contribution we have calculated to estimate the contribution per machine hour, the contribution per hour of labour, the contribution per £100 of materials used etc. Given that the fixed costs are fixed at £100, then we wish to maximise the contribution being made by A, B and C towards the fixed costs and profit. In short, our aim is to maximise contribution, and we can use our knowledge of fixed and variable costs as an aid to maximising contribution. This kind of analysis is sometimes called marginal costing, sometimes incremental analysis, sometimes break-even analysis, and sometimes variable costing. We simply refer to it as 'profit planning'.

	Total	A	B	C
Sales	500	200	200	100
Materials	250	100	75	75
Wages	100	35	50	15
Variable costs	350	135	125	90
Contribution	150	65	75	10
	(30%)	(32.5%)	(37.5%)	(10%)
Fixed cost	100			
Profit	50			

12   THE BUSINESS PLAN

The business plan is a major exercise in demonstrating your managerial competence. A plan is a list of activities, a 'to do' list. The business plan identifies everything which must be done to achieve the mission at a profit. It identifies with clarity the names of all the people who will carry out each part of the action plan. The business plan starts with the vision statement of an ideal future circumstance, followed by the mission statement along the lines 'to enrich the lives of our customers by ...'. The plan includes a complete industry analysis, identifying all the benefits of the product or service, and all its potential competition.

The part of the plan identifying the business strategy can be summarised under the headings specialisation, differentiation, segmentation and concentration. Our specialisation is our area of excellence, our core business. It describes our history and identifies our areas of expertise. Our differentiation is our competitive advantage, the way in which we are better, cheaper, faster and nicer than the competition. This section identifies with crystal clarity the reasons why customers will buy the benefit from us. We should then be able to identify our market segment or market niche, those people who care that we are better, cheaper, faster or nicer. Finally, we identify the resources we will need to concentrate hitting our market segment with our competitive advantage in our area of excellence. We need people, creativity, an advertising plan, plant and machinery, motor vehicles, finance etc. We shall need the co-operation of our partners, other shareholders and directors, customers, suppliers, employees, the bank manager, and even members of our own families.

Eventually, we shall be able to put together a sales plan. Our forecast level of sales will determine our purchases, our need to manufacture, productive wages etc. We shall need an investment in working capital, i.e., an investment in raw materials, work in progress, finished goods, debtors, and a minimum cash balance. We should be able to finance this in part by the use of trade credit, but no doubt we may well have to borrow, and raise equity. At this stage, we should now be able to compile our cash flow forecast, one of the critical documents required in the business plan. We can also forecast the profit and loss account for the first three months, six months and for the first year. We should also be able to forecast the statement of financial position, the balance sheet, at the end of the first trading period.

These forecast financial statements reflect our business plan, our list of activities. The business plan must also include a list of the key players in the management team. This list should include names, qualifications, previous experience, and a very precise statement of the contribution each person will make to carrying out the action plan. It should also list our most critical assumptions. Finally, we always recommend that business people examine at least three comprehensive business plans put together by their reference group, business mentors, mastermind alliance, or even somebody recommended by the bank manager.

13   WORKING CAPITAL

One of the major reasons for business failure is mismanagement of working capital, mismanagement of cash, stocks, debtors, and creditors. You will need to invest in raw materials, work in progress and finished goods. You will need to give credit to your customers and take credit from suppliers. You will need to operate within a cash constraint. Warehouses up and down the country are full of goods people do not want to buy. Firms all over the country are desperately chasing customers for cash, and are desperately trying to delay payment to creditors. We must all plan for these items.

Remember the first rule of thumb is that when you go into business it is quite normal to find that you need three times the amount of working capital you first thought you would need. The second rule of thumb is that it normally takes three times as long to break-even as you initially thought. If you expect to require to invest £10,000 in stock and debtors, plan for £30,000. If you think it will take four months to arrive at break-even, plan for one year. Set maximum amounts for the quantity of stock you will carry, give customers crystal clear guidelines as to your credit terms, chase up late payments, take credit from suppliers and explain your need to delay payments when necessary. Conserve cash, conserve cash, conserve cash!

Have a strategy for financial emergencies. You should consider delayed payments to creditors, loan facilities, additional equity, discounts to customers for immediate payment, sale of assets, sale and leaseback of property, reduction of directors' remuneration, delay tax payments, auctioning of stock, temporary suspension of production. Carry out a regular review of stock, prepare an aged list of debtors and creditors every month. Establish relationships with suppliers who are lazy in collecting cash, use different suppliers to gain extended trade credit. Beware of repeat orders where payment for previous orders has not been made. Think carefully about very large orders especially from new customers. Never do anything that could bankrupt the business.

14   CAPITAL EXPENDITURE

Capital expenditure has to be justified in terms of the additional or incremental cash inflows such expenditure will generate in the future. For example, a machine can be bought for £80,000 which is expected to generate incremental cash inflows of £10,000 per annum for the foreseeable future. If these cash flows are discounted back to the present at 10 per cent, then the present value of these cash flows is as follows:

Cash flow	£10,000	=	£100,000
10% discount	.1		

The net present value of the investment is £100,000 - £80,000 = £20,000, and the investment is theoretically worthwhile. If the same cash flows of £10,000 per annum are discounted back to the present at 20 per cent, then these cash flows have a present value of £50,000

Cash flow	£10,000	=	£50,000
20% discount	.2		

The net present value of the project is £50,000 – £80,000 = (£30,000), and the investment is not profitable in present value terms.

These discounting techniques are not popular with the vast majority of business people who tend to make decisions on the basis of the effect on earnings per share (EPS), effect on return on capital employed, additional profit generated, or the payback period. In the above example the payback period is eight years. At £10,000 per annum it will take eight years for the project to recover its initial investment of £80,000. Managers tend to look for payback periods within the range 2½–5 years.

15   MAXIMISING THE MARKET VALUE OF THE COMPANY

Economic and financial theory teaches that we should all strive to maximise the market value of our businesses. It is argued that the maximum well-being is achieved if individuals try to maximise market value. Furthermore, perhaps we should try to maximise the value of the business so that one day we can sell the enterprise and retire in comfort. You may well choose to do this. A brief glance around the real world reveals that the vast majority of people in business are not trying to maximise. We are all behaving in a manner consistent with our self concepts. We strive to achieve our self concept level of income, self concept level of wealth, self concept level of span of control. Almost everything that happens to us is determined by our self concepts, our bundles of beliefs about ourselves. You cannot set goals for other people. What is your exit plan? Do you sell the business after five, ten, twenty years? For how much do you sell? Is there a management buy-out? Do you sell to your existing partners? Is the business taken over by your children? Do you float the business on the Stock Market?

16   GOOD ACCOUNTING RECORDS

One pathetic reason for business collapse is the failure of the proprietor to keep satisfactory accounting records. In business it makes sense to keep lists of people who owe you money (debtors), lists of people to whom you owe money (creditors), lists of wages and payments for materials, payments for stationery and telephone, lists of assets acquired, and a running balance of cash at bank. These lists are called accounts. Some businesses actually fail because businessmen and women do not know who owes them money, what the cash balance is, or whether the company is making profits or losses. Many companies experience severe aggravation and even collapse from their experiences with VAT officers, PAYE inspectors, and the taxman. It is essential that you keep good accounting records and detailed records of contracts and agreements. Prepare profit and loss accounts and cash flow summaries on a monthly basis. Project cash flows every month for the following three months, six months and one year. Prepare statements of projected monthly profits, together with the projected balance sheet at the end of each month. Prepare these forecasts for one month, three months, six months and one year. If you hate maintaining accounting records, maintaining adequate documentation and preparing forecast financial statements, then either change your attitude or get somebody involved who will carry out these tasks on your behalf.

17   THE BANK MANAGER

You will probably need the co-operation of your bank manager. You may need an overdraft, a business development loan, hire purchase finance, letters of credit for overseas transactions, banker's drafts for immediate payment. It is important that you deal with a manager who can grant you what you want. If your contact at the bank has to keep referring your proposal to head office, then you are less likely to get what you want. Be sure you know the limits placed on your bank manager.

The key to success with your bank is relationship banking. The bank wants to establish a relationship with you, and you need to establish a relationship with your bank. You must keep your contact well-informed. A comprehensive business plan is essential for justification of your requests. Follow up every month with statements of actual profit and actual cash flows, together with forecasts for the following month, three months and twelve months. Your cash flow forecast is critical. Your bank manager needs this to justify the granting of your loan or overdraft request. Trust will be established between you and the bank as you meet the payment dates and learn to adapt to difficult situations. You will find that every cash flow problem/challenge imaginable arises in your business. Nobody ever said running a business is easy. Your bank manager can be an invaluable ally in difficult situations. Establish that relationship with the manager who can offer you what you want.

' A bank is a place that will lend you money if you can prove that you don't need it.' – *Bob Hope*

18   GROWTH

Organic growth

Rather than settle down into a comfort zone, many business people decide to go for growth. This could mean more sales, greater market share, more employees, more assets, a greater span of control. Organic growth arises when the business sells more of its existing products to existing customers or new customers, or develops more products for existing customers and new customers. Organic growth involves increasing the customer base and/or the product range.

Growth by acquisition

Growth by acquisition arises when we acquire shares in other companies, the products/skills of other companies, the customer base, the productive assets. Such acquisitions can lead to greater sales, higher profit growth, higher net profit and more positive cash flows. It can make good economic sense to buy a larger customer base, greater market share, better distribution channels, products which you can distribute through your existing distribution channels, savings in fixed costs, a more effective salesforce, etc. There are, however, considerable risks associated with buying other businesses. Frankly, we do not like conglomerates. If your area of excellence is the pizza takeaway, why buy an oil delivery service, an advertising agency, a hairdressing business, a hotel, travel agency, football club, newspaper, or airline? Where is the synergy? Where is the added value? If the pizza business is worth £2 million and the oil delivery business is worth £2 million, how can we add the two together to make £5 million? Some conglomerates have been justified on the grounds that there is a saving in fixed costs in that all these businesses can be run from one central office. Many conglomerates are now being broken up, each division being left to operate on its own, in its own area of excellence. We strongly advise business people to stick within their own area of excellence, i.e. 'stick to the knitting'. Of course, you may not care about the success of the business. One day you may be so wealthy that you decide to own a newspaper, or a football club, just for fun, for popularity, for influence. Running a football club may be entirely consistent with your self concept, even though the business does not make any money.

We are here emphasising that it is generally a mistake to buy into a business about which you know very little. Many former executives have wasted their redundancy pay buying into businesses about which they know very little. How can you establish competitive advantage without the knowledge available to the competition? Many people believe that throwing money at a business makes the business work profitably. Think of all the businesses you know where vast quantities of money have been 'invested' in disastrous enterprises. To be successful you must enter your area of excellence, establish competitive advantage, find your market segment, and focus all your resources on your customer, selling your benefit with your competitive advantage in your area of specialisation.

If you really do insist on buying into a business about which you know absolutely nothing, then at least buy into a business with three important characteristics. These are low technology, barriers to entry, and gross overstaffing. You can probably learn to understand a low-technology industry. Barriers to entry might include the presence of skilled labour, or access to a scarce material. Finally, one of the important reasons for business failure is that existing managers do not wish to reduce staffing levels. It may be possible to turn the business around simply by reducing fixed costs.

Most acquisitions are not commercial successes. It is very common for too much money to be paid for an acquisition. Always look for the fatal flaw when considering a business acquisition. There is a reason for everything, and there is most definitely always a reason why somebody wants to sell a business. You will always be told that the present owner is making so much money doing something else, that he or she does not have time to devote to the business. This probably means that the business is losing so much money it is dragging all the other businesses into liquidation. You may be told that the present owner has made so much money running the business that he or she now feels it is time to hand over to somebody else. Remember the general rule that it is unusual for anybody to sell a successful business. Is a management buy-out in prospect?

Once you have made the decision to buy, then as a general rule do not buy shares. Buy the customer base, the order book, the salesforce, the plant, the patents, the distribution channel, the assets, but not the shares. As a general rule, buy what you want, and leave the present owners with the fixed costs, redundant fixed assets, the workforce, legal battles, tax problems, VAT disputes, redundancy payments, etc. Always bear in mind that in mergers and acquisitions, the sellers are usually the winners, and the buyers are usually the losers.

19   COMPANY VALUATION

The value of a company is not available from the balance sheet. The real value of a company depends upon its ability to generate positive cash flows either from successful trading or from the disposal of its assets. At some stage you may wish to value your own business for disposal, or value somebody else's business for acquisition. Here are seven techniques you can use to try and establish the market value of a business where that business does not have a stock market quotation.

Present value analysis

In economic and financial theory we teach that the value of a company is the present value of its cash flows. Using this method, we forecast the company's operational cash flows into the future, and then discount them back to the present at a discount rate which reflects the volatility or riskiness of those cash flows. For example,

£100,000 worth of annual cash flows forever discounted back to the present at 10 per cent gives a present value of £1 million. Using a higher discount rate, £100,000 per annum forever discounted back to the present at 20 per cent gives a present value of £500,000. Although this method is appealing from a theoretical point of view, we all have great difficulty forecasting cash flows and estimating an appropriate discount rate.

Balance sheet values

One very practical approach is to examine the assets and liabilities (sources of finance) in the balance sheet. We can estimate the market value of the fixed and current assets, but then need to estimate a value for goodwill, or possibly for brand values. After deducting the loans, bank overdraft and creditors, this gives us the value of the business as far as the shareholders are concerned. This method is fairly practical, but the major dispute tends to arise over the value of goodwill.

Liquidation value

We can sometimes argue that the value of goodwill is more or less zero, when the business is not profitable. Under these circumstances we can value the assets, deduct the liabilities, and arrive at the market value of the equity.

Payback period

Over many years, simple rules of thumb have been established in many industries whereby the value of the business is deemed to be three years' profits, five years' profits etc. If the business is expected to generate £100,000 per annum, in an industry where the accepted payback period is five years, then that business would be valued at £500,000. In recent years, an interesting variation has arisen in that some businesses are selling on a multiple of turnover. A business with a turnover of £1 million per annum could be valued at £2 million, £3 million, or even £5 million, depending on the multiple accepted in that industry.

The price/earnings ratio

The price/earnings ratio method is similar to the payback method. If we wish to value a publishing business, then we can look at the price/earnings ratios for companies with a stock market quotation. We may find that in the publishing business price-earnings ratios are in the range 8–12. The price/earnings ratio is the price per share divided by the earnings per share. If the price per share is 100p and the earnings per share 10p, then it appears that the stockmarket is multiplying the earnings per share by 10 to arrive at a price per share of 100p.

Of course, stock markets do not multiply last year's earnings to arrive at a share price. In fact, we believe that the market discounts future cash flows. However, we can slot an unquoted publishing company into its industry group and estimate that if the unquoted company was in fact quoted on the stock market then we can expect that company to have a price/earnings ratio in the range 8–12. If the publishing company is earning £1 million per annum, then we can estimate that its market value is somewhere between £8 million and £12 million pounds. As with all these techniques, the final price is a matter for negotiation.

Dividend yield

Many companies coming to stock market for quotation appear to be valued on a dividend yield basis. For example, if the expected dividend yield is five per cent, then a company offering a dividend of £1m per annum would be valued at £20 million.

The market-value/book-value ratio

An interesting development in recent years has been the use of the market-value/book-value ratio. Once again, when we wish to value an unquoted company, we can look at companies in the same industry which are quoted on the stock market. For these quoted companies, we can calculate the ratio of the market value of the equity to the balance sheet/book value of the equity. We may find that in a particular industry the market value is, on average, about twice the book value of the equity. If the unquoted company we are attempting to value has balance sheet equity amounting to £3 million, then we can estimate its market value at £6 million. Again, we are fully aware that stock markets discount future cash flows. Stock markets do not multiply numbers in balance sheets to arrive at market values. However, this technique does allow us to slot a company into its industry group, and all other things being equal, arrive at a reasonable estimate of the likely market value.

We recommend that when you value a company for acquisition, you should make two calculations. Firstly, how much is the business worth as a stand-alone company, given its own products, distribution channels etc.? Secondly, how much is the business worth to us, given our distribution channels, our sales expertise? Can we make substantial savings in fixed costs, etc.? If the business is worth £3 million as an independent company, but £6m as an addition to our company, then we should be able to negotiate a deal to the satisfaction of all concerned in the range £3–6 million.

Remember, that companies usually pay too much for their acquisitions. It is not the only deal. Do not be afraid to walk away. Opportunities are like buses. You do not have to worry if you miss an opportunity because another one will come along in about 30 minutes. If you believe that life is full of opportunities, then you will see opportunities all around you.

20   SOLE TRADER OR LIMITED COMPANY

We strongly advise people to trade as sole traders or partnerships, rather than form a limited company, unless there is some reasonable possibility that the venture will collapse with considerable amounts of creditors unlikely to receive payment. There are three major advantages to trading in your own name.

1   Your drawings are not taxable at all. You are not subject to PAYE. You can draw as much money out of the business as you wish, providing the bank account can stand it, and all such withdrawals are completely tax free – even if you draw out £1 million. Business people have great difficulty in understanding this. Remember, you are taxed on your profits, not your cash withdrawals. The cash you take out of the business for your own use is not allowed as a tax deduction. You are taxed on your profits before charging your withdrawals. This can be important in the early stages of the business when you may not wish to hand over the cash to the tax man under PAYE, as you most certainly would have to do if you traded as a limited company. All directors and other employees must pay PAYE and contributions to the Department of Social Security on any remuneration. Your business may not make any taxable profits in the first year, but if you are a director or other employee of the limited company, then you must suffer PAYE etc. These tax payments would not be payable by a sole trader or partner.

2   For the sole trader or partner, there is no clawback on the company car. The taxman may not allow 100 per cent of your motor expenses as a tax deduction, if you are a sole trader, but this is negotiable, and in many proprietorships and partnerships, motor expenses are allowed 100 per cent as a deduction against profits.

3   As a sole trader, your accounts are sent only to the Inland Revenue. They are not available for public inspection. All limited companies must submit accounts to Companies House, where they are available to the general public. For only a few pounds, registration agents will send copies of your accounts to your suppliers, competitors, customers, employees and neighbours. Against all this the limited company does offer limited liability, i.e. if the company goes into liquidation with considerable debts then, as a shareholder, you cannot be called upon to supply additional funds, other than the amount you have agreed to pay for your shares. In a risky venture, this is important. As far as the bank is concerned, bank managers will generally ask you to pro-

vide personal guarantees for overdrafts and loans. The bank manager will not let you hide behind the 'veil of incorporation'. Other creditors may well lose their money, but do not think you can form a limited company, run up vast quantities of debts, and then simply walk away. The Department of Trade and Industry brings actions against people who run companies with the intention of defrauding creditors, and those who behave recklessly.

Many people are reluctant to give up their day jobs. Unfortunately, you cannot run a successful business 'on the side'. Your job suffers. The business suffers. It is a good idea to start small, establish a benefit, establish a competitive advantage, and find your market niche. In order to concentrate, you will soon find that running a business is a full time job, not the profitable hobby you wished it could be! Remember, you only have to work half the time, and you can please yourself which 12 hours per day you work 7 days a week. Nobody ever said that running a business is easy.

21   FORECASTING FINANCIAL STATEMENTS

(a comprehensive example for you to explore)

Allerton Traders Ltd: Example

The balance sheet of Allerton Traders Ltd at 30 June was as follows:

Employment of Funds		
Fixed Assets:		
Freehold premises (cost)		28,000
Plant and equipment (cost)	60,000	
Less depreciation	20,000	40,000
		68,000
Research and development		10,000
Trade and investment (cost)		18,000
Current Assets:		
Stock on hand	44,000	
Debtors	63,000	
	107,000	
Less Current Liabilities		
Creditors	22,000	
Bank overdraft	25,000	
	47,000	
Net Current Assets		60,000
		156,000
Sources of Funds		
Issued share capital		100,000
General reserve		35,000
Balance on profit and		
loss account		21,000
		156,000

This balance sheet is presented in vertical form, i.e. the current liabilities are deducted from the current assets, rather than being shown as an addition to the other sources of funds – share capital, general reserve and balance on profit and loss account.

From the following information prepare the cash forecast, forecast profit and loss account for the six months ended 31 December, forecast balance sheet as at 31 December, and a cash generation statement for the six months showing operational cash flows, non-operational cash flows and total cash flow.

1 Research and development is written off at the rate of £100 per month.

2 Depreciation of plant and machinery calculated at one per cent per month on cost.

3 The capital expenditure budget provides for payments for plant costing £4000 in July and £8000 in November (increase depreciation month after purchase).

4 Advertising budget – £120 per month.

5 Creditors at 30 June are for purchases.

6 Debtors at 30 June, May sales £27,500, June sales £35,500.

7 Credit periods are expected to be the same in the second half of the year, i.e. one month for suppliers, two months for customers.

8 Sales are forecast at £180,000 for the six months. August and September sales will be twice those in other months.

9 Fixed costs – £900 per month.

10 Additional variable costs – 10 per cent of monthly turnover.

11 Gross profit on turnover is budgeted at 20 per cent.

12 Closing stocks of purchases at cost are budgeted to be:
   31 Jul: £50,000   31 Aug: £30,000   30 Sep: £15,000
   31 Oct: £25,000   30 Nov: £35,000   31 Dec: £40,000

13 The annual dividend of 10 per cent on paid up share capital is payable on 31 December.

14 Income from trade investments is expected to amount to £1500 receivable on 31 December.

15 At 31 December, General Reserve to be increased from £35,000 to £40,000.

16 No expenditure on research and development is anticipated.

The answers are given in the following tables.

The forecast profit and loss account and balance sheet are as follows:

ANSWER   Allerton Traders Ltd: monthly trading accounts July–December

	July	August	September[a]	October	November	December	Total
Sales	22,500	45,000	45,000	22,500	22,500	22,500	180,000
Cost of Sales:							
Opening stock	44,000	50,000	30,000	15,000	25,000	35,000	44,000
Add purchases[b] (balance)	24,000	16,000	21,000	28,000	28,000	23,000	140,000
	68,000	66,000	51,000	43,000	53,000	58,000	184,000
Less closing stock	50,000	30,000	15,000	25,000	35,000	40,000	40,000
Cost of sales	18,000	36,000	36,000	18,000	18,000	18,000	144,000
Gross profit (20 per cent)	4,500	9,000	9,000	4,500	4,500	4,500	36,000
Note: Depreciation calculation[c]	600	640	640	640	640	720	3,880

[a] August and September sales are twice as high as in other months. Therefore, a 'normal' month's sales figure is £180,000 divided by eight = £22,500.

[b] The purchases figure is the balance amount in the monthly trading accounts.

[c] Depreciation at 1 per cent per month is increased one month after new plant is acquired.

The monthly trading accounts are based entirely on invoices, not cash.

The summary is for six months. The opening stock is the opening stock on 1 July. Managers often simply cast all the figures to the right as a check on the arithmetic.

Allerton Traders Ltd: cash flow for the six months ended 31 December

	July	August	September	October	November	December	Total
Opening Overdraft	(25,000)	(26,770)	(20,790)	(19,810)	920	6,650	(25,000)
Cash inflow:							
Sales (debtors)	27,500	35,500	22,500	45,000	45,000	22,500	198,000
Investment income	-	-	-	-	-	1,500	1,500
Total inflow	27,500	35,500	22,500	45,000	45,000	24,000	199,500
Cash outflow:							
Purchases (creditors)[a]	22,000	24,000	16,000	21,000	28,000	28,000	139,000
Fixed costs	900	900	900	900	900	900	5,400
Additional variable costs	2,250	4,500	4,500	2,250	2,250	2,250	18,000
Advertising	120	120	120	120	120	120	720
Capital expenditure	4,000	-	-	-	8,000	-	12,000
Dividends	-	-	-	-	-	10,000	10,000
Total outflow	29,270	29,520	21,520	24,270	39,270	41,270	185,120
Change[b] +	1,770	5,980	980	20,730	5,730	17270	14,380
–							
Closing Overdraft	(26,770)	(20,790)	(19,810)	920	6,650	(10,620)	(10,620)

[a] Creditors for purchases (from the monthly trading account) are paid one month after invoicing.
[b] A positive or negative cash flow for each month is calculated, and the opening balance adjusted to give the closing balance which is then carried forward to the start of the following month.
Cash is collected two months after invoicing.
No depreciation, transfer to general reserve, or research and development write-off as no cash flow is involved.

The forecast profit and loss account and balance sheet are as follows:

Allerton Traders Ltd: profit and loss account for six months to 31 December

Sales[a]		180,000
Less cost of sales:		
Opening stock 1 July[a]	44,000	
Purchases[a]	140,000	
	184,000	
Less closing stock 31 December[a]	40,000	
Cost of sales[a]		144,000
Gross profit on trading[a]		36,000
Less:		
Additional variable costs[b]	18,000	
Fixed costs[b]	5,400	
Research and development[c]	600	
Advertising[b]	720	
Depreciation[c]	3,880	
		28,600
Net profit on trading		7,400
Add income from trade investments		1,500
Net profit available for shareholders[d]		8,900
Less dividend (paid 31 December)	10,000	
Transfer to general reserve[e]	5,000	
		15,000
Increase in balance on profit		
and loss account (reduction)		(6,100)
Profit and loss account		
balance brought forward		21,000
		14,900

Notes
[a] These entries are reproduced from the monthly trading accounts summary.

dditional variable costs, fixed costs and advertising are taken direct
m the cash summary since there are no outstanding invoices.

esearch and development and depreciation are non-cash items but
ey are part of the cost of producing and selling goods to customers.

he net profit for shareholders is £8,900 against which a £10,000 divi-
nd paid in cash is charged. Dividends paid in cash must not exceed
e level of reported profit but we can pay the £10,000 dividend be-
use we have £21,000 of retained earnings from previous years against
hich no dividend has been charged in previous years.

he transfer to general reserve is inconsequential. Every £1 transferred
general reserve is £1 less balance on profit and loss account. No cash
involved. There is no money in a financial reserve. Such amounts rep-
esent accounting profits against which no dividend has been charged.
hese amounts show the extent to which the firm's fixed and current
assets have been financed from retained earnings.

The profit and loss account is based on invoices. Invoiced sales less
invoiced cost of sales and depreciation gives the profit which is then
allocated to either general reserve or balance on profit and loss account and against which dividends (paid in cash) are charged.

Allerton Traders Ltd: balance sheet as at 31 December

		December £		June £
Sources of funds				
Issued share capital		100,000		100,000
General reserve		40,000		35,000
Balance on profit				
and loss account		14,900		21,000
		154,900		156,000
Employment of funds				
Fixed assets:				
Freehold premises		28,000		28,000
(Cost)				
Plant and equipment[a]	72,000		60,000	
(Cost)				
Less depreciation	23,880	48,120	20,000	40,000
		76,120		68,000
Research and development[b]		9,400		10,000
Trade investments		18,000		18,000
Current assets:				
Stock on hand	40,000		44,000	
Debtors[c]	45,000		63,000	
	85,000		107,000	
Less				
Current liabilities:				
Creditors[d]	23,000		22,000	
Bank overdraft[e]	10,620		25,000	
	33,620		47,000	
Net current assets		51,380		60,000
		154,900		156,000

Notes
[a] Plant and equipment are shown at accumulated historic cost less accumulated depreciation.

[b] Research and development represents the amount of capitalised (put in the balance sheet) expenditure not yet written off to profit and loss account.

[c] Debtors are the November and December invoiced sales.

[d] Creditors are the December purchases.

[e] The bank overdraft is extracted from the cash flow forecast.

The balance sheet is a snapshot of the company's assets and sources of finance at one particular moment. The balance sheet does not show the value of the business, this being based on the company's ability to generate cash. For example:

- A successful hairdressing business may have a high market value because it generates excellent cash flows, although there may be very little in the way of balance sheet assets;
- An engineering company which makes trading losses can have a very low market value, but vast quantities of assets in the balance sheet.

'Funds' is a much misunderstood word in finance. It means cash or cash equivalent. An increase in trade credit is a source of funds, although it is not a source of actual cash.

Cash generation statement for the six months July–December

	Total	Funds from operations	Working capital	Fixed assets
	£	£	£	£
Funds from operations*	13,380	13,380		
Stock reduction	4,000		4,000	
Reduction in debtors	18,000		18,000	
Increase in creditors	1,000		1,000	
Purchase of plant	(12,000)			(12,000)
Operational cash flow	24,380	13,380	23,000	(12,000)
Non-operational cash flows:				
Dividend	(10,000)			
Total cash flow	14,380			
Opening cash	(25,000)			
Closing cash	(10,620)			
*Retained earnings for period	(6,100)			
General reserve (self generated)	5,000			
Dividend (self generated)	10,000			
Depreciation (non-cash)	3,880			
R&D (non-cash)	600			
	13,380			

Notes

This cash generation statement is based on balance sheet changes. Since the balance sheet balances at the beginning of the period and at the end of a period, then the differences from one period to another should cancel out to give the sources of funds during the period and the destinations or applications of those funds.

To the closing figure at the bottom of this year's profit and loss account we add back non-cash items such as depreciation and the research and development charge. We also add back appropriations of profit such as the dividend and transfer to general reserve to give the funds generated from successful trading. The amount of £13,380 represents funds generated from operations.

Additional sources of funds include reduction in stock and debtors, and an increase in trade credit.

Applications of funds include the payment of dividends, purchase of plant and equipment, and a reduction in the overdraft. The overdraft reduction is an increase in the stock of cash from negative £25,000 to negative £10,620.

NEVER DO ANYTHING
THAT COULD BANKRUPT THE BUSINESS.
THIS SOUNDS SO OBVIOUS, AND YET EVERY YEAR
TENS OF THOUSANDS OF BUSINESSES GO BUST BECAUSE
SOMEBODY DID SOMETHING,
OR FAILED TO DO SOMETHING,
WHICH LED TO CORPORATE COLLAPSE.
ALMOST EVERYTHING WE DO IN BUSINESS
HAS SOME EFFECT ON SALES, COSTS, PROFITS,
THE LEVEL OF INVESTMENT, THE GEARING, SOLVENCY,
GROWTH, SURVIVAL OR COLLAPSE.
BE SURE YOU UNDERSTAND
THE FINANCIAL IMPLICATIONS OF YOUR ACTIONS.

Nine

NEVER USE TIME
AS AN EXCUSE

How to focus on the 20%
that brings in the 80%

Life is time. The meaning of life is to enrich the lives of others. The way you manage your time is the way in which you manage your life. In fact, time cannot be managed, but you can manage the activities in your life. The actions you take determine your results. Never use time as an excuse. Everybody has 24 hours in each day. Losers blame time. Winners use their time to achieve their goals.

'Doust thou love life? Then do not squander time, that's the stuff life is made of.' – *Benjamin Franklin*

'All my possessions for a moment of time.' – *Last words of Elizabeth I*

'Life is short. Live it up.' – *Nikita Khrushchev*

'Where profit is, loss is hidden nearby.' – *Japanese proverb*

1   SET GOALS

The first step in time management is to set career goals, personal goals, and goals for your self-development. In essence, time management refers to the process by which we control the sequence of events which leads to the achievement of our goals. We need to use the law of control. Take control of your thoughts, control of your life, your time. You need to take control of your own mind, your thoughts, your feelings, your knowledge, your experiences, your attitude. Fortunately, nature gave you complete control over your own mind. Isn't nature wonderful?

Be careful how you use your time for time is the stuff of which life is made. Be honest with yourself. We all waste our time. We all waste our lives. To move forward in life we all have to change our habits. We have to get rid of yesterday before we can move on to tomorrow. We have to get rid of our negative emotions, self-limiting beliefs, negative attitudes, low expectations, visualising outcomes we do not want, making affirmations which are inconsistent with what we want, and spending time with people whose influence is inconsistent with achieving our goals, our priorities.

Life is a full-time job. We cannot control time, but we can control our activities. We can control the use to which we put our time. By setting goals you become a different person from the person you used to be who did not set goals. Life is an opportunity to help other people get what they want.

'Manage your future or someone else will.' – *Peter Drucker*

---

2   BELIEVE THAT YOU MANAGE YOUR TIME WELL

The law of belief tells us that we always behave in a manner consistent with our beliefs. Believe that you are excellent at time management. Believe that you are well organised. Visualise yourself managing your time well. Imagine how well you will feel if you manage your time well. Use the affirmation: 'I am managing my time well'. Get out of the habit of using time as an excuse. Everybody has 24 hours in the day. Yet we all say: 'I didn't have time.'

The simple fact is that some people use their time to achieve their goals, while others do not. Why do you not play the violin? Why do you not speak Russian? Why do you not earn £50,000 per annum? Why have you not yet completed the washing up? Why are you not running your own business? Why have you not completed that report? Why have you not written that book? The answer to all these questions is as follows: 'because I did not set it as a goal, and I did not resolve to pay the necessary price in advance'. In fact, you have had all the time in the world to go to the football match, spend evenings in the public house, and watch over 20 hours each week of television.

'Remember that time is money.' – *Benjamin Franklin*

---

3   SET GOOD TIME MANAGEMENT AS A GOAL

Set worthy goals. Set goals which make you feel a valuable and worthwhile person. Your self-esteem rises where there is consistency between your activities and your values, your worthy goals. Millions of people spend their lives in jobs which are inconsistent with their values/worthy goals. Millions of people find their jobs undemanding and unrewarding. Working hard at some activity which is inconsistent with our values can lead to stress, anxiety, worry and ill-health. Having established worthy goals, use desire, decision, determination and discipline to become excellent at time management. You must desire to become excellent at time management, make a decision to become excellent at time management, determine to become excellent at time management and be sufficiently disciplined to become excellent at time management.

'To fill the hour – that is happiness.' – *Ralph Waldo Emerson*

---

4   BE HONEST WITH YOURSELF

Make yourself fully aware of your own desires, your own goals. Analyse your starting point. Where are you now? How did you get there? What outcomes do you desire in the future? Where do you want to be three months from now, three years from now, 20 years from now? What are you strengths, weaknesses, opportunities and threats? Visualise yourself being at your destination, having achieved your goals. Use the law of reversibility to look backwards and identify the steps you must take to achieve your goals. What are you doing at the present time to achieve your goals? What are you doing right? What are you doing wrong?

Resolve to pay the necessary price to achieve your goals. Define your goals with clarity. Write down the dates by which each goal must be achieved. Identify the logical steps which must be taken to achieve your goals, and set target dates for the accomplishment of each part of the journey. The subconscious responds to clarity. Make each goal and each part of the journey clear, measurable, with its own deadline. Identify all those activities which can be delegated. You cannot do everything yourself.

Distinguish between activities and results. Most people focus on activities, high achievers focus on results. Be sure to understand the difference between efficient and effective. Efficient means doing things 'right', i.e. correctly. Effective means doing the right things. Millions of people spend all their lives working very, very hard at activities which do not yield the desired results. Millions of people spend all their lives becoming extremely efficient in activities which are extremely ineffective in achieving the desired result.

'The trouble with most of us is that we would rather be ruined by praise than saved by criticism.' – *Norman Vincent Peale*

---

5   SET PRIORITIES

Set priorities using the 80/20 rule. In just about all businesses we find that about 80 per cent of the sales is achieved from 20 per cent of our customers, 80 per cent of our stock is accounted for by 20 per cent of our products, 80 per cent of road accidents involve 20 per cent of our drivers, etc. We also find that 20 per cent of what we do accounts for 80 per cent of our results. Focus on the 20 per cent of what you do which yields 80 per cent of your results. Try not to focus on the 80 per cent of what you do which yields only 20 per cent of the desired result.

On a daily, weekly, monthly basis we can organise our tasks as follows. A tasks – must be done; B tasks – should be done; C tasks – could be done; D tasks – delegate to somebody else; E tasks – eliminate, file in the waste paper basket. Most managers admit that 80 per cent of their time is spent on tasks C, D and E. Unfortunately, we all tend to spend only 20 per cent of our time on tasks A and B which are the more important tasks. Make a decision to analyse your tasks, and to spend 80 per cent of your time/life on A tasks and B tasks. Tasks can be further classified as A1, A2, A3, etc.

Set priorities. Use the 80/20 rule.

6   CONTINUE WITH YOUR SELF-DEVELOPMENT

Wherever you are today is the result of your knowledge and attitude. If you wish to be in a different place in the future, then you must continue to learn more and continue to develop a positive mental attitude. You have to learn more to earn more. Review your personal, family and self-development goals every day. Read something every day. Review your goals every day. Reflect on your goals every day. Make a habit of using one hour each day for self-development. Your programme of self-development should include reading books and magazines, listening to educational tapes in the car, attending three/five courses per annum, and spending time with your mastermind alliance. Spend time with people from whom you can acquire knowledge and positive thoughts.

7 MAKE LISTS

Don't feel listless, make a list! Each weekend make a list of tasks to be completed during the following week. Each night make a list of tasks to be completed the following day. Each day focus on that list of three jobs which must be completed on that **Don't feel** day. All high achievers think on paper. Make lists, keep **listless.** lists in the in-tray until all tasks have been completed. **Make a list.** Catch each creative moment by making a note of the idea **Think on paper.** and dropping it in the in-tray. Alternatively, use a dicta-phone to catch the moment.

Every evening make that list of three jobs you will do tomor-row that will make a difference, an improvement in your life, your knowledge, your attitude, your expectations. It may be a telephone call, an approach to a potential customer, information relating to a job, an article you need to read, the development of an idea, pur-chase of a book, an offer to buy or sell. Make a decision that you will complete those three tasks regardless of excuses, pain, laziness, interruptions, avoidable and unavoidable delays, distractions, etc. Just think, in the course of a year that is over one thousand jobs, one thousand improvements. Be prepared to fail, fail and fail again until it becomes a new habit.

8 MAKE PLANS

Make detailed plans for the business, your personal goals and your own self-development. All successful people are planners. They think on paper. All failure in business results from taking action without planning. Failing to plan is planning to fail. A plan is a list of activities. Make lists of actions which must be **Failing to plan is** taken, and make a note of the person responsible for each **planning to fail.** action at each stage of the plan. Make a habit of reviewing each stage of your plans every day.

'Thinking always ahead, thinking always of trying to do more, brings a state of mind in which nothing seems impossible.'
– *Henry Ford*

---

9   IDENTIFY YOUR MOST COMMON TIME-WASTERS

Managers attribute their time wasting to the following causes: telephone calls; unexpected visitors; poor delegation; ineffective, prolonged, unnecessary meetings; no clarity of objectives, planning; fire fighting, being reactive rather than proactive; trying to juggle too many balls at the same time; too many pieces of paper on the desk; inability to make decisions, delayed decisions; failing to say 'no'; poor communications, unclear instructions; unclear responsibility/ authority; unavailable, inaccurate information; poor self-discipline; uncompleted jobs; incompetent staff; social 'business'. Make the necessary efforts to identify your own time-wasting activities.

TIME-WASTERS	
Indecision	Too many jobs
Telephone calls	Untidy desk
Visitors	Ineffective meetings
Firefighting	Socialising

'I recommend you to take care of the minutes; for hours will take care of themselves.' – *Lord Chesterfield*

---

10   ORGANISE YOUR WORKSPACE

Keep a clear desk. The only documents on your desk should relate to the task you are completing at the moment. Do one job at a time to completion. Use a dictaphone, which usually involves only 20 per cent of the time it takes to write.

Do one job at a time to completion.

11   BE EXCELLENT AT DELEGATION

You simply cannot do everything yourself. Don't insist on doing jobs which you enjoy doing. Focus not on what you can do, but on what you can achieve. Focus on desired results, not activities. Move from what you can do to what you can achieve.

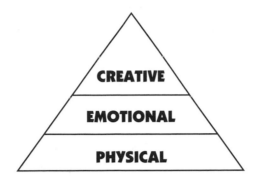

**TRY TO MOVE FROM BURNING UP YOUR ENERGY AT THE
PHYSICAL AND EMOTIONAL LEVELS TOWARDS THE CREATIVE LEVEL**

12   TAKE HIGH RISKS WITH YOUR TIME

'Our costliest expenditure is time. – *Theophrastus (370–287BC)*

You may not wish to take high risks with your money, but you can take high risks with your time. You will have far more available time if you delegate, stop watching television, stop propping up a bar, etc. You will have more time to chase new business, to attend trade shows, to win that big order, to go on courses, spend time with your mastermind alliance, listen to educational tapes, focus on cost-reduction exercises, make additional business contacts, focus on effective advertising and promotion, focus on long-shots that can yield very high financial rewards. One of the most rewarding things you can do is switch your time from activities to high-risk investments with your time, knowledge and positive mental attitude.

The authors of this book are involved at the present time in selling a substantial business on a commission basis, seeking a record contract for a pop group, franchising out our management-development programmes, putting together a management-development book which could sell one million copies, etc. These are all high-risk ventures, but if they all fail totally, it will cost us nothing in cash.

Make a list of five projects which you could undertake which would generate a great deal of cash if successful, but would cost you nothing in cash if it all comes to nothing. Even if you 'fail', just imagine what you would learn. Just imagine what you would accumulate!

TAKE HIGH RISKS WITH YOUR TIME

Self development	Identify rocks
New business	Team development
Trade shows	Promotion

YOUR COMPETITOR'S BIGGEST CUSTOMER

Take time out to visit the biggest customer of your competitor. When all else fails, ask this question:

'What would it take for you to switch from your present supplier to me?'

MAKE A LIST OF FIVE WAYS IN WHICH YOU COULD EARN £100,000 IN THE NEXT 12 MONTHS WITHOUT SPENDING MONEY.

What could you sell for a customer?

What/whom could you promote?

What could you franchise?

What could you write?

Could you write a book for another person?

What could you find/buy for a customer?

What could you design?

Do you sincerely want to be rich? You have been sentenced to death. Your execution will take place one year from today – unless you earn £100,000 in the next 12 months. Make a list of five ways in which you could earn £100,000.

Next time you hear somebody say that they could write a book about a certain subject, then offer to help, splitting the royalties fifty-fifty. Next time you hear somebody say 'we are thinking of getting out of such and such a business', then offer to sell the business on a five per cent commission. When somebody tells you they are thinking of entering such and such a business, then offer to find them an opportunity for a five per cent commission. Life is full of opportunities if you listen carefully to what people say.

13 TAKE TIME TO READ

All leaders are readers. Collect important articles together in a file to read while you are travelling. Carefully select the chapters you need to read in books. Read these when travelling. There will almost invariably be more important tasks requiring your attention during normal office hours.

14 IDENTIFY AND FOCUS ON YOUR KEY RESULTS AREAS

'For everything there is a time and season under the sun.'
– *Ecclesiastes*

In any job or any business, it is your ability to focus on priorities which determines your success. It is essential to focus on the important, not the urgent. It is essential to focus on the vital few, rather than the trivial many. Learn to say 'no'. Avoid the fire-fighting reactive approach to management. Keep asking those important questions: what is the most valuable use of my time at this moment? Why am I on the payroll? What can I, and only I, do that will make a big difference to the success of the business and to my own success? What are my key result areas? In every job, in every industry, people need measurable key results areas, the achievement of which raises their self-esteem and their perceived value to the business. In thinking about your own position, and when delegating to others, remember the golden rule: what gets measured gets done! We all have a strong tendency to do that which gets measured. We all have a tendency not to do those tasks which are not measured. We all have a strong tendency to do that for which we get rewarded. When employing other people, try to ensure that people are rewarded for achievement in key result areas. Try to avoid rewarding people for time. If you pay for time, then you tend to get time. Try to reward people on the basis of results, not time. Most people prefer to be rewarded on a time basis and, putting it bluntly, their time is worth nothing.

Identify and focus on key results areas for yourself and others.

15   OVERCOME PROCRASTINATION

'**Tomorrow is often the busiest day of the week.**'
– *Spanish proverb*

Procrastination is not just the thief of time, it is the thief of life. Make a habit of being proactive. Make it happen, take the initiative, do it now! It's a five-minute job. Do it now, and it will be completed in five minutes. Use deadlines. Make appointments with the boss, bank manager, employees, suppliers, to discuss your results. Never ask anybody to do a job 'when you've got a minute'. Put a deadline on every job. Break large tasks down into small achievable bits. This is called salami-slicing.

Writing a 240-page book sounds like a big job. However, if it is broken down into eight chapters of 30 pages each, and if the 30-page chapter is broken down into six sections of five pages each, then suddenly the job does not seem to be particularly big. Forty-eight sections of five pages each does not feel as big a job as writing a 240-page book. Use affirmations to change your attitudes towards awful jobs, e.g. 'I am really enjoying filling in my tax return. I am thoroughly enjoying chasing late payers for money, I am very happy dealing with customer complaints, I am really looking forward to negotiating a bigger overdraft facility with the bank manager, I am really excited about giving my next presentation.' Pretend that you enjoy it. Act the part. Develop a new habit. Develop a 'do it now' mentality. Remember that a little bit of self-discipline weighs ounces … but regret weighs tons.

'One of these days is none of these days.' – *Old English proverb*

'The first step in achieving your goals is to recognise that "someday" is not a day of the week.' – *Ed Bliss* (author of *Getting Things Done*)

HOW TO DO THINGS YOU DO NOT FEEL LIKE DOING

1 Mentally rehearse your sense of achievement when the job is done.
2 Imagine that someone who really loves/loved you is hovering over you, willing you to get the job done.
3 Make a list of all the milestones that must be reached with specified timings, e.g. every 15 minutes, every 30 minutes. It's a game. You are in a race at the Olympics. Play the game. Win the race.
4 At the completion of each stage, give yourself a little treat – a walk around the garden, a cup of coffee, 10 press-ups, one three-minute track of your favourite record/CD.

16   ORGANISE EFFECTIVE MEETINGS

Meetings are extremely expensive. If you work out the cost of all the salaries of all the people at meetings, then you very quickly realise that meetings are a substantial investment. What else could these people be doing? Is this the best use of their time? Make sure that there is a purpose to the meeting, and that a meeting is not held every Thursday afternoon because we always have meetings on Thursday afternoons. Set time limits for meetings, including time limits for each item on the agenda. Have you ever thought of stand-up meetings? They do not last as long as sit-down meetings. Have you ever thought of meetings without refreshments?

17   CONTROL INTERRUPTIONS

Use a 'do not disturb' sign to discourage interruptions. When uninvited guests turn up, stand up to leave the office. Meet surprise visitors outside the office. Use the expression 'I've only got five minutes'. Make a habit of saying 'no' to those activities and invitations which do not lead to the desired result.

With reference to telephone calls, screen out the unimportant calls. Make a habit of returning calls in batches. It is generally estimated that a 20 per cent improvement in managerial output is achieved by not answering the telephone. Experiment with a one-day free of telephone calls. This is generally associated with high achievement. Experiment with a one-day in the public library to perform tasks/organise work you have been avoiding.

18   DEVELOP BLOCKS OF TIME FOR SPECIFIC TASKS

From your own self-knowledge, you will know that at certain times of the day you are more creative than at other times. You will also know that you perform functional tasks more effectively at certain times of the day. For example, you may set aside one hour in the early morning to be creative, one hour in mid-morning to deal with telephone calls, one hour late morning for meetings, one hour around lunchtime for dealing with correspondence, one hour travelling to or from work to read, one hour after lunch 'do not disturb' to review plans, etc. Make a decision to set aside one hour very early in the morning to read your goals, identify the rocks that stand between you and the achievement of your goals, imagine 20 ways to overcome those rocks, to making progress every day. This is sometimes referred to as the golden hour. This is when you mentally programme yourself for high achievement.

19 BATCH YOUR TASKS

We all know from experience that there is a learning curve for similar tasks. We should all therefore develop the habit of batching our tasks. Dictate a dozen letters in one batch, make half a dozen telephone calls, organise eight interviews on the same day, etc. Batching is far more effective than switching from one task to another.

20 DO ONE JOB AT A TIME TO COMPLETION

Which is better if you are a builder: to have 100 houses half-completed, or 50 houses completed? Which is better: to have one report completed, or two reports half-completed? Both performances require the same amount of work. However, whatever the production process, the next person can do nothing until you finish your task. Do one job at a time to completion. Stay with the task to completion. One of the characteristics of successful people is that they carry out action plans to completion.

Winners use their time to achieve their goals

Losers use lack of time as an excuse

21 MEMORISE THE FOLLOWING SLOGANS

From the many slogans relating to time management, we have found the following to be particularly useful. When faced with any time-management situation, we suggest that you could find the answer you are looking for in the following statements. We always keep the following close to hand on a series of cards:

1 Life is so precious and so beautiful. Enjoy every minute.
2 Be careful how you use your time for time is the stuff of which life is made.

3   Learn what you need to know, be positive, and it will appear to others that you have all the luck in the world.

4   It's a challenge.

5   The more you do of what you do the more you get of what you've got.

6   I love uncertainty, I am thriving on chaos.

7   What one job can I do today that will make a real difference?

8   Success is a way of thinking.

9   We all tend to make the work fit the time, and pretend that we are busy.

10 Discipline weighs ounces, but regret weighs tons.

11 Is this the best use of my time right now?

12 Opportunities always come disguised as hard work.

13 Opportunities are like buses. Don't worry if you miss one, there'll be another one along in about 20 minutes.

14 When the going gets tough, the tough get going.

15 I am enriching the lives of my customers.

16 I am a valuable and worthwhile person.

17 I am swarming over the rocks that stand between me and the success I deserve.

18 Positive emotions give you energy, negative emotions drain you of energy.

19 Let it go! Forgiveness is totally selfish.

20 Face up to that which you fear, and fear is removed.

21 Focus not on what you can do, but on what you can achieve.

22 You have to get rid of yesterday before you can go on to tomorrow.

23 What is the quickest way to get this piece of paper off my desk within the framework of achieving my goals?

24 Because I know exactly what I want, shifting jobs off my desk is easy.

25 Do one job at a time to completion.

26 It's a five-minute job. Do it now and within five minutes it will be off my desk forever.

27 Be proactive.

28 Only action gets results.

THE DIFFERENCE BETWEEN WINNERS AND LOSERS
IS NOT THAT WINNERS HAVE MORE TIME.
EVERYBODY HAS 24 HOURS IN EACH DAY.
WINNERS USE THEIR TIME TO ACHIEVE THEIR GOALS.
LOSERS USE LACK OF TIME AS AN EXCUSE.

'Those who make the worst use of their time are the first to complain of its brevity.' – *La Bruyere, 1688*

'There are three things that can never be retrieved – the spoken word, time past and the neglected opportunity.' – *Old Muslim saying*

'As a well-spent day brings happy sleep, so life well used brings happy death.' – *Leonardo da Vinci*

ENJOY THE JOURNEY.
ENJOY EVERY MINUTE.

FURTHER READING

1 How to think creatively

Adair, J. (1990), *The Art of Creative Thinking,* Talbot Adair Press, Guildford.

Arnold, J.D. (1992), *The Complete Problem Solver: A Total System for Competitive Decision Making*, John Wilcy, Ncw York, NY.

Evans, R. and Russell, P. (1989), *The Creative Manager*, Unwin, London.

Firth, D. and Leigh, A. (1998), *The Corporate Fool: Doing the Undoable, Thinking the Unthinkable, Saying the Unsayable and Driving Your Sensible Organization Mad with Creative Folly*, Capstone, Oxford.

Foster, T.R.V. (1991), *101 Ways to Generate Great Ideas*, Kogan Page, London.

Isaksen, S.G. and Treffinger, D.J. (1988), *Creative Problem-Solving: The Basic Course*, Bearly, Buffalo.

Juniper, D.F. (1989), *Successful Problem Solving: The Organised Approach to Creative Solutions*, W. Foulsham, Slough.

Kuhn, R.L. (1988), *Handbook for Creative and Innovative Managers,* McGraw-Hill, Maidenhead.

Miller, C.M. (1987), *The Creative Edge: Fostering Innovation in Where You Work*, Addison-Wesley, Boston, MA.

Morgan, G. (1993), *Imaginization: The Art of Creative Management*, Sage, Newbury Park, CA.

Phillips, N. (1997), *Reality Hacking: Unusual Ideas and Provocations for Reinventing Your Work*, Capstone, Oxford.

Russell, P. and Evans, R. (1992), *The Creative Manager: Finding Inner Vision and Wisdom in Uncertain Time,* Jossey-Bass, San Francisco, CA.

2   How to set and achieve your goals

Borg, J. (1991), *The Inner Game of Selling ... Yourself: Mind-Bending Ways to Achieve Results in Business*, Mandarin, London.

Brennan, J.H. (1991), *How to Get Where You Want to Go: Dynamic Techniques for Achieving Success*, Thorsons, Wellingborough.

Calano, J. and Saltzman, J. (1990), *Career Tracking: The 26 Success Shortcuts to the Top*, Gower, Aldershot.

Calvert, R., Durkin, B., Gromdi, E. and Martin, K. (1990), *First Find Your Hilltop*, Hutchinson, London.

Goldratt, E.M. (1994), *It's Not Luck* (Sequel to *The Goal*), Gower, Aldershot.

Hopson, B. and Scully, M. (1991), *Build Your Own Rainbow: A Workbook for Career and Life Management*, Mercury, London.

Israel, R. and Crane, J. (1996), *The Vision*, Gower, Aldershot.

Megginson, D. and Whitaker, J. (1996), *Cultivating Self-development*, Institute of Personnel and Development, London.

Tulgan, B. (1998), *Work This Way: Inventing Your Career in the Workplace of the Future*, Capstone, Oxford.

Waitley, D. (1961), *The New Dynamics of Goal Setting: Flextactics for a Fast-changing Future*, Nicholas Brealey, London.

Wheeler, B. (1990), *The One and Only Law of Winning*, Shapolsky, New York, NY.

3   How to implement a winning business strategy

Beer, M. (1990), *The Joy of Winning*, Mercury, London.

Bland, W.A. (1991), *Creating Value for Customers: Designing & Implementing a Total Corporate Strategy*, John Wiley, Chichester.

Campbell, A., Devine, M. and Young, D. (1990), *A Sense of Mission*, The Economists Books, London.

Carling, W. and Heller, R., (1996), *The Way to Win: Strategies for Success in Business and Sport*, Warner

Heller, R. (1989), *Unique Success Proposition*, Sidgwick & Jackson, London.

Judson, A.S. (1990), *Making Strategy Happen: Transforming Plans into Reality*, Blackwell Publishers, Oxford.

Karloff, B. (1993), *Strategic Precision: Improving Performance through Organizational Efficiency*, John Wiley, Chichester.

Naylor, T.H. (1986), *The Corporate Strategy Matrix*, Harper & Row, London.

Shapiro, E. (1997), *Fad Surfing in the Boardroom: Reclaiming the Courage to Manage in the Age of Instant Answers*, Capstone, Oxford.

Shapiro, E. (1998), *The Seven Deadly Sins of Business: Freeing the Corporate Mind from Doom-Loop Thinking*, Capstone, Oxford.

Sewell, R. (1996), *The 12 Pillars of Business Success*, Kogan Page, London

Stein, J.D., Stone, H.L. and Harlow, C.V. (1990), *How to Shoot from the Hip without Gettng Shot in the Foot: Making Smart Strategic Choices Every Day*, John Wiley, Chichester.

4 How to implement a winning marketing strategy

Baker, M.J. (Ed.) (1993), *Perspectives on Marketing Management*, John Wiley, Chichester.

Christopher, M., Payne, A. and Ballantyne, D. (1991), *Relationship Marketing: Bringing Quality, Customer Service and Marketing Together*. Butterworth-Heinemann, Oxford.

Clutterbuck, D. and Kernaghan, S. (1991), *Making Customers Count: A Guide to Excellence in Customer Care*, Mercury, London.

Foster, T.R.V. (1992), *101 Ways to Get More Business*, Kogan Page, London.

Iyer, V. (1990), *Managing and Motivating Your Agents and Distributors*, Pitman, London.

Moore, G. (1998), *Crossing the Chasm: Marketing and Selling Technology Products to Mainstream Customers*, Capstone, Oxford.

Moore, G. (1998), *Inside the Tornado: Marketing Strategies from Silicon Valley's Cutting Edge*, Capstone, Oxford.

O'Hara, P.D. (1992), *The Total Marketing and Sales Plan*, John Wiley, Chichester.

Plowman, B. (1984), *High Value, Low Cost: How to Create Profitable Customer Delight*, Pitman, London.

Robinson, N. (1991), *Marketing Toolkit*, Mercury, London.

Van Mesdag, M. (1991), *Think Marketing: Strategies for Effective Management Action*, Mercury, London.

Wilson, J.R. (1991), *Word-of-Mouth Marketing*, John Wiley, Chichester.

5   How to be excellent at selling

Beer, M. (1991), *Break the Rules in Selling*, Mercury, London.

Beveridge, D. (1992), *Sales Management: Why the Best Are Better*, Walsworth, Marceline, MI

Cox, R. and Bolton, G. (1971), *Sales and Sales Management*, Butterworth-Heinemann, Oxford

Ellis, P. (1992), *Who Dares Sells: The Ultimate Guide to Selling Anything to Anyone,* Thorsons, London.

Fifield, P. (1997), *Making Customer Strategy Work*, Butterworth-Heinemann, Oxford.

Harvey, C. (1992), *Successful Selling in a Week*, Hodder & Stoughton, London.

Lidstone, J. (1991), *Manual of Sales Negotiation*, Gower, London.

Noonan, C. (1971), *Practical Sales Management*, Butterworth-Heinemann, Oxford.

Shook, R.L. (1991), *The Art of the Hard Sell: Subtle High Pressure Tactics that Really Work,* Piatkus, London.

Strafford, J. and Grant, C. (1993), *Sales Management*, Butterworth-Heinemann, Oxford.

6   How to negotiate better deals

Case, P. (1992), *That One Hour Negotiator*, Butterworth-Heinemann, Oxford

Fisher, R. and Ury, W. (1991), *Getting to Getting to Yes: Negotiating an Agreement without Giving in*, Business Books, London.

Fleming, P. (1992), *Successful Negotiating in a Week*, Hodder & Stoughton, London.

Hall, L. (Ed.) (1993), *Negotiation Strategies for Mutual Gains: The Basic Seminar of the Harvard Program on Negotiation*, Sage, London.

Johnson, R.A. (1993), *Negotiation Basics: Concepts, Skills and Exercises,* Sage, London

King, N. (1991), *The Last Five Minutes: The Successful Closing Moves in Sales, Business and Interviews*, Simon & Schuster, London.

Le Poole, S. (1991) *Never Take No for an Answer: A Guide to Successful Negotiation*, Kogan Page, London.

Mills, H.A. (1992), *Negotiate: The Art of Winning*, Gower, Aldershot.

Robinson, C. (1990), *Winning at Business Negotiations: A Guide to Profitable Deal Making*, Kogan Page, London.

Ury, W. (1991), *Getting Past No: Negotiating with Difficult People*, Business Books, London

7 How to lead a winning team

Adair, J. (1989), *Great Leaders*, The Talbot Adair Press, Guildford

Autry, J.A. (1991), *Love & Profit: The Art of Caring Leadership*, Chapmans, London.

Beer, M. (1989), *Lead to Succeed*, Mercury, London.

Bryman, A. (1986), *Leadership and Organizations*, Routledge & Kegan Paul, London.

Cohen, W.A. (1990), *The Art of the Leader*, Prentice-Hall, Englewood Cliffs, NJ.

Garratt, B. (1990), *Learning to Lead*, Fontana, London.

Henry, J., Johnson, G. with Newton, J. (Eds.) (1993), *Strategic Thinking: Leadership and the Management of Change*, John Wiley, Chichester.

Hitt, W.D. (1991), *Thoughts on Leadership*, Battelle Press, London.

Lundy, J.L. (1986) *How to Lead so Others Follow Willingly*, Kogan Page, London.

Strratt, R.J. (1893), *The Drama of Leadership*, The Falmer Press London.

Tulgan, B. (1997), *Managing Generation X: How to bring out the best in young talent*, Capstone, Oxford.

8 How to understand the financial implications

Dobbins, R. and Pettman, B.O. (1977), *European Insights in Managerial Finance*, MCB Books, Bradford.

Dobbins, R. and Witt, S.F. (1983), *Portfolio Theory & Investment Management*, Martin Robertson, Oxford.

Dobbins, R. and Witt, S.F. (1988), *Practical Financial Management*, Blackwell, Oxford.

Fenton, J. (1990), *How to Double Your Profits within the Year*, Mandarin, London.

Lewis, G. (1992), *Pricing for Profit*, Kogan Page, London.

Sales, G. (1988), *How to Deal with Your Bank Manager*, Kogan Page, London.

Secrett, M. (1993), *Successful Budgeting in a Week*, Hodder & Stoughton, London.

Simon, C. (1992), *The Role of the Accountant in Strategic Planning*, Gower, Aldershot.

Warner, A. (1992), *Beyond the Bottom Line: Advanced Financial Knowledge for Managers*, Gower, Aldershot.

Warren, R. (1988), *How to Understand and Use Company Accounts*, Hutchinson, London.

9 How to focus on the 20% that brings in the 80%

Adair, J. (1987), *How to Manage Your Time*, The Talbot Adair Press, Guildford.

Brown, P. (1993), *Managing Your Time*, Daniels, Cambridge.

Cormack, D. (1986), *Seconds Away: Fifteen Rounds in the Fight for Effective Use of Time*, Marc Europe, Bromley.

Humphrey, J. and Humphrey, F. (1990), *How to Get More Done: New Ways to Achieve Peak Performance at Work*, Kogan Page, London

Lakein, A. (1984), *How to Get Control of Your Time and Your Life*, Gower, Aldershot.

Maddux, R.B. (1990), *Delegating for Results*, Kogan Page, London.

Ollivier, D. (1994), *Prioritize Your Time*, Kogan Page, London.

Rudd, S. (1990), *Time Manage Your Reading*, Gower, Aldershot.

Seiwert, L.J. (1989), *Managing Your Time*, Kogan Page, London.

Walster, D. (1993), *Managing Time*, Neal-Schuman, London.

INDEX

Ackoff, Russell L. 126
acquisitions 117–18, 259–61
advertising 153–5
Aesop 147
Allen, Woody 34
Aquinas, St Thomas 50
Aristotle 31, 78
Armstrong, Louis 220
attitudes *see* positive/negative attitudes/
    cmotions
Aurelius, Marcus 32

Bacon, Francis 34
Bagehot, Walter 45
Beerbohm, Max 219
beliefs 4–5
    affirmation 50
    changing 44–45
    corporate 111–13
    emotionalisation 49
    law 43-50
    question 90
    visualisation of outcome 49
    see also mental laws
Bierce, Ambrose 208
Bilko, Sgt Ernie 40
Bono, Edward de 219
Boston Matrix 115–16, 124, 149
brain storming 20

Branson, Richard 61
Broille, Roger 63
Bronowski, Jacob 221
Buddha 63
business
    failure 128
        concentration 129
        differentiation 128
        segmentation 128
        specialisation 128
    industry analysis 109
    plan 253–5
    success
        concentration 130–1
        differentiation 130
        segmentation 130
        specialisation 130

Carnegie, Andrew 50
Carnegie, Dale 45, 59, 164, 220
Cato the Elder 112
Chesterfield, Lord 54, 284
Churchill, Sir Winston 225
Clements, John 38
Cocteau, Jean 47
competitive advantage 105–6, 109, 139–43,
      167–8, 184, 186
Confucius 47, 114, 172
Coward, Noel 88

creativity 1
  adaptive thinking 9
  alternative thinking 12–13
  ask focused questions 14–15
  ask innovative questions 23
  benefits for customers 25
  definition 3–4, 26
  determinants 4–5
  finish the statement 20
  goal setting 5–7
  20-idea method 18–19
  identifying rocks 7–8
  intelligence and genius 9–11
  lateral thinking 20–22
  make a new start 11
  mechanical thinking 8
  new ideas 24–5
  problem-solving 13–14, 16–17
  sources of innovation 23–4
  use three tiers of the brain 12
  zero-based approach 15–16
crisis management 121–22
Crisp, Quentin 69
customers
  benefits 25
  buyer-seller risk 151
  communication 186
  education 186
  identify 168–70
  marketing characteristics 146–7
  needs 149, 170–72, 187
  satisfaction 135

Descartes, René 43, 149
Dickens, Charles 241
Dionysius the Elder 220
Disraeli, Benjamin 88
Drucker, Peter F. 143, 221, 279

Edison, Thomas Alva 1, 59
education/learning 42–3, 81, 113–14
Einstein, Albert 26
Elizabeth I 277
Ellington, Duke 13
Emerson, Ralph Waldo 43, 280
emotions see positive/negative attitudes/
    emotions
entrepreneurs
  successful characteristics 231–32

acceptance of responsibility 232
commitment to success 232
excellence in selling 233
excellent communications 233
helicopter view 232
judgement 232
leadership skills 233
managing time effectively 233
persistence 233
resolution to pay the price 232
self-belief 232
sense of mission 232
Erskine, John 217
Esar, Evan 95
excellent companies
  autonomy and entrepreneurship 131
  bias for action 131
  closeness to customer 131
  hands-on, value-driven executives 131
  loose-tight properties 132
  productivity through people 131
  simple form, lean staff 132
  stick to the knitting 131

Feather, Vic 206
Ferguson, Marilyn 68
finance 235
  balance sheet 242–5
  bank manager 258
  business plan 253–5
  capital expenditure 256
  cash flow 239–42
  company valuation 261
    balance sheet values 262
    dividend yield 263
    liquidation value 262
    market-value/book-value ratio 263–4
    payback period 262–63
    present value analysis 261–62
    price/earnings ratio 263
  forecasting example 266–76
  gearing (leverage) 245–6
  good accounting records 257–8
  gross profit 238
  growth
    acquisition 259–61
    organic 259
  maximise market value of company 257
  net profit 237

overheads 238
product profitability analysis 251–53
profit and loss account 242
profit planning (marginal costing)
    249–51
ratios 246–9
sole trader/limited company 264–6
value added 246
working capital 255–6
Fix, Paul 59
Ford, Henry 45, 202
Franklin, Benjamin 74, 277, 280
Frost, Robert 4

Galbraith, John Kenneth 9
Gardner, John 219
genius 9–10, 70–72
    characteristics
        adaptive thinking 10
        clarity 10
        focus and concentration 10
        using systematic methodology 11
Getty, John Paul 8, 34, 72, 88
goals
    achieving 86
        analyse present position 87
        belief in fulfilling 87
        decision-making 86
        honesty with oneself 87
        identify people 87
        identify rocks 87
        identify skills 87
        make business plan 87
        patience and persistence 88
        use deadlines 87
        visualise, emotionalise, affirm 87
        write down goal 87
    setting 5–6, 27, 53, 76, 80–83
        career/business 6
        clarity 81–82, 83
        focus questions 82–83
        next promotion 79–80
        personal development 6, 29
        personal and family 7
        personal relationships 30
Goethe, Johann Wolfgang von 78, 222
Goldsmith, Sir James 137

Hacmillan, Harold 9

Holmes, Oliver Wendell 19
Hope, Bob 259
Horace 174
Hore-Belisha, Leslie 208
host-beneficiary relationship 150–51

Iacocca, Lee 30
innovation
    sources
        change in industry structure 24
        changes in values 24
        demographic change 24
        incongruity 23
        new knowledge 24
        process need to overcome difficulty 23
        unexpected events 23
intelligence 70–72
Internet 195

James, William 9, 49, 78
Johnson, Samuel 7, 39, 59, 174
Joyce, James 74
Jung, Carl 85

kaizen 57
Kennedy, John F. 197, 224
Kingsley, Charles 139
knowledge/skills 40–43, 112–14
Kruschev, Nikita 278

La Bruyère, Jean de 293
lateral thinking 20
    argue case for opposition 22
    fantasise 22
    random association 21
    reversal 20–21
    shift dominant idea 21–2
leadership 215
    basic skills 217–18
    becoming 230–31
    characteristics
        action 220–21
        continuous learning 224–5
        courage 221–22
        enjoyment of leading 223
        high expectations, commitment to
            winning 219
        high self-esteem 223–4
        integrity 225

listening skills 220
planning 222
results orientation 223
self-motivation 224
vision, mission, clear goals 218–19
definition 217
entrepreneur skills 233
in practice
build winning teams 227–9
communicate well 227
inspire/motivate others 225–6
put meaning/purpose into work 226
styles 230
learning organisation 112–14
Leonardo da Vinci 114, 293
limited company 264–6
Lincoln, Abraham 34, 85, 199
Lloyd George, David 222

McGannon, Donald H. 220
McGregor, Douglas 127
Magee, William Connor 167
marketing 133
advertising 153–5
benefits 147–9
buyer-seller risk 151
commodities 155–6
concentration 144–5
customer characteristics 146–7
customer needs 149
database 195
definition 137
differentiation 139–43
industrial 154–5
joint 150–51
major obstacle/rock 152–53
new products 156–7
opportunity gap analysis 150–52
overcome market ignorance 154
philosophy 135–6
product mix 149
product range 150
segmentation 143–4
specialisation 138
successful 158
Marshall, Colin 111
Maugham, William Somerset 55
mental laws
accumulation 56–8

attraction 47–48
belief 43–5
cause and effect 46–7
compensation 63–4
concentration 58–9
control 55–6
correspondence 48–50
emotion 61
expectations 54–5
expression 51–54
goal achieving 66–67
habit 61
inertia 65–6
reciprocity 65
reversibility 59–60
substitution 60–61
superconscious activity 62–63
mind storming 18–19
mission statement 110–11
Miyamoto Musashi 103
Morley, Christopher 34

Napoleon Bonaparte 226, 233
negotiation 197
agreement 212
bargaining
avoid emotion 208–9
incorrect assumptions 208
it's time to agree price 210–12
persuasion, reciprocation, social
proof 210
save important issues for the end
209–10
time is on your side 209
definition 199
establish friendly relationship 206
objective 199–200
outcomes 200
planning
develop options 204
everything is negotiable 203
power 204–5
situation reversal 205
use powers of love/suggestion 205–6
practice 213
preparation
define perfect outcome 202
four stages 203
statements of opening position 207–8

successful negotiators 200–201
niche markets 107–8, 143–5, 184
Nierenberg, Gerald I. 208
Nietzsche, Friedrich 10, 76, 225

Ohmae, Kenichi 110
Osler, Sir William 202

Pareto principle *see* 80/20 rule
Pasteur, Louis 158
Peale, Norman Vincent 281
Plato 45, 219
Player, Gary 59
positive/negative attitudes/emotions 38–43,
        41–42, 52–53, 60, 65–66, 72–78,
        94
price
    bargaining
        ask tough questions 211
        big order 211
        delegate negotiation 211
        do your homework 210
        low ball 211
        pull a face 210
problem solving 13–14
    systematic method 16–17
products
    benefits/competitive advantage 167–8
    mix 149
    new 156–7
    profitability analysis 251–53
    range 150
    strategy 123–4
profit and loss *see* finance

quality circles 19, 115

responsibility 35–6
Rickards, Tudor 19
Rogers, Will 66
Roosevelt, Eleanor 37
80/20 rule 162, 209, 277
Ruskin, John 140

sales 159
    basic skills 162–63
        be positive in attitude, love selling
            163–4
        close that deal 176–7

follow up, make the second effort
        177
    handle objections 174–6
    identify customer needs 170–72
    identify customers/prospecting
        168–70
    know your product, its benefit/
        competitive advantage 167–8
    make excellent presentations 172–74
    manage activities effectively 165–7
entrepreneurs 233
increase income (already considered)
    attitude 186
    check outputs of sales people 187
    close that deal 187
    develop a winning team 187
    establish clear standards of
        performance 187
    follow up 187
    formula for thinking about sales
        187–8
    identify customer needs 187
    improve presentation 187
    increase knowledge of competitive
        advantage 186
    learn how to handle objections 187
    manage activities 186
    more effective advertising 188
    offer credit 189
    outsource sales function 187
    prospecting for new customers 187
    public relations 188
    reactivate old customers 188
    reward structure for motivation 187
    sales training 187
    send Christmas cards 188
    separate price from terms 188
    stimulate competitors' inactive
        customers 188
    test different prices 188
    test everything 188
increase income (not considered)
    30-day trial 189
    commission-only sales 189
    complementary products 190
    cross sell 190
    endorsements 190
    extended guarantees 190
    first year free 189

franchising 191
free offer to lock-in sales in advance 191
free samples 189
guaranteed trade-in price on goods sold 190
joint ventures 192
licensing 191
networking 191
one-off irresistible offer 189
100 per cent money-back guarantee 190
point of sale sales 192
quantity discounts 189
reduction off next purchase 189–90
sell and sell again 191
telephone after mailing shots 192
telesales 192
upsell 191
use big distributor 191
your best customers are your customers 190
increase income (probably considered)
ask for referrals 186
better 184
caring, courteous, considerate 184
cheaper 184
commitment to excellence 183
communicate with customer 186
creatively imitate your competition 185
educate customer 186
fanaticism for service/quality 183
faster 184
love of the customer 183
make ordering/buying easy 185
market niche 184
market segmentation 184
mega credibility 185
more pressure 186
more promotion 186
nicer 184
overcome market ignorance 185
practise price discrimination 186
relationship selling 184
sell more units/increase the price 183
sustainable competitive advantage 184

unique selling proposition 184
use 80/20 rule 185
increase income (probably not considered)
acquire somebody else's Dog 194
ask your way to success 195
bring customers together 193
competitive product lists 192
complementary product lists 192
database marketing 195
exclusivity 193–4
fail, fail, fail 195
focus and concentration 196
Internet 195
invitation to the board 193
one store test 194
organise a conference 193
other businesses' inactive customer lists 192
proactive selling 195
profit on bankruptcy/liquidation 193
same product/new market 194–5
sell to other people's customers 194
special sales occasions 193
strategic alliances 194
switch risk from customer to self 193
use 10 per cent rule 194
use suppliers and bank manager 195
use your competitor 192
relationship selling 161–62
reward structure
achievement 181
financial 181
promotion 181
recognition 181
status 181
team members
basic needs 182–83
improvement/training 182
reward structure 181
winning teams 178
clear leadership 178
clear output responsibilities 179–80
clear strategy/planning 178
commitment to excellence 178
good communications 179
good counselling/review 180–81
people-development focus 178
selective player assignments 179

Sanders, Colonel 88
Schulz, Charles M. 43
Seneca 83
Shakespeare, William 241
Shaw, George Bernard 45, 78, 88
skills *see* knowledge/skills
Socrates 51
sole trader 264–6
Sophocles 30
Stephenson, Robert Louis 159
strategic business plan 126–7
strategic business unit 118–19
strategy 97
    basics 102–103
    Boston Matrix 115–16
    competitive/industry analysis 109
    concentration 107–8
    constant change 112–14
    corporate values/beliefs 111–12
    crisis management 121–22
    described 99–101
    differentiation 105–6
    driving force 119–20
    growth 117
        acquisition 117–18
        organic 117
    how to get rich quickly 122
        buy a Dog 124–6
        same product, different place
            123–5
        ten per cent rule 123
    mission statement 110–11
    quality 115
    reasons
        financial goals 101
        mission 101
        our ideal future 101
        repositioning the company 101
        SWOT 101
        to take action now 101
    responsibility 102
    segmentation 106
    specialisation 104–5
    zero-based thinking 120–21
success
    can-do suggestions
        accept responsibility for results 92
        ask for help 91
        avoid being aggressive driver 92

        avoid identification 92–93
        avoid victim language 92
        be a go-giver 91
        be patient 92
        carry out action plans to completion
            92
        do a great job 92
        emotionalise 91
        find key results areas 91
        I am in control 91
        I am responsible 91
        look for the good 92
        say 'no' 92
        set priorities 91
        stop hurrying 92
        stop justifying yourself 92
        use affirmations 91
        visualise perfect outcome 91
    difficult suggestions
        access the superconscious 94
        acquire self-knowledge 94
        attend three to five courses per
            annum 93
        avoid negative emotions 94
        avoid the words 'try' and 'wish' 94
        be consistent 94
        be creative 93
        be proactive 93
        form a mastermind alliance 93
        listen to educational tapes 93
        look after your health 95
        read one book per month 93
        set goals 93
        set worthy goals 93
        tape your affirmations 93
        use all mental laws 94
        use blind faith/belief 94
        use powers of love/suggestion 94–5
        value your relationships 95
    formula 40–43
    mental laws of achievement 43–66
    personal goals 29–30
    personal importance 30
        adequate finance 31
        excellent health 31
        happiness/peace of mind 31
        loving relationships 31
        self-fulfilment 32–4
        self-knowledge 32

worthy goals 31
personal responsibility 35–6
self-concept 4–5, 68–70
simple suggestions
    acquire self-knowledge 91
    develop self-improvement plan 91
    don't be late 89
    don't use time as excuse 89
    dress for success 89
    earn self-concept level of income 90
    focus on outcomes 90
    I am a valuable/worthwhile person 90
    I feel marvellous 89
    look at pictures 89
    question assumptions 90
    question beliefs 90
    remember law of reciprocity 90
    today 89
    tomorrow 89
    U X E = R 90–91
    understand that failing equals
        succeeding 90
    use deadlines 89
    use law of reversibility 90
    use lists 90
stop making excuses 37–40
successful/unsuccessful differences 84–5
Sun Tzu 212
SWOT (strengths, weaknesses,
        opportunities, threats) 101

teams
    building 227–8
    developing 187
    sales 178–83
    winning characteristics
        clear leadership 228, 229
        clear strategy/planning 228
        commitment to excellence 228
        good communications 228
        output responsibilities 228
        people-development focus 228
        selective player assignments 228
Thatcher, Margaret 78
Theophrastus 285
Thoreau, Henry David 27

time 277
    batch your tasks 291
    be excellent at delegation 284
    be honest with yourself 279
    believe that you manage time well
        279–80
    continue with self-development 282
    control interruptions 290
    develop blocks of time for specific tasks
        290–91
    do one job at a time to completion 291
    don't use as excuse 89
    effective management 233
    identify most common time-wasters
        283–4
    identify/focus on key results areas
        287–8
    make lists 283
    make plans 283
    memorise suggested slogans 291–92
    negotiation bargaining 209–12
    organise effective meetings 289–90
    organise workspace 284
    overcome procrastination 288–9
    read 287
    set goals 279
    set good time management as a goal 280
    set priorities 282
    take high risks with time 285–7
Timm, Paul R. 88
TUPSY (totally unemployable public sector
        yanker) 136
Twain, Mark 32
Type A/Type B people 126

Virgil 45

Waitley, Denis 83
Wallis, Barnes 10
Walton, Izaak 34
Watson, Thomas J. 167
Weldon, Joel H. 52
Wilde, Oscar 68, 69
Wilson, Earl 47

zero-based approach 108, 120–21